Connectivity in Antiquity

Approaches to Anthropological Archaeology

Series Editor: Thomas E. Levy, University of California, San Diego

This series recognizes the fundamental role that anthropology now plays in archaeology and also integrates the strengths of various research paradigms that characterize archaeology on the world scene today. Some of these different approaches include 'New' or 'Processual' archaeology, 'Post-Processual', evolutionist, cognitive, symbolic, Marxist, and historical archaeologies. Anthropological archaeology accomplishes its goals by taking into account the cultural and, when possible, historical context of the material remains being studied. This involves the development of models concerning the formative role of cognition, symbolism, and ideology in human societies to explain the more material and economic dimensions of human culture that are the natural purview of archaeological data. It also involves an understanding of the cultural ecology of the societies being studied, and of the limitations and opportunities that the environment (both natural and cultural) imposes on the evolution or devolution of human societies. Based on the assumption that cultures never develop in isolation, anthropological archaeology takes a regional approach to tackling fundamental issues concerning past cultural evolution anywhere in the world.

Forthcoming titles in the series:

Archaeology, Anthropology and Cult
The Sanctuary at Gilat, Israel
Edited by: Thomas E. Levy

Hunter-Gatherers of the Southern California Coast
Edited by: Brian F. Byrd

Dawn of the Metal Age
Jonathan Golden

Israel's Ethnogenesis
Settlement, Interaction, Expansion and Resistance
Avraham Faust

New Approaches to Old Stones
Recent Studies of Ground Stone Artifacts
Edited by: Yorke M. Rowan & Jennie Ebeling

Structured Worlds
The Archaeology of Hunter-Gatherer Thought and Action
Edited by: Aubrey Cannon

Connectivity in Antiquity

Globalization as a Long-Term Historical Process

Edited by Øystein S. LaBianca and

Sandra Arnold Scham

Routledge
Taylor & Francis Group
LONDON AND NEW YORK

First published 2006 by Equinox, an imprint of Acumen
Paperback edition published 2010

Published 2014 by Routledge
2 Park Square, Milton Park, Abingdon, Oxon OX14 4RN
711 Third Avenue, New York, NY 10017, USA

Routledge is an imprint of the Taylor & Francis Group, an informa business

British Library Cataloguing-in-Publication Data

A catalogue record for this book is available from the British Library.

ISBN 978 1 84553 947 4 (paperback)

Library of Congress Cataloging-in-Publication Data

Connectivity in antiquity : globalization as a long-term historical
process / edited by Øystein Sakala LaBianca and Sandra Arnold Scham.
p. cm. -- (Approaches to anthropological archaeology)
Includes bibliographical references and index.
ISBN 1-904768-13-X
1. Civilization, Ancient. 2. Economic history--To 500. 3.
Commerce--History--To 500. 4. Economic history--Medieval, 500-1500. 5.
Commerce--History--Medieval, 500-1500. 6. Mediterranean
Region--Antiquities. 7. Middle East--Antiquities. I. LaBianca, Øystein
Sakala. II. Scham, Sandra Arnold. III. Series.
CB311.C75 2004
382'.09'02--dc22

2004013027

Typeset by ISB Typesetting, Sheffield

Contents

List of Contributors

Jenny Cashman is a research student at Lincoln College, Oxford.

Manuel Castells is Professor of Sociology and Professor of City and Regional Planning at the University of California, Berkeley.

William Collins is Professor at California State University and Doctoral Candidate, Department of Near Eastern Archaeology, University of California, Berkeley.

Sheldon Lee Gosline is Associate Professor of Egyptology and Director of the Hieratic Font Project, History Department, Northeast Normal University, Changchun, China.

Øystein S. LaBianca is Professor of Anthropology and Senior Director, International Development Program, at Andrews University, Michigan.

Thomas E. Levy is Professor in the Department of Anthropology and Director of the Judaic Studies Program at the University of California, San Diego.

Leif Manger is Professor of Social Anthropology at the University of Bergen.

Paul J. Ray, Jr. is the Director of Publications, Institute of Archaeology, Andrews University.

Sandra Arnold Scham is Lecturer and Research Development Specialist, Department of Anthropology, University of Maryland and Coordinator, Negev Bedouin Identity Project, Howard University.

William R. Thompson is Professor of Political Science at Indiana University, Bloomington and President-elect of the International Studies Association.

Bethany J. Walker is Assistant Professor of Middle East History at Grand Valley State University in Allendale, Michigan.

Introduction—Ancient Network Societies

> The dream of the enlightenment, that reason and science would solve the problems of humankind, is within reach... There is no eternal evil in human nature. There is nothing that cannot be changed by conscious, purposive social action, provided with information and supported by legitimacy. If people are informed, active and communicate throughout the world; if business assumes its social responsibility; if the media become the messengers rather than the message; if political actors react against cynicism, and restore belief in democracy; if culture is reconstructed from experience; if humankind feels the solidarity of the species throughout the globe; if we assert intergenerational solidarity by living in harmony with nature; if we depart for the exploration of our inner self, having made peace among ourselves. If all this is made possible by our informed, conscious, shared decision, while there is still time, maybe then we may, at last, be able to live and let live, love and be loved.

Thus did Manuel Castells end the final volume of his masterwork *The Rise of the Network Society*. As we edit this volume, during what seems to be a dawning of a new phase of globalization where the initial promise of solidifying human bonds throughout the world seems to have been replaced by the wide and rapid dissemination of destructive technology, the 'dream of the enlightenment' seems more elusive than ever. Western politicians and political writers assure us that technology is still the key—the more 'connected' societies are, according to a recent interview with Thomas Barnett of the US Naval War College, the less danger they pose to world peace. He goes on to say, 'Show me where globalization is thick with network connectivity, financial transactions, liberal media flows, and collective security, and I will show you regions featuring stable governments, rising standards of living, and more deaths by suicide than murder.' This is what he calls the 'new security paradigm that shapes this age' (Barnett 2004).

Disregarding the implication in this pronouncement that world peace is synonymous with online banking, there is, in fact, some comfort to be gained from the knowledge that the ties that bind societies together, which postmodernists have been wont to dismiss as Western hegemonic control, can augur well for global stability. It is also obvious that Barnett, whether he acknowledges the debt or not, has been strongly influenced by Castells—who may well become the most imitated and unwittingly referenced theorist of the millennium.

Is this, however, a 'new' paradigm, as Barnett suggests, or do those who have a sense of déjà vu about these ideas, stretching back to the first historical imperialist enterprises, have a valid point? The answers to this query are as varied as the disciplines that have been strongly influenced by Castells' work. Communications specialists and students of modern politics and international affairs will inevitably stress the essential modernism of *The Network Society* and argue that adding the dimension of the past to Castells' body of theory, would unnecessarily obfuscate some of the author's essential premises. His work is, after all, meant to be *uber*-historical and so firmly rooted in postmodernity and the information technology revolution that it appears to exist beyond time as well as physical space. Further, throughout the three volumes, the author suggests that each phenomenon he describes in such detail is distinct from anything that might have gone before.

Nevertheless, students of the past including historians, archaeologists, social anthropologists and political scientists who take the long view tend to agree with the writer of Ecclesiastes that 'there is nothing new under the sun'—or, rather, human phenomena remain more constant than the terms used to describe them. Networks dependent upon new technology, identity versus collectivization issues and globalization itself, they would argue, are features of many ancient and historical civilizations. Those of us who work in these disciplines can hasten to assure Castells that, while his theoretical framework is wholly innovative, the trends he explicates are quite typical of cultures and societies from previous millennia.

On a smaller scale, for example, Castells' 'space of flows', the non-substantial dimension in which information is transmitted and transactions conducted without physical proximity, was prefigured by trade networks that may have begun as far back as human prehistory. With the exchange of goods came an exchange of ideas that often moved far beyond the areas or regions of the world where the physical exchanges took place. The 'ripple effect' of these exchanges is just beginning to be known to students of the past. Certainly, technology can facilitate such networks but the technology in this case may amount to something as simple as the domestication of pack animals. The 'space of flows' is not established by mere technology, however, and important influences can be transmitted across cultural and physical boundaries—expanding and redefining the 'territory' of human contact. This phenomenon can be mapped in physical space but physical space is not its boundary.

Ancient empires were the original globalizing forces along with the spread of the world's great religious traditions. So powerful were some of these institutions that they could forcefully establish languages of transaction, not unlike today's globalization and informationalization through the medium of English. Aramaic became the enforced mode of speech and writing for those under the control of the Persian Empire and the Inca managed to spread the Quechua language throughout the Western half of the South American continent. The expansionist compulsions of historical states and empires may stem originally from their commercial transactions and 'hearts and minds'—and purses—have historically been won before conflict and conquest ever enter the picture, suggesting that the corporate and national 'tyranny' of flows that is implicit in globalization processes today are not new.

Finally, that great postmodern concept that, for Castells, operates to balance and challenge information technology, 'cultural identity' as opposed to the 'individualization of identity' of the network society, is inextricably embedded in the past as he readily admits: 'A cultural community, organized around language and a shared history...is not an imagined entity, but a constantly renewed historical product, even if nationalist movements construct/reconstruct their icons of self-identification with codes specific to each historical context, and relative to their political projects' (Castells 1997: 49–50). People are conscious of their past before they become conscious of their collective or individual identities and, logically, it is that past which is used to construct and legitimate those identities.

Many scholars will be understandably suspicious of what may appear to them to be a hyper-diffusionist perspective inherent in the papers here. For a vital connector between Castells' theories and modern archaeology the contributors have turned to the great French historian Fernand Braudel and in particular Braudel's first major work, *The Mediterranean and the Mediterranean World in the Time of Phillip II*. First of all, cognitive history and archaeology have made great use of one important Annales concept—*mentalités* (mentalities). The suggestion that historical cultures, societies and people can only be considered in the context of their contemporaries—and not as viewed in relation to moderns—is not unique to this school, but it is in the application of mentalities that cognitive archaeologists have made their mark. For example, there are similarities at the outset between the Annales historical school represented by Braudel and others and the work of today's archaeology with its recent emphasis on region, landscape and gradual processes. Braudel's concept of time is sufficiently different from that of traditional historians to make it particularly functional for

Figure 1.1 Hong Kong, China, 19th-century church amid modern skyscrapers.

archaeologists who seldom deal with events and often deal with spans of time totaling a century or more. Braudel defines three types of historical time—*événements* (events), *moyenne durée* (medium duration) and *longue durée* (long duration). Although dividing history into short-, medium- and long-term processes hardly qualifies as revolutionary, the Annales concept of time is more complex than it first appears.

At the short-term level of historical events, chance occurrences and individual men and women comprise what Braudel viewed as the traditional approach to history. He played down the importance of this level, seeing events and individuals as the 'ephemera' or 'trivia' of the past, as the following passage illustrates:

> When I think of the individual, I am always inclined to see him imprisoned within a destiny in which he himself has little hand, fixed in a landscape in which the infinite perspectives of the long term stretch into the distance both behind him and before. In historical analysis as I see it, rightly or wrongly, the long term always wins in the end (Braudel 1972:244).

Braudel's middle level is concerned with what economists call conjunctures. By this he means the wave-shaped cycles of change of middling duration, seen in economic and social history, such as population cycles, agrarian cycles and economic cycles. Archaeology and history has mostly operated within this level of time with its emphases on quantitative analyses, styles and periods, the growth of hierarchical levels of organization and settlement pattern studies.

For the purposes of our explorations the *longue durée* is the venue of choice. The long-term or *longue durée* has begun to define time in a way that traditional historical models never could. The permanent, the gradual and the recurrent aspects of life on earth—geography, climate, technology, the limits of human physical capability—all represent almost timeless constraints on human behavior.

These are the structures that Castells' seeks to redefine for the 'Information Age' and these are the structures that have shaped the economy, society and culture of the distant past.

The papers contained in this volume are the results of an interdisciplinary exploration of Castells' theories as applied to societies of the past. They vary in scope from regional and quite time-specific explorations to analyses that span civilizations and millennia. The papers were originally presented in 2001 at the annual meetings of two professional societies—the American Anthropological Association and the American Schools of Oriental Research. Contributors were informed of Castells' trilogy in the call for papers and were asked to address the theme of 'Connectivity in Antiquity' against the background of the analytical constructs employed in Castells' work.

None of the authors could have predicted the startling events of September 11, 2001, that occurred between the original planning of the sessions and their presentations in November and December of 2001. Nevertheless, these sessions brought together three concepts that have great immediacy. Globalization, the Middle East and long-term historical processes have indeed become the current watchwords for the media as well as for academia. As CNN and C-SPAN aficionados tune in to witness the endless parade of distinguished theorists attempting to understand, to explain and to predict, our contribution to the debate is being made in the hope that the 'clash of civilizations' and *Jihad Versus McWorld* discussions will pave the way for more serious and in-depth examinations of the economic, social and cultural factors of the past that created today's newspaper headlines.

All of the papers address, in some form or another, the historical bases for the existing relationships between the East and the West. All of the authors are western-born and educated people who have spent substantial time living or working in the Middle East which has given them a unique understanding about what a long-term historical process truly implies. Each author has dealt with

Figure 1.2 View of the New city of Xian, China, from ancient walls.

different aspects of Castells' monumental work—whether they address cultural identities, both ancient and modern, trade networks and the development and dissemination of technology in the past or globalization in general—and they would more or less conclude that while these are all the prime movers of modernity these three conceptual spheres were also strongly influential in past cultures. Just as the Net connects disparate identities and simultaneously reinforces both individualism and collectivism, other institutions like trade networks and religious pilgrimage have over the centuries had the effect of or been used to support either particularist or universalist views.

These papers take us beyond the typical contrast between 'tradition' and 'modernity' that has become a fixture in our interpretations of other cultures and propose that it is history and our notion of history that is the more relevant comparison to tradition. We know, intuitively that there is nothing really contradictory about the use of up-to-date technology by Islamic Fundamentalists, despite the ubiquitous humor about this phenomenon. A far more intransigent concept than history, tradition can continue to exist alongside obvious contradictions. 'History' that contradicts the present will almost certainly cease to exist or be substantially revised. Tradition that contradicts the present can be justified, explained or simply, and tenaciously, embraced.

In the last part of his trilogy, *The End of the Millennium,* Castells speaks of the dilemmas of modernity and of nation-states in crisis and suggests that a synthesis of the processes that are attendant to globalization, technology and identity construction—that is, the demise of statist capitalism, the advent of the cyberspace revolution and the formation of particularist social and cultural movements—have created the 'new society' we live in today. The authors of these papers have established that these processes have taken other forms in the past—the establishment and demise of trade routes and monopolies, other technological revolutions and, most assuredly, cultural and social movements.

References

Barnett, T. (2004) *The Pentagon's New Map: War and Peace in the Twenty-First Century*. New York: G.P. Putnam.

Braudel, F. (1972) *The Mediterranean and the Mediterranean World in the Age of Philip II*. 2 vols. New York: Harper and Row.

Braudel, F. (1995) History and the social sciences: the *longue durée*. In *Histories: French Constructions of the Past*, edited by J. Ravel and L. Hunt. New York: New Press.

Castells, M. (1996) *The Rise of the Network Society: The Information Age: Economy, Society and Culture* 1. 3 vols. Oxford: Blackwell.

Castells, M. (1997) *The Power of Identity: The Information Age: Economy, Society and Culture* 2. 3 vols. Oxford: Blackwell.

Castells, M. (1998) *The End of the Millennium: The Information Age: Economy, Society and Culture* 3. 3 vols. Oxford: Blackwell.

Section One: The 'Space of Flows' in Antiquity

Introduction to Section One: The 'Space of Flows' in Antiquity

For cognitive archaeologists it has long been considered axiomatic that material goods transmit both information and meaning. When those goods flow outside of a society and culture, some of the meaning may be lost but the information remains and interacts with new cultures to form new meanings. In this section our authors examine the long-term processes of metal technology and urbanization within the framework of Castells' theories.

This section introduces three visions of the 'space of flows' and its stimuli in antiquity—including technology, politics and commerce. All of the authors have looked to deep time to address the fundamental alterations in the relationship between the Middle East and the West that we are witnessing today. The kinds of technological and social structures that Levy has looked for in the prehistoric Levant and that Collins and Thompson have dealt with in their discussions of emerging states and trade in early states concern different aspects of Castells' monumental work but all, essentially, deal with transactions that took place in the 'space of flows' of their time.

Figure 2.1 Roman columns at Jerash.

Levy proposes that technology and technological changes, often couched in the language of 'revolutions', can produce significant transformations in social structure and that we can view the development of metallurgy as analogous to the development of information technology covered in Castells' work. Fundamental changes in production and consumption wrought by the discovery of pyro-technology combined with other factors produced a 'new society' composed of controlling elites, specialists and non-elites engaged in systems of monopoly and reciprocity that had far-ranging effects in the Chalcolithic Period. Collins, similarly, suggests that the second great urban revolution in the Near East, with the rise of late third millennium west Syrian trading networks resulted in the first great web of interstate communication and widened the exploitation of human and material capital in facilitating the first global model of connected social hierarchies. Thompson's innovative study of trade pulsations looks at the conjunctures of the *moyenne durée* as leading to long-term restructuring within a new global model of trade and economy.

All of these essays emphasize that Castells' vision is essentially materialist and, emanating from this conclusion, their investigations look at material remains as representative of the age-old relationship between human beings and their creations through the alliance of knowledge and resources.

Grand Narratives, Technological Revolutions and the Past: Deep-Time Studies of Metallurgy and Social Evolution in the Eastern Mediterranean

Thomas E. Levy

Introduction

Meta-accounts of social evolution have the power to make very complex interrelated social phenomena understandable in terms of answering the 'how' and 'why' questions related to the emergence of new socio-political institutions. These accounts transcend time and space and are cross-cultural in approach. Broadly speaking, interest in culture change is one of the central issues that crosscuts disciplines as diverse as anthropology, archaeology, economics, history, political science, sociology, urban studies and other fields. Archaeologists have been strong proponents of the application of meta-accounts to describe distinct cultural phenomena such as the emergence of agriculture and the rise of states. These are fundamental cultural transitions that had profound transformative power in restructuring human societies on global scales. Castells' (Castells 2000a, 2000b, 2000c) powerful trilogy *The Information Age: Economy, Society and Culture* provides a new grand narrative for understanding the current restructuring of societies worldwide into ever increasingly complex social formations based on technological revolutions introduced by electronic networked communication media. This paper explores some of the processual implications of Castells' model and seeks to explain the rise of a 'new society' based on structural transformations brought about through technological change. Øystein LaBianca is to be congratulated for bringing Castells' work to the attention of this group of archaeologists and providing a forum for discussing the implications of *The Information Age* for our field.

How can anthropological archaeologists contribute to Castells' project on 'The Information Age', especially when technology may be the truly distinctive feature of modernity (Marx 1992)? First we have to realize that technology is, as Robert McC. Adams has stated, 'intimately embedded in the entire field of forces constituting society at large' (Adams 1997). In Adams' *Paths of Fire*, taking an anthropological view he examines the impact of technological change on major policy issues today through a holistic perspective. By refusing to be reductionist in approach, Adams (1996) suggests three reasons why anthropology offers important 'deep time' perspectives on how technology can fundamentally restructure societies. These include the fact that anthropological archaeology: 1) is relatively open to examining the complexities of interaction that are not readily reducible to simple regularities or precisely measurable quantities; 2) tries to maintain a consistently integrative, contextual emphasis—to understand specific paths of change and continuity, we focus on context, which leads to an inductive approach that eschews causal determinism; and 3) searches out diverse, improbable kinds of patterning that is skeptical of commonly accepted categories or boundaries, and employs varying temporal and geographic scales as tools of inquiry. Thus, archaeology, armed with an anthropological perspective, offers the only 'deep time' database for examining technology's role in social transformations that spans the entire human experience from prehistoric to historic times. Castells' focus on the triad of 'Technology—Society—and Historical Change' reawakens interest and makes archaeological investigations particularly germane to understanding the oscillations of these relationships through time.

Revolutions and Punctuated Technological Change

At the heart of Castells' (2000:1) meta-account of social change is his concern with the effects of a technological revolution on reshaping, altering the speed of change and reconstituting the nature of societies at the end of the 20th and beginning of the 21st centuries AD. In this sense, Castells' framework follows on a number of meta-narratives concerning the profound impact of technology on social change. The identification of technological revolutions in human history are not new; however, Castells' analytical framework which links technological change with social change profoundly demonstrates the centrality and relevance of materialist perspectives on the study of social evolution, the formation of ethnic and social identities, and the processes that promote change for both the present and the past.

Castells' identification of the latest technological revolution, the 'information technology revolution' is of importance for those of us studying 'deep-time' processes of material culture change. It demonstrates the profound importance of how technological change can fundamentally reconstitute the fabric of human social organizations over relatively short periods of time. Castells builds on Melvin Kranzberg's (Kranzberg and Pursell 1967) and Joel Mokyr's (1990) idea that that there were two industrial revolutions: the first, which was not science-based, relied on the use of information to develop pre-existing knowledge in the development of new sources of energy—essentially the development of the steam engine. The second industrial revolution, after 1850, was characterized by the shift from the steam engine to electricity and perhaps even nuclear power. What separates these two industrial revolutions is the decisive role of science in giving birth to innovation—a process epitomized by the emergence of research and development laboratories in Germany and other parts of Europe and the US. However, there were earlier technological revolutions in human history. It was V.G. Childe, writing in the 1930s, whose volume *Man Makes Himself* (1936) made the concept of technological revolutions popular in both academia and in the public media. Childe, writing about the fundamental changes that occurred in human social evolution, built on the concept of the 'Industrial Revolution'—a term first made popular in reference to the British Industrial Revolution in the late 18th and early-to-mid-19th centuries. As Andrew Sherratt (1997b:59) points out, just as the Industrial Revolution marked a crucial turning point, so prehistory too was punctuated by periods of sharply accelerated growth. Accordingly, Childe (*ibid.*) argued that the transitions from hunting to farming during the Neolithic period, and from farming to urban society (in the ancient Near East around mid 4th–early 3rd millennia BC), represented two analogous 'revolutions', which he called the 'Neolithic' and 'urban' revolutions. For Childe, the Neolithic revolution represented the profound social change from what the 19th century anthropologist Lewis Henry Morgan had called 'savagery' to 'barbarism' and it took place in both the Old and New Worlds with the domestication of cereal crops. Similarly, the Urban Revolution represented the shift from 'barbarism' to 'civilization'. While Childe's conceptual models represented a return to certain Enlightenment ideas of progress, it was the first time that hard archaeological evidence was used to demonstrate these fundamental changes in his social organization and subsistence.

Recently, in a deep-time study of Paleolithic technology and human evolution spanning over 2.5 Ma, S.H. Ambrose (2001) made a case for an evolutionary process of exponential rapidity that led to the leap from the first bow and arrow c. 12,000 years ago to today's International Space Station. It is suggested that the Oldowan and Acheulean industrial complexes represent an extraordinary slow pace of progress between 2.5 and 0.3 Ma that is characterized by restricted mobility and limited regional interaction. Ambrose asks if the challenges posed by the increasingly variable, severe, and hazardous environments of glacial/interglacial cycles over the past 800,000 years as well as more dramatic short-term climatic events, influenced behavioral and biological evolution? However, he argues that with the appearance of near-modern brain size, anatomy, and perhaps of grammatical language c. 0.3 Ma, the role of punctuated change in human evolution was the exception, rather than the rule. Behavioral changes were increasingly autocatalytic (2001:1748), driven by language and by cultural systems of knowledge and understanding of nature and society. Could this characterize an 'Upper Paleolithic' revolution that ushered in the modern humanity that was early on responsible for such conceptual and artistic achievements as the painted caves of western Europe in the Perigord and Pyrenees in southwest France and Cantabria in northern Spain dating from around 30,000 BC.

Following on the heels of the 'Neolithic Revolution', perhaps the most significant feature of Childe's Urban revolution, and one that is a precursor of the IT revolution, was the adoption of writing systems by early pristine states in both the Old and New Worlds. The shift from rural settlement systems to urban life was associated, for the most part, with a loss of village autonomy and the personal freedoms associated with egalitarian and rank level societies. Corvée labor and taxation by the urban elites became the norm. Why people would abandon autonomy for the 'urban revolution' is beyond the scope of this paper. However, walled towns and cities did offer food surpluses, security and opportunities that village based societies could not provide. With the rise of archaic states in Egypt (Baines and Yoffee 1998) and Mesopotamia (Wright 1998), for example, new opportunities developed for the exchange of preciosities and staples between distant ecosystems that specialized in distinct resources such as timber, ores, minerals, foodstuffs, and other products. These exchanges led to the development of extensive, pan-regional, trade networks that led to the emergence of new economic systems embedded in culture core-periphery relations (Champion 1989) and sometimes referred to as 'world systems' (Wallerstein 1974). In both Egypt and Mesopotamia, the rise of urbanism and archaic states was enmeshed in new developments in administrative organization, craft production and the innovation of writing systems. Writing began in the 4th millennium in both these areas primarily for economic administration of the newly formed urban centers as a means of organizing these sizeable pan-regional polities. However, with Mesopotamian cuneiform, it quickly evolved from pictographic forms into a mixed ideographic and syllabic system that eventually approximated the grammatical structures of ordinary language. As Adams (1997: 952) points out, these marked technological changes represent a single complex that served as a stimulus and response to major changes in social scale an complexity that evolved in the wake of the 'urban revolution' and in a generic sense, resemble the onset of today's information technology age some five millennia later.

The information technology revolution, the most recent in the sequence of fundamental socio-technical movements in human history, must be viewed as the melding of not only technology but also its deep relationship with science. Advances in both technology and science cannot be separated today. In a metaphor proposed by Harvey Brooks (1994), he says 'while science and engineering can exist independently, like DNA strands, they are tending today to become meaningful only when they are paired'. A similar link between technology and other dimensions of culture can also be made. For example, the advances made by the adoption of domesticated plants and animals and the subsequent creation of food surpluses fundamentally changed the ways societies organized themselves. This is why many scholars, when describing the nature of cultural systems, often use terms like 'socio-technic' (Binford 1983; White 1949) or 'sociotechnological systems' (Marx 1997) simply because technology does not stand alone from culture. In this sense, it is imperative to examine technological revolutions in their social context. In the case study below, this is achieved through the examination of changes in the mode of production (metal craft specialization) used at different points in time in association with a specified technological system. However, there are several other technological revolutions in the Old World that need to be mentioned before examining the case of ancient metal production in the Levant.

Recently Identified Ancient Technological Revolutions in the Old World

Since the 1980s, Old World archaeologists have identified two additional fundamental techno-subsistence changes that reflect punctuated changes. These technological 'revolutions' created multi-faceted alterations that forever modified the structure of numerous societies around the world. Following the Neolithic revolution when plants and animals were domesticated and the creation of agricultural surpluses spurred on sedentary lifestyles and the beginnings of institutionalized social inequality, Sherratt (1981) has identified another meta-account for subsistence change across the prehistoric Old World, which he has called the 'secondary products revolution'. The major difference the Old and New Worlds with regard to the 'Neolithic revolution' rest in the role animal domesticates played in ancient subsistence economies. In the New World there were few domesticated animals—only the turkey in North America and only the guinea pig and Andean camelids (which functioned much like sheep, cattle and equids in Eurasia) in South America. The fundamental difference in agrarian development between the Old and New Worlds was the close interaction between plant and animal domesticates in the Old World. Simply put, the secondary products revolution refers to the shift from the Neolithic mode of exploiting domestic animals primarily for meat to a new mode of production several millennia later in which the secondary products (milk, hair, wool and traction) of herd animals (primarily sheep, goat and cattle) were systematically exploited. The development of wool in sheep, following their initial domestication, created a new source of fibers suitable for the production of textiles. The harnessing of animal-power (primarily from cattle) for traction enabled the application of the plough as well as the use of the cart. Both of these technological developments led to intensification of farming and the transportation of goods that were a direct result of a new application of domesticated cattle. Similarly, around the same time, equids were used as draught and pack animals. Thus, the secondary products revolution spurred on the emergence of new pastoral-based societies and new trade networks (Levy 1983) in the Levant and other parts of the Old World (Sherratt 1997b).

Recognizing the singular importance of textiles in cementing social relations in human societies, Joy McCorriston (1997) has unpacked Sherratt's notion of the secondary products revolution further to suggest that the transition from reliance on animal skins and plant fibers for clothing and apparel to animal fibers linked to the intensive exploitation of mostly sheep wool, warrants an additional period of punctuated technological change which she refers to as the 'fiber revolution'. Accordingly, McCorriston suggests that one of the most important transformations in the rise of complex societies was the emergence of social groups with differential access to proactive resources. In this model, empirical data is garnered suggesting that women have disproportionately lost access to productive resources following the domestication of plants and animals that harbored the Neolithic revolution. Based on the identification of textile workshops in early Mesopotamian civilization, McCorriston argues that women producers were progressively alienated in urban societies setting the stage for the role of women that has been characteristic since the 'urban revolution'.

With the shift from relatively autonomous village sites to the highly integrated rural and urban settlement systems that characterized the Early Bronze Age, a significant shift took place from the use of cultivated flax to the use of wool for the majority of textile production. This technological shift had tremendous socioeconomic ramifications for agricultural production, the division of labor and social interactions. Thus, the 'fiber revolution' goes further than 'secondary products revolution' by promoting the role of wool fibers in the genesis of what may have been the first dependent labor force—women textile workers (cf. Sherratt 1997a). Based on surveys and early historical documents, Robert McC. Adams (1974) explains how the early Mesopotamian economy was articulated and textile workshops certainly played a key role in the emergence of early social stratification and temple elites. As Sherratt (*ibid.*) highlights in his critique of the fiber revolution model, whether the beginnings of wool use (as opposed to flax) can be invoked, as a *deus ex machina* for initiating the process of social inequality is questionable. However, the role of fiber production in ancient Near Eastern ritual centers and temples was significant and it did play a role in the promotion and maintenance of early complex societies (cf. Levy 2005).

The Dangers of Technological Determinism: The Legacy of Leslie White

The links between technology, society and historical change run deep. Today, the web of new economic, social and cultural structures that have emerged under the power of globalization can all be traced back to the information technology revolution. For Castells (2000a:5), the information technology revolution provides an 'entry point in analyzing the complexity' of these new socioeconomic structures. While eschewing any suggestion that technology determines society, he does highlight that 'the dilemma of technological determinism is probably a false problem, since technology is society, and society cannot be understood or represented without its technological tools'. Still, the overriding explanation for the explosion in new social structures that have evolved around the world in the wake of globalization at the end of the 20th century is the new information technologies and their large-scale impacts. Although not explicitly stated in his three-volume treatise, underlying Castells' view of human culture is the idea that culture can be conceptualized as a system made up of various component parts such as ideology, interaction, social organization, subsistence and technology. In this he is not far from processual archaeologists who view human culture as made up of different interrelated parts, each of which can be examined like a lens for understanding the evolution of culture (cf. Levy 1998; Renfrew and Bahn 2000). The profound socioeconomic changes that have accompanied technological change do make it the idea locus of investigating so many other transformations in human culture.

There is a danger when researchers focus solely on technology and ignore the other dimensions of cultural systems alluded to above. This problem is closely examined by contributors to M.R. Smith and L. Marx's (1994) volume entitled *Does Technology Drive History?* Modernity, especially when viewed from the Euro-American perspective, is closely linked to envisioning technological power as a crucial force in promoting socioeconomic change. It is important to look at the intellectual roots of technological determinism in anthropology because it will help explain why the field moved away from technology-focused investigations in the early 1980s. The deterministic perspective is epitomized in the work of the American cultural anthropologist, Leslie White. White's most influential work was carried out in the aftermath of the Second World War and in the wake of the 'Thermodynamic Revolution' that ushered in the 'Nuclear Age'. As part of White's concept of 'General Evolution', he viewed progress as an essential ingredient of culture. As Trigger (1992) points out, White modeled cultures as elaborate thermodynamic systems. Accordingly, cultural systems are composed of techno-economic, social and ideological components 'determined by technological systems, and philosophies and the arts express experience as it is defined by technology and refracted by social systems' (White 1949). For White, technological determinism was encapsulated in terms of a 'basic law of evolution' that states, all things being equal, culture evolves as the amount of energy harnessed per capita increases or as the efficiency of putting energy to work increased. The following formula characterizes this law:

$$Culture = Energy \times Technology \; (C = E \times T)$$

White's thinking evolved in the post-war atmosphere of American technological prowess and optimism in which he privileged the link between technology and society at the expense of other kinds of relations, such as social interaction, the relation between society and environment, and the role of ideology on social transformations. However, White's thermodynamic modeling of energy capture as a reflection of social complexity is highly reductionist and ignores issues of contingency in social change (Gould 1999). A number of researchers have pointed out that there is no teleological trajectory between advances in technology and social change. Social filters can both enhance and hinder the acceptance of technology resulting in differential rates of social change. This is a crucial concept that must be factored into any study concerning the role of technology on social evolution. R.W. Buillet's (1975, 1994) penetrating study entitled *The Camel and the Wheel* explores the reasons why in the Middle East, where some of the earliest evidence for the invention of the wheel is found, its use for transportation was abandoned throughout the Middle East and North Africa sometime between the 3rd and 6th centuries AD. During this period, the wheel was abandoned for the pack camel that dominated transport in these regions until the early 20th century AD. The link between the emergence of new nomadic pastoral groups who used the camel to penetrate the vast desert zones of North Africa and the Middle East to dominate trade networks with the settled world is shown to be the main 'cultural filter' which led to the abandonment of non-motorized wheel-based transport. Similar cultural filters are evident in totalitarian states, such as formerly in Afghanistan, where the Taliban government banned a wide range of electronic devices (e.g. personal computers, the use of the Internet, radios, etc.) in an effort to maintain their ideological system. The denial of women's rights by the Taliban and other regimes can also be viewed as a 'cultural filter' that prevents the adoption of new technologies by large segments of a population.

'Punk Eek'—Punctuated Equilibrium and Major Social Transformations

Some would argue that there is no such thing as a technological revolution. For example, IBM's then-chief scientist, R. Gomory (1983) argued that at IBM technological development tends to be 'much more evolutionary and much less revolutionary or breakthrough-oriented'. Nevertheless, this is the perspective of someone deeply rooted in today's 'technological trenches' who, on a day-to-day, basis strives to push the 'technological envelop' for financial gain within a human lifespan. For these individuals, the adoption of their new inventions, ideas and discoveries seems slow. However, seen from a deep-time Braudelian (Braudel 1974) perspective, the crystallization of fundamental technological advances that might take 100 or 200 years are indeed revolutionary. Some years ago, researchers from Michigan State University (Elena and Lenski 1996), observed evolutionary changes as a family of bacteria passed through 3,000 generations in their laboratory experiment in the space of only 4 years. As J. Horgan points out in *Scientific American*, conducting an analogous experiment with *Homo sapiens* would require roughly 60,000 years, a timeline too long for most granting agencies. The Michigan State researchers reported in the June 21, 1996 issue of *Science* that their observations support the punctuated equilibrium theory proposed by Stephen Jay Gould and Niles Eldredge, and sometimes known by its nickname 'punk eek'.

Punctuated equilibrium challenged the traditional view of Darwinian evolution as a gradual, stately unfolding. Gould and Eldredge (1977) argued that the fossil record still shows species persisting unaltered for eons before giving rise to new species almost overnight and that those apparent sudden changes in the geological record were a real indicator of the pace of evolution. They suggested that species experience long stretches of general stasis interrupted by the abrupt emergence of new evolutionary forms in the space of a 'few' generations. Punk eek has been critiqued (Prothero 1992). The theory was adopted by creationists as 'proof' that the theory of evolution was not universally accepted. However, Gould and Eldredge (1993) responded that their model does not deny evolution but rather shows a processual alternative to the Darwinian model. In that paper, Gould and Eldredge acknowledged that their model was merely one of many recent ideas in science that emphasize the role of discontinuity and randomness in nature—what anthropologists refer to as 'contingency' (Bintliff 1999) in social change.

For more than two decades biologists and other researchers have debated over Punk Eek and the hypothesis that most morphological evolution occurs during relatively brief episodes of rapid change that punctuate much longer periods of stasis. The Michigan State research presents a clear and unambiguous case of punctuated evolution for cell size in a population of *Escherichia coli* evolving for 3,000 generations in a constant environment (Elena 1996). They have shown that 'punctuation is caused by natural selection as rare, beneficial mutations sweep successively through the population'. As J. Holladay (1998:371) points out for archaeology, 'archaeologically attested social evolution seem to follow a pattern of "punctuated equilibrium" ... Long stretches of time characterized by relative sameness or only minor change are punctuated by sudden and often violent episodes eventuating in wholesale paradigm changes, implying new levels of social organization and cultural expression.' In the context of punk eek, the different archaeological revolutions outlined above do indeed represent relatively short periods of time during which formative technologically based changes occurred since this end of the last ice age. From the perspective of Castells' discussion of the Information Age, each of these 'revolutions' promoted the rise of 'new societies' based on structural transformations brought about through technological change. In what follows, a case study is presented which examines the advent of metallurgy in the southern Levant and its profound impact on creating structural changes in different cultural groups that inhabited the region from c. 4500–2000 BC.

The Original Network Society: The Emergence of Metallurgy during the Chalcolithic and Early Bronze Age in the Southern Levant, c. 4500–2000 BC

As Castells (2000a:38) points out, technological revolutions (here he refers to the industrial revolutions) create processual change in the socioeconomic fabric of societies by acting on the power to produce, distribute and communicate technology's products. In this sense, archaeology provides the only source of data to test models related to the deep-time technological revolutions that began with the appearance of anatomically modern humans and grew exponentially from the Neolithic revolution to the advent of the Information Age in less than 12,000 years. In the wake of the information technology revolution, Castells has shown how the rapidity of change, what Gould (Gould and Eldredge 1993) would call 'punctuated' change, creates disaffected social movements who cannot cope with modernity or the 'New Global Order'. Globalization, which is closely linked to the IT revolution, represents the birth of a new technological system which has created a digital divide—those with complete access to the new technology and those who are excluded for either real or imagined reasons. The point is that new technological systems have the effect of creating punctuated social change. It is possible (but beyond the scope of this paper) that each of the prehistoric and early historic technological revolutions discussed above were also associated with marked social readjustments. While today these can be identified as social movements, social outcasts and high-tech elites, in the past there were also winners and losers who gained or lost power in the wake of the rapid technological changes that appeared in their lifetimes. The dawn of metallurgy in the southern Levant presents an ideal case study for examining the impact of a new technology on social change. Perhaps the apex of prehistoric advances in pyrotechnology was the invention and spread of metallurgy. The ability to control increasingly high temperatures allowed humans to produce synthetic materials for the first time. The most important early non-ferrous metal was copper. While metallurgy cannot be separated from the other dimensions of cultural systems (e.g. ideology, social organization, trade and exchange, and subsistence), the technology of metal production played a profound role in the emergence of some of the earliest rank or chiefdom societies in the Levant during the Chalcolithic period [c. 4500–3600 BC; Levy 1998]. Similarly, punctuated changes in the distribution, control and production of early metallurgy helped contribute to the collapse of these once vibrant chiefdom organizations and the emergence of a new power structure during the following Early Bronze IA (c. 3600–3300 BC). Cathy Costin has shown that (1991: Figure 1) some of the best analytical tools to monitor these processes are based in the anthropological study of craft specialization.

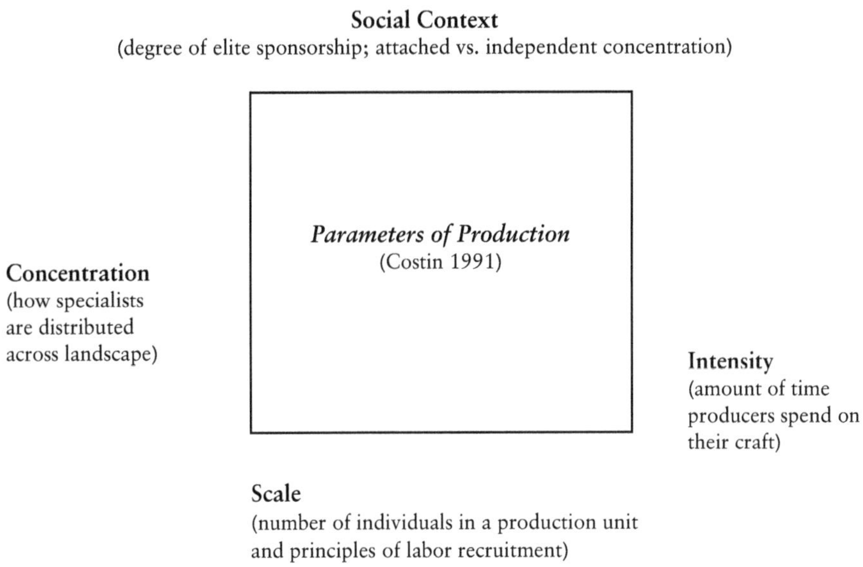

Figure 3.1 The organization of craft specialization.

The Organization of Craft Specialization

Changes in the organization of craft production provide an important analytical lens for monitoring changes in the scale of society (Table 1). In very generic terms, scalar differences in social organizations run from small band level societies, to segmentary societies, to chiefdoms or rank societies, to state level organizations (Johnson and Earle 1987). By studying the degree of elite sponsorship in craft production, how specialists are distributed across a landscape, the number of people in a production unit and the amount of time people spend on their craft, it is possible to measure the ebb and flow of changes in social complexity. This model is applied to two phases of social change in the southern Levant (Table 2): the Chalcolithic period (c. 4500–3600 BC) when the first identifiable chiefdom organizations emerged in the Levant (Levy 1998) and the period following the collapse of Chalcolithic societies called the Early Bronze IA (EBIA, c. 3600–3300 BC). While the term 'Bronze' is used to define this period, tin alloys were not known in the Levant until the beginning of the Middle Bronze Age (c. 1750–1550 BC).

The Dawn of the Metal Age in the Levant—Chalcolithic

In the southern Levant, the earliest conclusive evidence for the smelting of copper ore dates to the Chalcolithic period (Hauptmann *et al.* 1992). The appearance of metal production coincides with a number of new socioeconomic developments during the Chalcolithic period. These include (Levy 1986): the emergence of a two-tier settlement hierarchy with centers that coordinated social, economic and ritual activities; increases in human populations; craft specialization in metal, ivory, pottery, basalt and other materials; the growth of distinct regional cultures which mostly settled along drainage systems in different parts of the country; the rise of pan-regional ritual centers; the first formal cemetery sites established away from settlements; new developments in agro-technology; and other features. Taken together, these features indicate the emergence of some of the earliest chiefdom organizations in the eastern Mediterranean. The appearance of metalworking some 4500 years after the 'Neolithic revolution' is rapid, well developed and seems to appear toward the end of the Chalcolithic period. What role did the development of this new pyro-technological system based on the production of metal have in the Chalcolithic societies of the southern Levant? Recently, J. Golden (2005) presented a synthetic view of the birth of metallurgy in the southern Levant. Table 2 highlights the organization of metal working in the late 5th–4th millennia based on the analysis of the parameters of craft production.

One of the most salient features of metal production during this formative period is the fact that evidence for the detritus of metalworking activities is limited to only one Chalcolithic settlement system for the entire region (Levy and Shalev 1989). This focuses on the Wadi Beersheva in Israel's northern Negev desert, some 150 km from the nearest copper ore sources in the Faynan district of southern Jordan (Hauptmann 2000). Alternative Chalcolithic ore sources were probably located around Timna (Rothenberg 1990: Figure 2). Chalcolithic metal production was characterized by two broad production systems: one based on the smelting of malachite ores and casting of the metal into 'utilitarian tools' such as axes, chisels, and awls; and another system which utilized alloyed

Table 1. Deep-time study of cultural evolution through the lens of copper ore procurement, metal production and social interaction—the Jabal Hamrat Fidan Project, Jordan.

Period	Dates	JHF	Timna	Social change in the southern Levant
PPNB	c. 7500–6000 BC	x	-	Settled villages
PN/Chalcolithic	c. 6000–4500 BC	x	-	Autonomous villages
Chalcolithic	c. 4500–3600 BC	x	?	Rise of 1st Chiefdoms
Early Bronze IA	c. 3600–3300 BC	x	-	General social collapse
Early Bronze IB	c. 3300–3000 BC	-	-	1st Egyptian Colonies in Palestine
Early Bronze II	c. 3000–2700 BC	x	-	1st Urban, Fortified Towns
Early Bronze III	c. 2700–2200 BC	x	x	Expansion, Consolidation of Urbanism
Early Bronze IV	c. 2200–1950? BC	x	x	General social collapse
Middle Bronze IIA/B	c. 1950–1550 BC	-	-	Resurgence of Urbanism
Late Bronze I–IIB	c. 1550–1200 BC	-	x	Internationalism/Mediterranean LB 'Dark Age' Collapse
Iron Age IA/B	c. 1200–1000 BC	x	x	Small regional state formation
Iron Age IIA/C	c. 1000–586 BC	x	x	Consolidation of small regional states, imperial intervention in the southern Levant

Table 2. The organization of Chalcolithic (c. 4500–3500 BC) metallurgy craft specialization: Shiqmim and Beersheva Valley

Parameters of Production

Social context (degree of elite sponsorship)

- Workshops found in association with corporate buildings in village centers perhaps linked to leading 'chiefly' lineages/attached production. Metalworking occurred in 'secrecy' of corporate courtyards.

Concentration (how specialists are distributed across landscape)

- Metalworking occurred away from copper ore source area.
- Beersheva valley settlements possessed 'monopoly' on production.

Scale (number of individuals in a production unit and principles of labor recruitment)

- Relatively small number of craftspeople; residence pattern unknown, however, cemetery excavations reveal possible presence of metalworkers.

Intensity (amount of time producers spend on their craft)

- Small quantities of slag, density of production debris imply periodic production.

Figure 3.2 Early copper mines at Timna, Israel, thought to date to the Chalcolithic period (Rothenberg 1990).

Figure 3.3 Early Bronze 1a (c. 3600–3300 BCE) metal production village at Wadi Fidan 4, Jordan. Aerial photo by T. E. Levy (UCSD Levantine Archaeology Laboratory).

metal (arsenic, etc.) to produce 'prestige metal work' including mace heads, crowns, scepters and other decorative objects (Bar Adon 1980). To date, evidence of metal working in the Beersheva valley has been exclusively linked to the production of 'utilitarian tools' made from Faynan ores (Golden *et al.* 2001). It is ironic that in the copper ore rich Faynan district, which is the source area for most of the copper used in the Beersheva settlement system, there is a virtual absence of Chalcolithic sites. This observation has been confirmed by a number of intensive surveys in the Faynan district (Barker *et al.* 1997; Levy *et al.* 1999). This has led us to suggest the Chalcolithic inhabitants of the Beersheva valley essentially had a monopoly on metal production in the southern Levant at this time (Levy 1998).

The rapid appearance and control of the new metal technology by the Chalcolithic chiefdom in the Beersheva valley worked mostly as part of an elaborate gift giving system (Mauss 1954), effectively helping to create what Gosden (1989) has called 'debt-based societies'. By circulating prestigious metal objects (both 'utilitarian' and 'prestige' metalwork), elites in the Chalcolithic chiefdom solidified social ties, obligations and social debt. The knowledge needed to procure ore, transport it across the Arava and Negev deserts, smelt the ore, cast it into useful objects and finish the work seems to have been a carefully guarded secret. No doubt there was a great deal of magic or ritual involved in formative metalworking (Eliade 1978) as evidence of actual smelting and casting activities has been found only in the confines of the settlement sites in the Beersheva valley. Based on the excavations at the Shiqmim settlement center (Levy *et al.* 1991), metalworking is closely associated with large corporate buildings which all contain evidence of prestige metalwork foundation deposits or offerings. Thus, Chalcolithic metal production seems to have been controlled by elite individuals or, possibly, elite lineages that resided in the large settlement sites.

The collapse of the Beersheva Chalcolithic chiefdom cannot be attributed to a single factor. Instead, it relates to a number of variables that worked together and these factors may only be applicable to the Beersheva system discussed here. To date, there are four main factors that may have caused this once vibrant system to implode. These include: 1) climatic factors and a possible drying out of the environment that promoted the erosion of rich valley bottom soils (Goldberg and Rosen 1987); 2) Warfare between other Chalcolithic polities and, possibly, with growing Pre-dynastic Egyptian military organizations (Levy 1998); 3) commercialization and Pre-dynastic Egypt's usurpation of Chalcolithic trade networks; and, finally, the attenuation of the socio-political system that was rich in symbols, concerned with territoriality, and engaged in the procurement of copper and other preciosities for the local Chalcolithic elites (Joffe 1991). The Beersheva metal monopoly, like the digital divide today, must have fostered animosity with other contemporary societies. When the valley was finally abandoned, there was a fundamental reorganization of the metal industry in the southern Levant.

Figure 3.4 Distribution of copper related artifacts at Wadi Fidan 4, Jordan.

The Reorganization of Levantine Metal Production during the EBIA (c. 3600–3300 BC).

With the abandonment of the major Chalcolithic settlement systems in the Golan, Jezreel valley, lower Jordan valley, Beersheva valley and other northern Negev wadis, and other regions, during the following EBIA period, there was a marked decrease in social complexity and period of social reorganization that is reflected in metal production (Table 3). In most parts of western Palestine, the well-planned rectilinear architectural lay-outs that characterized so many villages, were abandoned for more ephemeral settlements which reverted to autonomous village sites with small pit houses or cave occupations (Joffe 1991). Most of the achievements of the previous Chalcolithic period lapsed into oblivion. While prestige metalwork disappeared in the EBIA, there was actually an increase in the scale of 'utilitarian metalwork' associated with the new aspects of production (see Table 2). Perhaps the greatest changes were associated with ore procurement strategies in the copper ore resource zones. Recent excavations in the Jabal Hamrat Fidan (JHF), the 'Gateway' to the Faynan copper ore district in southern Jordan, provide the most conclusive evidence for the fundamental change in the organization of metal production during this period of reorganization (Levy *et al.* 2001). Whereas during the proceeding Chalcolithic period the distant Beersheva valley chiefdom controlled the production and, presumably, exploitation of copper ore and metal production, during the following EBIA, for the first time, local residents took control of the ore extraction and metal production in the Faynan copper ore district. Intensive surveys in the Faynan district have failed to identify any 'normative' Chalcolithic site with affinities to the copper producing Beersheva valley sites. Instead, in a survey along the Wadi Fidan in the JHF, the only Chalcolithic site found in the area (Site WFD 51) dates to the earliest phases of the Chalcolithic period (Levy *et al.* 2001) with no temporal or cultural links to the Beersheva complex.

However, in the following EBIA period, while Palestine was experiencing a major period of social collapse (Table 1), the social dimensions of metal production underwent a major transformation in that, for the first time, the local population in the Faynan district took control of the extraction, processing and production of metal. This has been evidenced through the excavations at the site of Wadi Fidan 4 most recently by Levy and Adams (Adams and Genz 1995; Levy, Adams and Najjar 1999: Figures 3 and 4). In an extensive open-air excavation, evidence was found for (Table 3): a) workshop found in separate courtyard/building complex near domestic household structures suggesting that production was attached to on-site residents; b) first time metal production occurs in resource zone; regional survey indicates WF4 primary site, surrounded by other regional hamlets, and metallurgy within the contexts of the village environment; c) in terms of scale, the centrality of metalworking activities on-site may indicate village industry (van der Leeuw and McGlade 1997) where recruitment was possibly based on village membership, and d) a relative increase in production debris, especially crucibles, implying longer term and larger quantities of metal production than the previous Chalcolithic period.

In Castellian and peer-polity interaction terms (cf. Renfrew 1986), we can assume that the existence of the 'copper production divide' or monopoly on production during the Chalcolithic period, when one culture (Beersheva valley) controlled metal technology which probably led to tension with the excluded mass of contemporary cultures. When the Chalcolithic production system collapsed (for whatever reasons—see above), during the following short period of time associated with the reorganization of societies in the EBIA, the local population in the Faynan district quickly took charge of local production. By rapidly restructuring themselves, the local EBIA population in

Table 3. The organization of Early Bronze IA (c. 3600–3300 BC) metallurgy craft specialization: Wadi Fidan 4

Parameters of Production

Social Context (degree of elite sponsorship)

- Workshop found in separate courtyard/building complex near domestic household structures = Production attached to on-site residents.

Concentration (how specialists are distributed across landscape)

- First time metal production occurs in resource zone; regional survey> WF 4 primary, highly specialized site for smelting and casting metal with some nearby hamlets production agricultural products.

Scale (number of individuals in a production unit and principles of labor recruitment)

- Centrality of metal-working activities on-site may indicate village industry. Recruitment possibly based on village membership.

Intensity (amount of time producers spend on their craft)

- Relative increase in production debris, especially crucibles, implies longer term and more hours.

Faynan was able to build a well-planned village at WFD 4 that had more elements of complexity than most contemporary settlements in Palestine that previously had dominated the social landscape of the southern Levant. Thus, a society that had previously been excluded from access to a dynamic new technology, suddenly gained control and dominance of it.

Conclusion

Castell's work is rooted in a materialist analysis for explaining what he has identified as the 'information technology revolution'. Seen in neo-evolutionary terms, this could be viewed as the present apex of human abilities to harness technology. While technology should not be seen as a 'prime mover' in promoting social change, the deep-time prehistory and history of technological revolutions (cf. Upper Paleolithic, Neolithic Revolution, Secondary Products Revolution, Fiber Revolution, Urban Revolution, Industrial Revolutions and the IT Revolution) should be seen as important processual forces working with other dimensions of culture to promote change and social reorganization. Adams (Adams 1997) is cautiously hopeful that—'technology is overwhelmingly "a reservoir of underutilized promises rather than threats".' This, however, is a western perspective. As we currently see with the disaffected groups identified in Castells trilogy—the Islamists, US militias, and other groups—rapid technological change is precisely a threat to those who feel disenfranchised from it. Given the opportunity, as seen in the late 5th–4th millennium Levantine example discussed here, the excluded will consistently work for change or at least take advantage of weakness when a previously vibrant, technologically centered, society flounders

While technology is not a prime-mover of social change, it does have a momentum of its own. As Adams points out (1997:950) 'over the very long run it has tended to prove unique among human cultural achievements in being cumulative and irreversible'. Advances have not been constant or continuous, but are rather characterized by a series of punctuated changes. What separates the IT revolution from its prehistoric and historic predecessors is that technological improvements are now consistent and almost continuous.

References

Adams, R. B. and Genz, H. (1995) Excavations at Wadi Fidan 4: a copper village complex in the copper ore district of Feinan, southern Jordan. *Palestine Exploration Quarterly* 127: 8–20.

Adams, R. (1996) *Paths of Fire: An Anthropologist's Inquiry into Western Technology*. Princeton, NJ: Princeton University Press.

Adams, R. (1997) Social contexts of technology. *Social Research* 64(3):947–64.

Ambrose, S. (2001) Paleolithic technology and human evolution. *Science* 291: 1748–53.

Baines, J. and Yoffee, N. (1998) Order, legitimacy, and wealth in Ancient Egypt and Mesopotamia. In *Archaic States*, edited by G. M. Feinman and J. Marcus. Santa Fe, NM: School of American Research, pp. 199–260.

Bar Adon, P. (1980) *The Cave of the Treasure*. Jerusalem: Israel Exploration Society.

Barker, G., Creighton, O., Gilbertson, D., Hunt, C., Mattingly, C., McLaren, S. and Thomas, D. (1997) The Wadi Faynan Project, southern Jordan: a preliminary report on geomorphology and landscape archaeology. *Levant* XXIX:19–40.

Binford, L. (1983) *In Pursuit of the Past: Decoding the Archaeological Record.* New York: Thames and Hudson.

Bintliff, J. (ed.) (1999) *Structure and Contingency: Evolutionary Processes in Life and Human Society*. London: Leicester University Press.

Braudel, F. (1974) *Capitalism and Material Culture, 1400–1800*. New York: Harper and Row.

Brooks, H. (1994) The relationship between science and technology. *Research Policy* 23: 477–86.

Bulliet, R. (1975) *The Camel and the Wheel*. Cambridge, MA: Harvard University Press.

Bulliet, R. (1994) Determinism and pre-industrial technology. In *Does Technology Drive History? The Dilemma of Technological Determination*, edited by M. R. Smith and L. Marx. Cambridge, MA: The MIT Press, pp. 201–15.

Castells, M. (2000a) *The Rise of the Network Society: The Information Age: Economy, Society and Culture* 1. 3 vols. 2 edn. Malden, MA: Blackwell Publishers.

Castells, M. (2000b) *The Power of Identity: The Information Age: Economy, Society and Culture* 2. 3 vols. 2 edn. Malden, MA: Blackwell Publishers.

Castells, M. (2000c) *End of Millennium: The Information Age: Economy, Society and Culture* 3. 3 vols. 2 edn. Malden, MA: Blackwell Publishers.

Champion, T. C. (ed.) (1989) *Centre and Periphery: Comparative Studies in Archaeology*. London: Unwin Hyman.

Childe, V.G. (1936) *Man Makes Himself*. London: Watts.

Costin, C. (1991) Craft specialization: issues in defining, documenting, and explaining the organization of production. *Archaeological Method and Theory* 3:1–56.

Elena, S. and Lenski, V. (1996) Punctuated evolution caused by selection of rare beneficial mutations. *Science* 272:1802–04.

Eliade, M. (1978) *The Forge and the Crucible: The Origins and Structures of Alchemy*. Chicago: University of Chicago Press.

Goldberg, P. and Rosen, A. (1987) Early Holocene Paleoenvironments of Israel. In *Shiqmim I*, edited by T. E. Levy. BAR International Series 356. Oxford: British Archaeological Reports, pp. 22–33.

Golden, J. (2005) *Dawn of the Metal Age*. London: Equinox.

Golden, J., Levy, T. and Hauptmann, A. (2001) Recent discoveries concerning Chalcolithic metallurgy at Shiqmim, Israel. *Journal of Archaeological Science* 28:1–13.

Gomory, R. (1983) Technological development. *Science* 220:576–80.

Gosden, C. (1989) Debt, production and prehistory. *Journal of Anthropological Archaeology* 8:355–87.

Gould, S. (1999) Introduction: the scales of contingency and punctuation in history. In *Structure and Contingency: Evolutionary Processes in Life and Human Society*, edited by J. Bintliff. London: Leicester University Press, pp. ix–xxii.

Gould, S. and Eldredge, N. (1977) Punctuated equilibria: the tempo and mode of evolution reconsidered. *Paleobiology* 3:233–37.

Gould, S. and Eldredge, N. (1993) Punctuated equilibrium comes of age. *Nature* 366:223–7.

Hauptmann, A. (2000) *Zur frühen Metallurgie des Kupfers in Fenan*. Der Anschnitt Beiheft 11. Bochum.

Hauptmann, A., Begemann, F., Heitkemper, G., Pernicka, E. and Schmitt-Strecker, S. (1992) Early copper produced at Feinan, Wadi Araba, Jordan: the composition of ores and copper. *Archeomaterials* 6(1):1–33.

Holladay, J. (1998) The Kingdoms of Israel and Judah: political and economic centralization in the Iron IIA–B (c. 1000–750 BCE). In *The Archaeology of Society in the Holy Land*, edited by T. E. Levy. London: Leicester University Press, pp. 368–98.

Joffe, A. (1991) *Settlement and Society in Early Bronze I and II in the Southern Levant: Complementarity and Contradiction in a Small-Scale Complex Society*. Monographs in Mediterranean Archaeology. Sheffield: Sheffield Academic Press.

Johnson, A. and Earle, T. (1987) *The Evolution of Human Societies: From Foraging Group to Agrarian State*. Stanford: Stanford University Press.

Kranzberg, M. and C. Pursell (eds) (1967) *Technology in Western Civilization*. New York: Oxford University Press.

Levy, T. (1983) The emergence of specialized pastoralism in the southern Levant. *World Archaeology* 15:15–36.

Levy, T. (1986) Archaeological sources for the history of Palestine: the Chalcolithic period. *Biblical Archaeologist* 49:83–108.

Levy, T. (ed.) (1998) *The Archaeology of Society in the Holy Land*. 2nd edn. London: Leicester University Press.

Levy, T. (1998) Cult, metallurgy and rank societies: Chalcolithic period (c. 4500–3500 BCE). In *The Archaeology of Society in the Holy Land*, edited by T. E. Levy. London: Leicester University Press, pp. 226–44.

Levy, T., Adams, R. and Najjar, M. (1999) Early metallurgy and social evolution: Jabal Hamrat Fidan. *ACOR Newsletter* 11(1):1–3.

Levy, T., Adams, R., Witten, A., Anderson, J., Arbel, Y., Kuah, S., Moreno, J., Lo, A. and Waggoner, M. (2001) Early metallurgy, interaction, and social change: The Jabal Hamrat Fidan (Jordan) Research Design and 1998 Archaeological Survey: Preliminary Report. *Annual of the Department of Antiquities of Jordan* 45:1–31.
Levy, T. (ed.)(2005) *Archaeology, Anthropology and Cult: The Sanctuary at Gilat (Israel).* London: Equinox.
Levy, T, Alon, D., Grigson, C., Holl, A., Goldberg, P., Rowan, Y. and Smith, P. (1991) Subterranean Negev settlements. *Research and Exploration* (Nov.).
Levy, T. and Shalev, S. (1989) Prehistoric metalworking in the southern Levant: archaeometallurgy and social perspectives. *World Archaeology* 20:353–72.
Marx, L. (1992) Letter to the editor. *Technology and Culture* 33:407.
Marx, L. (1997) Technology: the emergence of a hazardous concept. *Social Research* 64(3):965–88.
Mauss, M. (1954) *The Gift: Forms and Functions of Exchange in Archaic Society.* London: Routledge.
McCorriston, J. (1997) The Fiber Revolution: textile extensification, alienation, and social stratification in ancient Mesopotamia. *Current Anthropology* 38(4):517–48.
Mokyr, J. (1990) *The Lever of Riches: Technological Creativity and Economic Progress.* New York: Oxford University Press.
Prothero, D. R. (1992) Punctuated equilibrium at twenty: a paleontological perspective. *Skeptic* 1:38–47.
Renfrew, C. and Bahn P. (2000) *Archaeology: Theories, Methods, and Practice.* 3rd edn. New York: Thames & Hudson.
Rothenberg, B. (ed.) (1990) *The Ancient Metallurgy of Copper: Archaeology-Experiment-Theory.* London: Institute of Archaeology, University College, London.
Sherratt, A. G. (1981) Plough and pastoralism: aspects of the secondary products revolution. In *Patterns of the Past: Studies in Honour of David Clarke*, edited by I. Hodder, G. Isaac and N. Hammond. Cambridge: Cambridge University Press, pp. 261–305.
Sherratt, A. G. (1997a) Comment on McCorriston: the fiber revolution. *Current Anthropology* 38(4):539.
Sherratt, A. G. (1997b) *Economy and Society in Prehistoric Europe: Changing Perspectives.* Princeton, NJ: Princeton University Press.
Smith, M. R. and Marx, L. (eds) (1994) *Does Technology Drive History? The Dilemma of Technological Determinism.* Cambridge, MA: The MIT Press.
Trigger, B. G. (1992) *A History of Archaeological Thought.* Cambridge: Cambridge University Press.
van der Leeuw, S. and McGlade, J. (eds) (1997) *Time, Process, and Structured Transformation in Archaeology.* London: Routledge.
Wallerstein, I. (1974) *The Modern World System I.* San Diego: Academic Press.
White, L. A. (1949) *The Science of Culture.* New York: Farrar and Straus.
Wright, H. T. (1998) Uruk states in southwestern Iran. In *Archaic States*, edited by G. Feinman and J. Marcus. Santa Fe: School of American Research.

Emerging State Connectivity: Dynamic Urban and Economic Growth in Fourth and Third Millenium BCE West Syrian Societies

William Collins

Introduction

Exchange of goods among settlements of the ancient Near East has been a long-term historical process since the Neolithic era. By the Ubaid and Uruk periods the exchange evolved into systems of trade including a complexity of products which reached a multiplicity of urban centers. For the first time settlement systems could be seen to be linked in networks of interaction spheres and trade systems. These networks evolved and devolved with the rise and ebb of political dynasties in Sumeria, Babylonia and upper Mesopotamia. Work by Algaze (1989, 1993) and others has brought special attention to the idea of long-distance trade linking these networks as a world system. Their view classifies the elements of these networks as parts of a core population interacting with, and in some sense, economically manipulating a resource rich periphery.

The relationships between 4th millennium population centers and the networks integrating them are an excellent example of Castells' (1996) dialectic between the leveling effects of networks and the resistant inertia of human identity with locality. The progressively increasing connection of places through the mechanisms of trade advanced the complexity and interaction of places over greater distances and through time. These successive iterations of connectivity evoked the earliest forms of long-distance economic integration. I define 'connectivity' as a measure of social and economic interaction. A place may have vertical connectivity with smaller urban places, which exhibit fewer social and economic functions or with larger places which have a wider range of functions. Also, that place may have horizontal connections with places of equal rank.

But an understanding of this evolving system of linkages, their increasing complexity and the effects on place identity (viewed as changes in place functionality) has been strongly biased in the literature. Most of the work on 4th millennium trade systems has been on the Uruk network and has emphasized a narrow set of settlement sites, is strongly oriented to one principal river corridor and to the apparent settlement hierarchies found along that corridor. The immediacy of salvage archaeology operations along the upper Euphrates may have given rise to models of settlement systems, network interactions and site functional classifications that fall prey to the 'accident' of geographic biases. It may also have led to a 'far-sighted' view of interaction at a distance and between simplified views of singular poles of population demand and resource supply.

It is proposed here that trade connectivity in the 4th millennium BC was not a river corridor based system of outposts and enclaves nor an axial system connecting lower and upper Mesopotamia. Rather, it was a sectoral system of independent producing regions, each with its own internal economic functionality, yet economically interrelated with adjacent and distant centers. Upper Mesopotamia especially was an interconnected system with strong off-corridor elements and competing adjacent regions including, on the west, independent city-state sectors of western Syria.

Antecedents

Antecedents to Uruk contact in northern Mesopotamia, include at least two millennia of interchange with the Ubaid society. These interactions are not well studied, yet regionally interconnected networks did exist. Lupton (1996) has identified, in upper Mesopotamia, three clearly distinct and overlapping pre-Uruk interaction spheres defined by ceramic associations. Each represents a sectoral set of somewhat integrated settlements unified in some social, political or economic way, yet marked by a common ceramic repertoire. On the east, a region including the north Jazira, upper Tigris, upper Khabur and Keban valley defined one sphere showing parallels between stamped and impressed wares. Centrally, an interaction sphere included the upper Balikh (including Hammam et-Turkman), the central and western Khabur and parts of the upper Euphrates (including Arslantepe). This interaction sphere was characterized by shallow bowls, grooved rim, or carinated bowls. On the west, a region running from western Syria through the Karababa basin and to the Keban Valley defined a sphere characterized by Coba bowls and chaff-tempered bowls with beaded rims. Each of the three interaction spheres included crude flaring bowls which overlapped at Norsuntepe in the Keban Valley.

Oates (1993) also notes a very extensive region of interaction radiating from the Altinova plain to Tells Brak and Gawra in the southeast and clay sealings from the Altinova appearing in private houses. Later shared symbolism is discovered at Hassek Hoyuk to the south and al Kowm, below the Euphrates bend (Oates 1993:410–11).

What is distinctive about these regions is not only their distinctive ceramic traditions but also the variation in the hierarchical relationships of their settlement systems. The Keban Valley settlements in the Altinova demonstrated no obvious regional center. There seemed a high degree of place autonomy among the sites of Norsuntepe, Tepecik, Tulintepe, Korcuntepe and Degirmetepe. This would be an example of Castells' strong identity instrumentality in the maintenance of local social development identity. The valley was a common place of regional interaction yet comprised of independent polities.

The Karababa basin, by contrast, was dominated by the primate center at Samsat, a highly centralized settlement system, probably managed by a central authority. It is likely that strong connections with long-distance trade partners existed. This, then, would be an example of Castells' network instrumentality in the social order.

Uruk Contact

With initial Uruk contact it is presumed that agents of the Uruk society relocated to most of the larger populated settlements in the sectors of upper Mesopotamia. Increasing hierarchical settlements organization and increased connectivity would have resulted in the existing urban pattern. The work of Algaze (1993), Stein (1999) and others characterizes this 4th millennium contact as the establishment of colonies, enclaves and stations along the river courses of the eastern two regions in Lupton's scheme. It follows that the Uruk expansion then is an initial form of world economic system employing a string of settlement centers along the river corridors of upper Mesopotamia. This becomes an overly simplistic model of resource acquisition of a material rich and socially disconnected north by a socially complex core in the south. It ignores the reality of pre-Uruk contact relationships, the true complexity and identity of local sectors and their traditional interactions and of the economically connected settlement systems outside the corridors. Connectivity and independent contemporary economic activity may well have existed outside of the corridor model in Western Syria.

A Case for the Connectivity of Western Syria

Connectivity in Western Syria, it might be argued, was equal to that east of the Euphrates. In the late 1950s the Braidwoods discovered true Uruk pottery in the Amuq at the end of phase F and the beginning of phase G (Braidwood and Braidwood 1960). Red-slipped wares and beveled-rim bowls in those levels and at the sites of Catal Hoyuk, Alalakh and Tell Judeideh (Roaf 1996) indicate as much an Uruk presence in the western Syrian Amuq as in north Syrian sites where these markers appear. Among other probable indicators of Uruk period relationships, beveled-rim bowls were also found at Hama on the upper Orontes in western Syria, the most extreme southwestern point in Syria from Habuba Kabira-South. Also, finds of beveled-rim bowls at el-Kowm in the Syrian Desert at least 100 km south of Habuba Kabira and the Euphrates suggest a trade route linkage west from the Khabur-Euphrates confluence (Moorey 1990). A direct link west would bring a caravan out of the desert at Hama.

Habuba Kabira-South remains the least well-explained link in the Uruk chain of Euphrates settlement 'colonies'. Its function and source of support remain in question unless it is viewed as a critical link as a connection, and break-in-bulk station, to a westward sector of the regional network, that of western Syria. Its location was near the traditional western terminus, as was Emar later, for access to the Mediterranean. It is the nearest point to an overland connection with Aleppo and at that point to the Amuq Plain and a north-south route connecting Arslantepe, Aleppo, Afis, Ebla and Hama. Oates (1993) also considers this westward link to be the critical link in Mesopotamian connectivity to the Levant and Egypt.

Evidence of the Uruk culture at Buto (Tell el Faraìn) in the western Egyptian Delta has led Moorey (1987) to suggest a maritime and overland linkage with the Uruk through Syria. These have made it clear that material culture transmission was taking place during Naqada II in Egypt and the Late Uruk, a remarkable range for Urukian enterprise. Distinctive Uruk-type terracotta wall pegs found at Buto adds weight to the argument for the Mesopotamian influence on the monumental mudbrick architecture of Egypt and of connections between Mesopotamia and Egypt that facilitated this interchange. Additional finds at Buto include sherds identified from western Syrian Amuq F levels (von der Way 1987). At the west Syrian end of this linkage, Sürenhagen (1986) has identified rim fragments at Habuba Kabira-South that are similar to those found in graves in Egypt and Nubia. In the same levels ceramics were found which were attributed to the Late Chalcolithic Palestinian repertory, the first evidence for Egyptian imports into Syria and Mesopotamia at this time (Moorey 1990).

Beatrice Teissier, Helen Cantor and Holly Pitman have documented the motifs of Susa II as inspiration for alien decoration in Egyptian luxury objects. These were modeled from Uruk style seal cutting in Iran and Syro-Mesopotamia. The inspiration lingered into the third millennium in Egypt. Teissier argued a route of transmission across northern Mesopotamia and western Syria, then via the Lebanese coast to Egypt (Teissier 1987). She argues for linkages in the western network to Byblos. Other work with glyptic evidence indicates a possible connection between Byblos and Ugarit (Ras Shamra level IIIB) in the fourth millennium (De Contenson 1970). Kay Prag (1986) also argues for linkage between Byblos and Egypt during Naqada II and Naqada I periods. Moorey (1990) suggests a possible shipment connection from some as yet undiscovered port serving the Amuq plain (Moorey 1990:67).

Figure 4.1 View of Jazr Plain north from Tell Afis.

There is also evidence of Late Chalcolithic and Early Bronze urbanization and a connected settlement network along a north–south route between the Amuq and Hama. Excavations at Ebla, itself an 'accidental' discovery, show Late Chalcolithic settlement, but perhaps more impressive evidence has been revealed at Tell Afis, about 10 km to the north of Ebla (Mazzoni 1998). By the late 4th millennium the tell was fortified by a massive stone wall, implying some significant administrative and/or economic function in the region. Stamp and cylinder seals of local style were encountered in the earliest levels. The ceramic corpus has strong parallels with northern Syrian and eastern Anatolian Late Chalcolithic assemblages including chaff-faced ware. Also, diagnostic coarse, shallow, mass-produced Coba bowls were included in the assemblage. These are in the style and name attributed to the site of Coba Hoyuk in Anatolia (Mazzoni 1998:10–11). Most interestingly, the Late Chalcolithic ceramics included chaff-faced painted ware with simple patterns attributed to the Syrian Late Ubaid tradition. The pottery suggests that the Late Chalcolithic levels at Afis were correlated with Early, Middle and Late Uruk periods, though not likely influenced by them.

Many small import finds demonstrate links with bordering regions during the period. The remains of equids in the Late Chalcolithic at the site, implying local use of pack animals, suggest economic linkages from longer distances (Barbara Wilkens, personal communication).

Surveys conducted by the University of Pisa in 1993 and 1995 in the plain north of Afis (Figure 1) identified a uniform to random pattern of Late Chalcolithic settlements lying along that northern 25 km axis. The pattern includes at least seven tells of the period. The largest of these, Tell Nuwaz, lies at the natural junction linking the Jebel Barishi, the Jebel Sam'an, the Amuq plain and the lower course of the Orontes and 'Afrin rivers. It is possible that the growth of Afis depended on the control of the northern area, both for the exploitation of its natural and agricultural resources and access to the road network linking it to the copper and obsidian trade (Mazzoni 1998:13).

Fewer traces of occupation in the Early Bronze I did yield a cylinder seal, and cups and jars painted in Ninevite 5 styles. The site was reoccupied and flourished during the Early Bronze IV A and B (2400–2000 BC) after the destruction of Ebla. It clearly had an industrial function with evidence in a private residential unit of pottery and flint working installations and benches alongside hearths. Fragments of imported Egyptian alabaster bowls were recovered from the latter phases of the period (*ibid.* 15).

Mazzoni believes that the urban revolution took place simultaneously throughout the Fertile Crescent during the middle of the fourth millennium. This would have included local centralization, social stratification, specialization and unequal distribution of wealth derived from unequal control over local food and fiber resources. The process began with the Ubaid culture, facilitated by its interaction with different regional societies, rapid population increases (Mazzoni 1998) and the effects of reflexive long-distance trade.

At the beginning of the Uruk connections with upper Mesopotamia the Levant was already marked by a stable network of settlements linked by cross-cultural interactivity and structured by highly integrated polities. The occurrence of stamp and cylinder seals and massive fortifications are evidence of the emergence of local forms of urbanization, economic development and complex social organization. With the emergence of Ebla and its ability to expand an interaction sphere to include Afis, Aleppo Alalakh and other city-states, west Syria emerged as an independent political and economic region alongside similar regions to the east of the Euphrates. The wealth of the Syrian steppe was in its flocks, herds and grain production capacity. Wool became the basis of Ebla's prosperity in the third millennium (Oates 1993:413.).

Conclusion

In conclusion, trade connectivity in the 4th millennium and 3rd millennia BC, therefore, was neither a river corridor based system of outposts and enclaves nor an axial system connecting lower and upper Mesopotamia. Rather, it was a sectoral system of independent producing regions, each with its own internal economic functionality, yet economically interrelated with adjacent and distant centers. Upper Mesopotamia especially was an interconnected system with strong off-corridor elements and competing adjacent regions included, on the west, independent city-state sectors of western Syria.

Western Syria and the early rise of its centralized urban society lay at a strategic center of local exportable resources and at the geographic tangent and in some sense a hub, for interconnected trade patterns between upper Mesopotamia, south central Anatolia, the Amuq and the Levant. It was a participating region in the system of trade connectivity during the 4th and 3rd millennia BC as a part of emerging city-state economies of upper Mesopotamia.

The strength of sectoral evidence supports participation or local management of the economy and marshals against a model of Uruk domination or Uruk centrality to Mesopotamian trade. The plural state integration of the 4th and 3rd millennia fostered an expanding regional/global trading and politically interactive system. The rise of western Syrian trading centers was key in the formal integration of Mesopotamian with Levant, Egyptian and Mediterranean connections as historic centers of local production. Yet little is known of the role and connectivity dynamics of west Syrian states in the supra-regional network.

The west Syrian trade sector offers an opportunity to view economic connectivity differently from the core-periphery and corridor model. It may be viewed as a network stimulated by local opportunity rather than external exploitation. Rather than seen as a resource-rich region controlled for strategic purposes, the principal assumption may be one of the primacy of local commodity and craft production. The production and export of animal, food, fiber and crafts becomes the multiplier for development of local and regional economic and political success.

What is needed is further evidence of settlement hierarchies and economies from sites west of the great bend of the Euphrates. Evidence is necessary to link that regional system of economies to the larger Mesopotamian framework of trade systems during the 4th and 3rd millennia BC. Such an examination of a west Syrian interaction sphere and its international economic connectivity will be forthcoming.

References

Algaze, G. (1989) The Uruk expansion: cross cultural exchange as a factor in Early Mesopotamian civilization. *Current Anthropology* 30:571–608.

Algaze, G. (1993) *The Uruk World System: The Dynamics of Expansion of Early Mesopotamian Civilization.* Chicago: University of Chicago Press.

Braidwood, R. and Braidwood, L. (1960) *Excavations in the Plain of Antioch I: The Earlier Assemblages Phases A-J.* Oriental Institute Publication 61. Chicago: University of Chicago Press.

Castells, M. (1996) *The Rise of Network Society: The Information Age: Economy, Society and Culture*, 1. 3 vols. Cambridge, MA: Blackwell Publishers.

De Contenson, H. (1970) Sondage sur l'acropole de Ras Shamra. *Syria* 47:1–23.

Lupton, A. (1996) *Stability and Change: Socio-Political Development in North Mesopotamia and South-East Anatolia 4000-2700 B.C.* BAR International Series 627. Oxford: Hadrian Books.

Mazzoni, S. (1998) *The Italian Excavations of Tell Afis (Syria): From Chiefdom to an Aramaean State.* Pisa: University of Pisa, Edizioni ETS.

Moorey, P.R.S. (1987) On tracking cultural transfers in prehistory: the case of Egypt and Lower Mesopotamia in the Fourth Millennium B.C. In M.Rowlands *et al.* (eds), *Centre and Periphery in the Ancient World.* Cambridge: Cambridge University Press, pp. 36–46.

Moorey, P.R.S. (1990) From Gulf to delta in the fourth millennium BCE: the Syrian connection. *Eretz-Israel* 21:62–9.

Oates, J. (1993) Trade and power in the fifth and fourth millennium BC: new evidence from northern Mesopotamia. *World Archaeology* 24(3):403–22.

Prag, K. (1986) Byblos and Egypt in the fourth millennium BC. *Levant* 18:19–74.

Stein, G. (1999) *Rethinking World-Systems: Diasporas, Colonies and Interaction in Uruk Mesopotamia.* Tucson: University of Arizona Press.

Sürenhagen, D. (1986) The dry farming belt: the Uruk period and subsequent developments. In *The Origin of Cities in Dry-Farming Syria and Mesopotamia in the Third Millennium B.C.*, edited by H. Weiss. Guilford, Connecticut: Four Quarters Press, pp. 7–43.

Teissier, B. (1987) Glyptic evidence for a connection between Iran, Syro-Palestine and Egypt in the fourth and third millennia. *Iran* 25:27–53.

von der Way, T. (1987) Tell-el- Faraìn-Buto 2. Bericht. *Mitteilungen des Deutschen Archäologischen Instituts abt. Kairo* 43:241–50.

Trade Pulsations, Collapse and Reorientation in the Ancient World

William R. Thompson

Castells' vision of the 'space of flows' seems to have relevance only to societies whose citizens are connected through modern technology. Castells organizes his social theory of the space of flows on the basis of its material support. The first layer of support is exchange that is implemented by technology. Technology forms the material basis in this sense for the transmission of ideas, trends, ideologies and systems of ideologies between cultures and civilizations. The second layer of support is the network nodes and hubs. The third layer is the spatial organization of societal elites, that is, where the 'orders' are coming from. These three layers of support, however, were characteristic of ancient societies and civilizations that were closely connected to each other through trade. Thus, an ancient 'space of flows' can be posited in which the material basis for these exchanges consisted of trade goods, the 'network' nodes and hubs were ports and inland cities dependent upon early trade, and the social elites were the primary stimuli for the movement of goods, services and thoughts.

International political economies pulsate to a number of rhythms varying from the very long to the very short variety. We are all quite familiar with the shorter ones. It is the longer ones that remain contested. This analysis focuses on two hypothesized patterns of the longer stripe—one is about millennium-long movements toward and away from center concentration and center deconcentration, while the other addresses the implications of slightly shorter, periodic crises in the ancient world. The main questions are whether the hypothesized patterns appear to fit southwest Asian trade fluctuations in the ancient world, whether the two hypothesized patterns seem compatible, and whether they tell us anything about long-term systemic change. To address these questions, we also need an information base on which we can peg the evaluations. This database is constructed by creating a bird's eye narrative view of southwest Asian trade between the 8th and 2nd millennia BC. Who trades with whom, when, and where do they trade, and at what level? Such a narrative can at best function as a very crude time series on which we can impose patterns of concentration, diffusion and crisis. As usual, the problem reduces to the typical social science problem: how well do the hypothesized patterns seem to fit the observed data?

How does this analysis fit within a volume concerned with Manuel Castells' (2000) ideas about post-industrial transformations? In a long prologue to his first volume, focused on the contemporary rise of a network society in response to radical technological change, Castells argues that the advent and diffusion of information technology will produce changes as sweeping as the advent of industrialization. He also contends that governments are critical to this process of change—both as accelerants and blocking forces. This second argument is illustrated initially by reference to Chinese history and what he describes as a near-industrialization in the 1400s that was thwarted by conservative bureaucratic forces.

There is certainly no problem with suggesting that paradigmatic shifts follow (or can follow) radical technological change. This is a perspective that should be more central to the deciphering of

Figure 5.1 Chinese emperor's tomb at Xian.

collective behavior than it is.[1] But there are two other problems with Castells' approach. One is that by starting with contemporary changes, there is a 'presentism' tendency to compress history into a narrow straitjacket. Thus, Castells implies that the past can be viewed as a pre-industrial, industrial and post-industrial sequence even though he recognizes that there was more than one wave of technological change within the industrial era. The problem here is one of matching sources of change with the outcomes. If one sees just two basic transformations in the past (industrialization and post-industrialization), there is some likelihood that any consequent analysis will reflect this presumption by embellishing the extent of transformation. If, on the other hand, one imagines multiple waves of technological change in which the current information age represents a fifth industrial transformation that was itself preceded by a number of commercial-political-economic transformations that can be traced back to prehistorical times, contemporary changes may be seen as radical in nature but somewhat less than unprecedented. This chapter will examine some transformations and paradigmatic changes that took place thousands of years before the present as part of a longer-term investigation of the history of globalization—a developmental process that has been ongoing for millennia.

One hypothesis on the arrested development of China is an inward turn taken in the 15th century AD prompted by bureaucratic conservatism and the fear of uncontrolled societal change. Still another, however, is that Sung China did experience something approximating the first contemporary industrialization transformation in the 12th and 13th centuries AD only to be overwhelmed and defeated by the Mongols. From this perspective, the 15th century inward turn reflected a Ming obsession with ensuring that a Mongol takeover could not recur.[2] The point here is not that governmental strategies play no role in accelerating or de-accelerating societal change—they certainly do—but only that we need to be careful in assessing the relative contribution of any actor. By looking at earlier times, the idea that epochal transformations tend to overwhelm everyone's strategies can be examined more neutrally.

Figure 5.2 Chinese emperor's tomb at Xian.

The Rhythm Problem(s)

Before reviewing the anticipated patterns to be tested in the ancient world, some interpretation problems may be avoided by specifying an embarrassingly long list of issues that will not be discussed. First, the Polanyi question of whether ancient economies operated on different principles than modern economies is of rather limited interest here. A second question with some cachet in the anthropological literature is whether one can fit world-system arguments about modern core-periphery relations to the ancient world. While I will proceed without hesitation to assume that the ancient world can be viewed as a world system (without the hyphen), the argument that cores become wealthy and stay that way only by exploiting peripheries that must remain underdeveloped is also not at explicit risk here.[3]

A related question is the one about whether we should spend time tracking the flow of luxury commodities for elite consumption when some analysts have argued strongly that it is only the flow of basic commodities that lead to mass consumption that have the potential of shaping political-economic relationships. This analysis will proceed on the assumption that restrictions against analyzing elite luxury trade have been put to rest. Fourth, an even more interesting question is the pattern of economic expansion and contraction. Was the ancient world characterized by regular long waves of prosperity and depression along lines not dissimilar to the modern world (Frank 1993; Gills and Frank 1993)? Regrettably, considerations of space suggest that this is a project that should be postponed to a future venue. Any attempt to look simultaneously at all possible rhythms might easily become bogged down with too many tangents to pursue efficaciously.

A fifth evasion pertains to the question of precisely which units belonged to this first world or international system, and when they did so. This question probably should not be evaded but it is more complex than it seems and space simply does not permit its exploration. Suffice it to say that the panoramic view of southwest Asian trade patterns has been conducted without any preconceived boundaries. The picture that emerges is quite suggestive about who is in and who is not in the system. It is also a picture that does not correlate closely to some others suggested, in comparison, seem either too narrowly defined and/or slow to acknowledge the existence of substantial interdependencies.[4] But this topic, like most of the others that are being ducked, deserves separate treatment.

Sixth, no attempt will be made here to answer questions of ancient world fact that have so far gone unanswered or unexplored. I do not know to what extent domestic problems in southern Mesopotamia at the end of the 4th millennia were responsible for the retrenchment of the Urukian trading network. I do not know whether Mesopotamian/ Elamite traders first approached Upper Egypt from a southern/ Red Sea approach. Nor do I know whether Indus traders first penetrated the Mesopotamian circuit or whether Mesopotamians (or Dilmunites) first co-opted Indus into a Persian Gulf trading circuit. I do not know where Ahhiyawa was.[5] These are questions that archaeologists and ancient historians have yet to resolve. Quite possibly, they will never be resolved. All I can hope to do is to take what appears to be known about ancient trade patterns and fluctuations and put this information to use in developing a hopefully coherent and consistent panorama of several millennia of ancient trade. That some effort is required to create this panoramic view should not be too surprising. Archaeological and historical professional practices do not encourage foci on long-term changes. Thus, we have a fair amount of information about trade in specific locales and at specific times. What is needed is an effort to weave a longer-term and wider scale tapestry of the various threads—without making too many gross errors of interpretation. Still, one cannot spin and weave thread at the same time. Moreover, some of the prevailing threads, no doubt, will prove to be invalid as more information is revealed by ongoing and future fieldwork. But the prospects of better information in the future should not caution against making the effort to utilize what we know (or think we know) now. We may not know all of the details but we do know enough about the basic contours of ancient international political economy to look for long-term patterns.

Finally, it should be acknowledged at the outset that any effort to put together a panoramic view of ancient southwest Asian trade interactions will inevitably cut some spatial corners. Assuming that southwest Asia was the central economy of the ancient world is one of them. Frank (1998:130) argues that world (economic) history can only be comprehended as a single global process studied everywhere at the same time simultaneously.

It is difficult to disagree with this dictum but it is something else to live up to it. In ancient times, there were numerous regional economies—some of which were poorly connected and also less interesting as foci for the gradual emergence of a planetary-wide world economy. The Near East constituted the first world economy and it is from this acorn that the oak of the contemporary world economy eventually evolved—or so it is assumed in this analysis. There is no denying that other people were involved in trade between 4,000 and 1,000 BC but their impact on subsequent developments seem less critical to long-term changes. Should someone demonstrate that this assumption is entirely misconceived, so much the better for our understanding of how things work and how they once worked.

But there is another dimension to the problem of studying everywhere simultaneously. We simply lack information on a variety of ancient connections. If Indus traders were linked to the Mesopotamian-centered circuit, how wide was the Indus acquisition network in its own right? Did it extend as far as Southeast Asia or East Africa as Tosi (1993) suggests? How far into Central Asia did the Harappans penetrate?[6] Then, too, there are certainly migration and diffusion relationships linking the Near East to the greater Black and Caspian Sea areas. Troy, or better, the different generations of Troy, was situated in an area that not coincidentally linked multiple trade routes presumably covering all points of the compass. Troy definitely impacted Anatolian political economy and therefore must have been at least an intermittent, fringe player in Near Eastern trade, even if only as an alternative option for obtaining desired commodities from Mesopotamian (or central Eurasian) sources. But there are limits to our current information base and one of them is that as you move away from the alleged Near Eastern center(s) of activity, the quality and quantity of information becomes less available. If faced with a choice of expending energy on capturing the main contours of what we think was the center of the action or sketching hypothetical possibilities on the full extent of the frontiers of the system, the current analysis will be biased towards the former. Once we have the main contours in sight, it may be more appropriate (and obvious) that those contours can be extended further in space at various times and places. But first we need to establish those main contours over a *longue durée*. We also need some conceptual abstractions to facilitate this contour establishment mission.

Production Concentration, Diffusion and Crisis

Modelski and Thompson (1996, 2002; Modelski 1999, 2000) suggest a periodization of world economy evolution that focuses on very long, alternating periods of concentration and deconcentration, as delineated in Table 1. Production concentration phases are periods in which new forms of economic productivity and growth are innovated. The number of innovators is not great and they earn political-economic centrality as one of the rewards for pioneering and consolidating new ways of doing things.[7] Trade diffusion phases are periods in which those new forms are diffused to adjacent areas, although not necessarily evenly. One of the expectations of the model is that trade volume is greater in a trade diffusion phase than in a production concentration phase. Thus, this model of systemic development is one predicated on a very long-term and specific type of leapfrogging. A focus on innovative production is followed by an emphasis on increased interaction and diffusion which, in turn, is followed by another period of production innovation and so on.[8] Each successive pair of phases should also be expected to encompass a wider scale of interaction as long as there is room for the system to grow.

Table 1. The production concentration-trade diffusion alternation pattern.

Iterations	Production	Trade
Ancient	3400–2350 BC	2350–1200 BC
Classical	1200–100 BC	100 BC–930 AD
Modern	930–1850	1850–

In Table 1, the principal foci of the ancient world were Sumer and Egypt, although these two centers were not equally salient at the same time. In the succeeding classical world, the general nuclei were China, India and a Near Eastern/Mediterranean complex. In the modern world, the nuclei encompassed a string of successive Eurasian innovative economies from Sung China in the 10th century AD through Genoa, Venice, Portugal, the Netherlands, and Britain.[9] In the 20th century, the United States was the latest in this modern line of innovators but the first one located outside of Eurasia. The explanation for this economic leapfrogging is overtly evolutionary. Periods of experimentation, some of which are successful, consolidate themselves and then spread through trade interaction and adaptation processes. Confronted with innovations, people may choose to ignore them or to adopt them without changes but it is more likely that they will adopt some with modifications while they reject others. New rounds of experimentation then take place in novel or altered settings, leading again to selective diffusion. None of this model is meant to suggest that diffusion is either the exclusive or even the principal process of change; rather, only that it is one of the principal processes of systemic change in which some experimentation is more successful, earlier and, therefore, more influential than the experimentation of others. In this fashion, world economic development spread from urbanization and agrarian innovations first in the Near East, to several key Eurasian regions, and then swung back from east to west before moving outside of Eurasia.

Granted, an emphasis on diffusion is not currently in vogue. Archaeologists and anthropologists are more comfortable emphasizing endogenous processes (Renfrew 1978, 1987).[10] But it is rather difficult to ignore Andrew Sherratt's (2000:132, fn. 7) take on this question:

> The Near East (western Asia) has successively given rise to: behaviorally modern humans (Upper Paleolithic), farming (Neolithic revolution), copper metallurgy, animal traction (secondary products revolution), the first cities (urban revolution), the first empires, the first maritime states, iron metallurgy, the first metropolitan cities, and three of the major world religions. Yet in spite of this, diffusionism has for the last half-century been vilified as an interpretative framework!

The point is that we should not be too quick to reject the existence of diffusion when it is so obviously present. Of course, it does not follow from this observation that everything diffuses, without modification, and in all directions. Ultimately, we need to develop ways to juggle exogenous and endogenous processes and influences simultaneously. But since other analyses have stressed endogeneity, a bias toward exogeneity in this paper is not out of place.

Modelski and Thompson (2001) examine some evidence in terms of population growth, urbanization spread patterns, and the timing of innovations in such areas as metallurgy, writing/languages, and Sherrat's (1997:155–248) secondary products revolution, as well as co-evolutionary developments in migrations and center-hinterland interactions, that pertain to this thesis. Arguably, the crude evidence examined is initially supportive of an alternating pattern in innovation and diffusion but the nature of the argument does not lend itself to a once-and-for-all, definitive test. Much more work remains to be done and one of the most obvious testing grounds is the evolution of trade patterns. While a full test of the model needs to encompass behavior over the five to six millennia between the 4th millennia BC and the 2nd millennium AD, generating appropriate trade information is a labor-intensive process. In this analysis, the test will be restricted primarily to the ancient world and the first two phases of production concentration and diffusion. The basic empirical question is whether a plausible case can be made for imposing the hypothesized, double-gaited rhythm on ancient world trade. Does there appear to be a phase of production concentration and consolidation that is followed by a phase stressing the diffusion of trade?

Yet reality, even ancient ones, are more complex than binary phases of consolidation and deconcentration suggest. Another model (Chernykh 1992) contends that a second pattern characterized the ancient and classical worlds in Eurasia. Focusing especially on structural changes in the production of metal tools and weapons beginning in the middle of the fourth millennium, Chernykh advances seven periods of crisis and transformation, shown in Table 2, in which societal and ecological changes generated periods of destabilizing migrations and turbulence. At the core of this argument is the assumption that socioeconomic and political structures were tied to metallurgical developments. Surpluses from metal trade monopolies financed temples and palaces and enabled chiefdoms to transform themselves into states from at least the 5th millennium onward. Moreover, trade itself was predicated to a considerable extent on the tendency for metallic ores to be located in one place, specialists in transforming the ores into metal products to reside elsewhere, and metal consumers to be spread quite widely. Trade networks were organized around bringing these three areas into contact with one another. Therefore, changes in metal extraction and working were fundamentally disruptive, leading to shifts in trading network orientations and the displacement of skilled metal workers and other people on an increasingly large scale.

Table 2. Chernykh's seven great migration crises.

Timing	Scope	Comments
3500–3000 BC, peaking in 3500–3200	Carpatho-Balkans to Iran and Afghanistan	First wave of Indo-European migrations around Black Sea area
2600–2400 BC (peak)	Throughout metal producing cultures	Aegean-west Asian Minor destruction; early Bronze Age towns in Syria and Palestine collapse; Old Kingdom crisis onset in Egypt
1800–1500 BC	Eastern Europe to China	Spread of tin-bronze; middle–late Bronze Age transition in Eurasian steppes; Kassites in Mesopotamia; Hyksos in Egypt; Harappan collapse in Indus; Hsia collapse and rise of Shang in China
1200–900 BC	Pan-Eurasian	Spread of iron; second wave of Indo-Aryan and Indo-Iranian migrations; Phrygians in Asia Minor; Sea Peoples in eastern Mediterranean
400–200 BC, peaking in 300–200	Pan-Eurasian	Celts moving east and Sarmatians moving west; Alexander the Great; warring States in China
300–700 AD	Pan-Eurasian	Successive waves of Huns and Turks from Pacific Ocean almost to Atlantic Ocean
1000–1300 AD, peaking 1200s	Pan-Eurasian	Crusades, in Near East; Mongol conquests from Indonesia to central Europe

Thompson (2002) has examined the impact of the shocks outlined in the Chernykh model in the ancient Near Eastern context. The evidence suggests that increasing hinterland attacks on urban areas, and the fall of political regimes (e.g. transitions from Old to Middle to New Kingdoms in Egypt and Uruk to Jemdat Nasr, Early Dynastic I–III, Akkadian, Ur III, Old Babylonian, and Kassites in Mesopotamia) coincided in time and space with at least three of the four ancient Chernykh crises, as delineated in Table 3.[11] Chernykh's 2600–2400 BC crisis does not appear to correspond very well to Near Eastern political conflict which becomes highly turbulent only toward the end of the 3rd millennium, and not in its middle. But if there is some degree of correspondence between the crises and political-economic unrest, one should also expect significant implications for trading systems. Periods of economic crisis and political disorder should be highly disruptive for trading networks, whether or not the trading network is biased toward metallurgical developments. Yet the succession of political regimes suggests that these disruptions need not be terminal or permanent. Trade should resume with the return of economic prosperity and political order—assuming these other processes do resume.

Since we know that trade must have resumed at some point after these periods of crisis, it would not pose a very interesting question to simply ask whether trading relationships of some sort were resurrected after a patch of bad times. A more interesting twist, however, is to ask whether trade resumed along the same lines as before. Or, were these crises opportunities, whether desired or not, for reorienting trade networks? We know that the ancient Near Eastern world first turned east (to Indus) and then west (to the Mediterranean) in seeking trade partners.[12] Were these reorientations geared (in timing) to the tendency for occasional system-wide crises as delineated by Chernykh (1992)? Did they contribute in some way to the production-diffusion pattern—assuming that support is first found for that pattern? Did serial crises contribute to the likelihood that production concentration would be followed by deconcentration, and vice versa?

From an evolutionary perspective, trading networks can be viewed as solutions for the problem of acquiring commodities not locally available. Other strategies are conceivable. Raiders can seize what they need by force (at least sometimes). The imposition of imperial hierarchy can establish a tribute process. Import substitution policies can be pursued. But trade is a rather old form of cooperative

Table 3. Systemic crises in the ancient world.

Systemic Crises	Mesopotamian Transitions	Mesopotamian Center-Hinterland Conflict	Egyptian Transitions	Egyptian Center-Hinterland Conflict
3500–3000	Uruk-Jemdat Nasr	Uruk retreat	unification	
2600–2400	Akkadian Takeover (2350)	Guti/Amorite pressure (2200–2000)	First Intermediate (2150–1980)	Libyan/Bedouin pressure
1800–1500	Old Babylon Kassite Takeover (1590s?)	Kassites	Second Intermediate/ Hyksos Takeover (1720–1550) New Kingdom	Hyksos
1200–900		Aramaean pressure (1000s on)	Third Intermediate Period (1070 on)	Sea Peoples/Libyan pressure (late 1200s–1100s on)

strategy for acquiring desired commodities that seems to have had appeal throughout historical times and in all parts of the world. Still, at the outset, there is no guarantee that an exploratory expedition will either find the goods that are being searched for or, if they are found, that some sort of exchange network can be established. Once such networks are established and they become more or less routinized, what happens when they collapse? A new round of experimental problem solving ensues to either reconstruct the old acquisition network or to develop a new one. In the sense of punctuated disequilibrium in biology, recurring crises in international political economy could thus serve as a vehicle for both consolidation and dispersal, but especially the latter.

The empirical question here then is whether deconcentration occurs and, if it does, does it occur in a smooth and gradual fashion or is it characterized by marked discontinuities in which the system switches from one type of trade orientation to another—all the while expanding the field of play as much as is feasible and shedding old connections that no longer work very well? If the latter pattern prevails, is it well correlated with the timing of the system-wide crises already found in center-hinterland conflict and regime transitions? If trade collapses and reorientations occur randomly or independently of other types of crisis, we will have found rather surprising evidence for substantial autonomy between internal and external structures and relations. Far more likely is that internal and external affairs were no more autonomous than in other (classical, modern) periods of time. We should anticipate that system-wide crises encompass trading relations as well as center-hinterland relations and political institutions. The real question is to what extent are trade collapses and reorientations dependent on system-wide crises in the ancient world? A high degree of dependence would mean that they only occur when other subsystems are also in crisis. If that is the case we will have found strong evidence for not treating economic, social, political, military and environmental problems as if they were somehow well insulated from one another. We will also have gained some new understanding of long-term historical changes and the role they have played in human affairs.[13]

The Ancient Southwest Asian Trade Configuration

To first recapitulate, the design of this analysis is to piece together a continuous narrative of ancient southwest Asian trade to serve as a crude time series. As far as I know such a narrative has rarely been attempted.[14] The more normal (and admittedly saner) approach is to bite off smaller chunks of time and space. But the types of questions that are being raised in this analysis do not permit a more specific focus on say Urukian expansion and retrenchment or Egyptian trade patterns before and after the Second Intermediate Period. We need several thousands of years worth of information and if it does not already exist, the only recourse is to first piece together in longitudinal fashion what appears to be known. One of the empirical questions to keep in mind in reading through the trade configuration narrative is whether there is some plausibility for a concentration/diffusion alternation roughly before and after the rise of the Akkadian empire in Mesopotamia and in the waning years of the Egyptian Old Kingdom. Given the nature of the data, this first exercise must be a fairly subjective undertaking. The second exercise is less subjective. Are substantial collapses and reorientations in trade highly correlated with four previously identified and sequential crises in the Near East that occurred toward the end of the 4th, and 2nd millennia, and in the middle of the 3rd and 2nd millennia, as Chernykh (1992) might suggest? Or, did they occur at other times, such as the end of the 3rd millennium, as Thompson (2002) argues in modifying the Chernykh crisis list for Near Eastern purposes?

Turning to the who, when, where trade narrative summarized in Table 4, an effort has been made to document as many descriptive generalizations as feasible.[15] This practice does not make it easier to follow the narrative, but it should help to bolster the interpretations being advanced. The fact that there are sources for these generalizations does not render them carved in stone in terms of their indisputable accuracy. However, the documentation will serve to distinguish an attempt to synthesize what is known as neutrally as possible from a new, idiosyncratic interpretation of what happened. Even so, sometimes one has to make choices between alternative interpretations that can be found in the historical and archaeological literature. If the available evidence seems to favor one interpretation over another, that interpretation became part of the narrative. Where the evidence is lacking or hard to evaluate, suitable hedging accompanies any descriptive generalizations that are advanced. Most important, the reader must keep in mind that this interpretation of ancient trading patterns is not based on an ample, well-substantiated information base. What evidence we have must usually first be reconstructed from slim and elusive clues. This admonition certainly applies to the period before historical documentation begins to become available (roughly before the 3rd millennium) when the clues are even more few and far between than after actual trade records begin to be preserved for posterity. But even after some historical records have survived, there remains a high degree of uncertainty in being able to make precise statements of fact.

Table 4. Reconstructing ancient southwest Asian trade.

8th–6th Millennia BC	
	A long-distance exchange network for tool-making obsidian linked eastern Anatolia and Mesopotamia (but not Egypt) in a limited, indirect, down-the-line, overland network through the 4th millennium (Culican 1966:11-12; Zarins 1989:342; Moorey 1994:12; Stein 1999:84–9).
Late 6th and 5th Millennia BC	
	Initially northern and southern Mesopotamia were not in direct contact but Halafian penetration from the north into the Zagros overlapped in timing with the expansion of Ubaid influence into northern Mesopotamia and southeast Anatolia (Marfoe 1987:28; Hole 1994:135; Lupton 1996:1). Ubaid long-distance networks linked southern Anatolia, the Zagros, northern Syria, Mesopotamia, the Arabian coast and may have reached to southern Syria, Palestine and Egypt. It remains unclear the extent to which the Ubaid network constituted a cohesive trade network, the diffusion of a cultural style, or both (Wright 1968:248, 252; Marfoe 1987:28; Porada *et al.* 1992:88; Oates 1993:408–9; Roafal and Galbraith 1994; Mark 1998:6-7 122–3; Stein 1999:84–5). Peaking roughly mid-5th millennium, there is a retraction in Ubaid influence

	that resembles the Urukian retrenchment at the end of the 4th millennium (Wright 1968; Oates 1993:410; Kuhrt 1995:22). A Palestinian network (4500–3300 BC) linked the Sinai, the Red Sea, southern Syria, Anatolia, and possibly Egypt (Mark 1998:8, 122–8). Egypt was obtaining material from northeast Africa via the Red Sea and possibly Nubia, Palestine and Syria (Zarins 1989:342; Kantor 1992:12; Mark 1998:12, 122–8).
4th Millenium BC	
	Urukian expansion began on a small scale in 2700 and increased toward 3100. Based on increased demand for raw materials in southern Mesopotamia, the acquisition network was composed of large settlements in the north where local population density was limited and trading enclaves situated along the principal, river-centered trade routes (Algaze 1993:46, 117; Hole 1994:136; Lupton 1996:41; Mark 1998:122–8; Stein 1999:91–2). By the middle of the millennium, the initially northern thrust was augmented by links from the eastern Mediterranean to the Gulf (Moorey 1994:6). Egyptian overland connections with Syria, Palestine, the Sinai and Nubia increased. Maritime links probably via Byblos connected Egypt to Anatolia and Mesopotamia. Sumerian influences in Egypt ended with the Urukian retrenchment and collapse of the Syrian colonies (Adams 1977:165–6; Trigger 1983:39; Marfoe 1987:26; Moorey 1987, 1994:235; Zarins 1989:368; Kantor 1992:3–4, 13–14; Stager 1992:41; Potts 1994:74; T. Potts 1994:161; Mark 1998:16, 19–20, 122–8, 130; Joffe 2000:116, 119.
Late 4th–Early 3rd Millennia BC	
	North-south Mesopotamian trade broke down around 3100 due to a combination of problems, including social disruptions in southern Mesopotamia, a trans-Caucasian influx from the east, and immigration into Syria by Semitic groups (Algaze 1986:289; Postgate 1986:96; Kelly-Buccelati 1990:122; Steinkiller 1993:115–16; Lupton 1996:72, 105). The Urukian contraction made space for local substitutes to continue some levels of overland trade flow (Chavalas 1992; Crawford 1992; Algaze 1995:96) even while Sumerian contacts were increasingly focused on Iran and Persian Gulf areas and Dilmun (Potts 1990:90–2, 1994:225; Moorey 1994: 245; Mark 1998:10, 12).
Mid-3rd Millennium BC	
	Exchange between southern Mesopotamia and the north may have become extensive again in the Early Dynastic I period, with cities in northeastern Syria operating as gateways and the southern cities competing for access to trade routes (Kelly-Buccelati 1990:123; Algaze 1993:107–8; Moorey 1994:8). By the second quarter of the 3rd millennium, Mesopotamian trade was increasingly coming from the east via south Asia, Dilmun and the Gulf, peaking between 2600 and 2230, and leading to the collapse of the overland network linking Central Asia, Afghanistan, Iran, Baluchistan and Indus around 2500 (Muhly 1969:593, 595–6; Dales 1976; Rattenagar 1981:208–9, 238–9; Frank 1993:392–3; T. Potts 1993:396; Potts 1994: 159, 281). Akkade attempted to reconstruct the Urukian expansion formula and managed to link the Gulf to southern Anatolia and the Levant, but encountered more resistance than earlier had been the case (Edens 1992:125–6; Algaze 1993:2–3, 108). Dilmun's entrepot functions between the Indus and Mesopotamia had been relocated away from the Arabian mainland to Bahrain by the 24th century (Potts 1990:182, 189). Central Asian raw materials began appearing in the Aegean via the Gulf route during the Akkadian period (Cline 1994:25). Cypriot trade mediation with the Asian mainland began in the last quarter of the 3rd millennium (Muhly 1968:84). Byblos appears to have provided Egypt with its principal Mediterranean connection before and after the trade interruptions associated with the First Intermediate Period (Culican 1966:19; Kantor 1992:21; Stager 1992:41; Butzer 1997:259; Watrous 1998:19). A Cretan connection was also established by 2600 (Warren 1995:12). Stronger maritime connections implied less overland trade via Palestine (Marfoe 1987:27; Stager 1992:41).

Late 3rd Millennium BC	
	Mesopotamian trade increased its reliance on Dilmun's Gulf middleman role, even though Indus merchants were established in Sumerian cities as trading agents (Muhly 1968:72; Porada *et al.*, 1992:78; Tosi 1993:369). Urban collapse was experienced throughout Central Asia between 2200 and 2000 (Kohl 1987a; Tossi 1993:373). In response to Akkadian attacks on Egypt's Syrian trade monopoly, Egypt appears to have attempted to hold on to its position in Palestine by force, leading to widespread urban destruction in Palestine, thereby further weakening the Egyptian regional economy (Kantor 1992:21; Butzer 1997:281–2). The Egyptian Delta was infiltrated by Bedouin in the First Intermediate Period, interfering with overland trade between Egypt and Palestine-Syria, but not maritime trade (Muhly 1969:617; Ward 1971:49). Minoan trade with the Levant and Egypt may have begun to expand after 2050 (Watrous 1998:20–1).
2nd Millennium BC	
	Overland routes into Mesopotamia had been reopened by the beginning of the millennium (Muhly 1969:603; Potts 1990:258; Algaze 1993:116). By the end of the millennium's first quarter, trade via the Gulf seems either to have come to a halt or declined substantially in volume, and roughly at the same time as the Indus collapse and a marked decline in Mesopotamian productivity (Muhly 1969:582, 585; Rattenagar 1981:235–7; Potts 1990:258; Edens 1992:130–2; Shaffer 1992:450; Moorey 1994:246). The subsequent Kassite control of trade moving through southern Mesopotamia is not well documented but they probably attempted to maintain the Old Babylonian flow of eastern goods into the Mediterranean economy (Leemans 1960:120–1, 136; Piesinger 1983; Potts 1990:298; Kuhrt 1995:340). Cretan-Syrian and Egyptian-Cretan contacts increased early in the millennium (Culican 1966:27; Muhly 1968:84; Kantor 1992:4: Klengl 1992:42; Cline 1994:32; Merrillees 1998:154; Watrous 1998:21). Egyptian-Aegean exchange, via Syrian entrepots, actually increased in the Second Intermediate Period, with Egyptian goods increasingly becoming the central focus of exchange in the eastern Mediterranean (Culican 1966:10; Redford 1992:130; Cline 1994; Knapp and Cherry 1994:128–34; Kuhrt 1995:180; Warren 1995:11). Cyrus became an increasingly important trading actor after 1700. Minoan Crete's role declined after the Mycenaean takeover of eastern Mediterranean trade routes without affecting the flourishing of trade in the 1400–1200 era. Egyptian relations with Nubia in the Middle Kingdom era stressed the protection of a Nile-based trading system, anchored by a string of fortified trading posts (Adams 1977:166). This approach moved into direct colonial enterprises focused on mineral extraction during the New Kingdom period. Adams (1977:232) compares the role of Nubian gold in financing Egyptian foreign policy in Asia as similar to the later role of Mexican silver in subsidizing Spanish wars in 16th century Europe.
Late Second Millennium BC	
	Kassite Mesopotamia fell to an Elamite invasion in 1155 (Zettler 1992). The Hittites and a number of Syrian trade entrepots were destroyed by Sea People attacks. Mycenaean and Minoan exports appeared to have ceased during this crisis period (Cline 1994:37). Piracy increased. Palace-originated trading ventures collapsed. In general, the political infrastructure making long-distance trade possible disintegreated (Liverani 1987:70; Muhly 1992:19; Sherratt and Sherratt 1993:363). Egyptian foreign contacts also contracted after the early 12th century to the 10th century before re-expanding (O'Connor 1983:254, 270; Weinstein 1998:188–9).

Data Evaluation

An even more abridged version of the ancient world trade panorama sketched above might read as follows. A southwest Asian trade network, focused on commodities such as obsidian and lapis lazuli was in place considerably prior to the emergence of urbanization and states. The early leaders in urbanization, the Sumerians, created in the 4th millennium an ambitious acquisition network for raw materials and luxury goods that were absent from southern Mesopotamia. The network encompassed Mesopotamia, Syria, parts of Iran and Anatolia, and Egypt until toward the end of the 4th millennium when this network was forced to retrench by new, less cooperative people moving into parts of the Sumerian resource acquisition area. Restricted access to desired commodities in the north and east encouraged an opening to Oman and Indus through the Gulf beginning in the late 4th/early 3rd millennia that became increasingly important through the end of the 3rd/early 2nd millennia, prior to the probably interrelated decay in Mesopotamian wealth and collapse of the Indus civilization.

The other growth node of the ancient world, Egypt, had also begun to develop its own acquisition networks into Nubia and Palestine in the 4th millennium, and also became linked to the Mesopotamian network in that same period.[16] While its maritime connection to Mesopotamia was broken towards the end of the 4th millennium, a now-unified Egypt continued to expand its contacts on land into Palestine until its Byblos maritime connection rendered the land caravans essentially non-competitive. Eventually, however, Akkadian coercive expansion temporarily severed the functioning of the Byblos connection toward the end of the 3rd millennium. Egypt's maritime connections to the Levant were restored in the 2nd millennium and Egypt's linkages, whether direct or indirect remains unclear, with Minoan Crete expanded significantly.

In the 2nd millennium, trading activity was particularly intense in the Levantine/Assyrian area as the central intermediaries linking a southwest Asian-eastern Mediterranean trade now connected to Cyprus and Crete with stronger than ever Egyptian participation. The Gulf area trade languished. The movements of hinterland peoples, imperial warfare, and natural disasters (e.g. earthquakes in Crete) influenced trade patterns somewhat, but did not stop trade volumes ascending to new heights in the last two centuries before the multiple catastrophes occurring around 1200 BC and the consequent collapse of trade networks in the ancient world. However, these trading networks soon re-emerged with new actors, a more pronounced western tilt (toward the western Mediterranean), and a wider playing field in the 1st millennium BC.

Both of these abridged overviews of ancient world trade leave much to be desired. We may sense when volume and levels of interaction increase and decrease, and in which direction these changes occur, but there are a number of restrictions on any attempt at capturing trade fluctuations with precision. Still, we do not require a fully specified, International Monetary Fund-style matrix of trade flows stated in some constant, current currency to be able to make some judgments about hypothesized general patterns in the timing of dispersal and on the impact and implication of serial crises.

The Production-Trade Hypothesis

The first hypothesis is that ancient southwest Asian trade can be divided into an early period of production concentration that is followed by a period of diffusion and increased trade. The expected temporal framework differentiates 3400–2350 BC (production concentration) from 2350–1200 (trade diffusion). More recent changes in dating the Uruk phenomenon suggest that we might push the 3400 date further back in time to 3800 or 4000.[17] None the less, a 3400–2350 interval captures the initial, most innovative periods of the two growth nodes in the ancient Near Eastern system: the Sumerian Uruk to Early Dynastic phases and the Unification to Old Kingdom era in Egyptian history.

These are the prime developmental periods of urbanization, writing, agrarian innovations such as plows and canal building, and pyramid building. It does not matter to the first hypothesis that the Sumerians became politically more fragmented while the Egyptians became more unified within a single state in this time period. What matters is the timing of their maximal innovations in production. Nor is the argument that no more innovations were to be developed after the end of the first production concentration period—only that subsequent innovations (in production but not in trade) should pale in significance to what was accomplished in the first period. Finally, the fact that Mesopotamians and Egyptians attempted periodically to repeat the achievements of their predecessors, thereby spawning intervals of concentrated political power and politico-economic-military expansion after 2350 should also not distract from support for the hypothesis. By and large, these subsequent efforts were imitative of the earliest periods, borrowing their symbols and strategies, and often relying on more coercive resources in attempts to achieve or re-achieve a form of consolidation.[18] In Mesopotamia, they were short-lived imitations in part due to a generally declining productivity base thanks at least in part to a heavy reliance on irrigation and subsequent soil salinity problems. They were longer lived in Egypt because the way in which the Nile functioned required less dependence on irrigation and, therefore, high agrarian productivity levels could be sustained—all other things being equal. The Egyptians were also less vulnerable to serious hinterland attacks than were the Mesopotamians.

But this we already knew. Can 2350–1200 BC be described as a period of diffusion? Indus joined the southwest Asian trade circuit prior to 2350 but its peak involvement appears to be captured by this period. So is its collapse by the 18th century. But if the Gulf trade declined after the mid-1700s, compensatory gains appear to have been made in the west with the development or redevelopment of Assyrian trade routes throughout Anatolia (albeit also relatively short-lived), the flourishing of trading entrepots in the Syrian-Levant area (Ugarit, Mari, Byblos, Ras Shamra), the apparent rise in Egyptian trade volumes, and the emergence of Crete, Cyprus and Mycenae as major participants in the Near Eastern trade circuit.

The coming-on-line of multiple new players seems to be a hallmark of this dispersal period. It is also precisely what one should expect in a period of diffusion or deconcentration. In comparison, the principal increase in trading activity in the production concentration period appears to be traceable largely to the growth poles of the ancient Near Eastern system, Mesopotamia and Egypt.

We can take this argument one step farther by tracking what might be called a 'trade yeast model' which can be discerned as being operative in both phases of production and diffusion, although perhaps more prominently in periods of diffusion. The metaphor of trade yeast is meant to imply that there are various local processes interacting to bring about development and greater organizational complexity. The added stimulus of trade with the outside world is not some sort of pixie dust that magically creates development where nothing was taking place before, but it does appear to be a very interesting additional stimulus, and possibly even an accelerating factor.

One of the reasons that we continue to debate about what drives socio-political development in prehistory and in the ancient world is that we do not have as much information as we would like to sort out developmental causalities. Hence, various scholars promote the effects of circumscription, warfare, technological change, hydraulic demands, population growth, and so forth. No solution to this analytical controversy will be advanced here. However, the panoramic view of ancient Near Eastern trade suggests an intriguing pattern. Not all, but a large number of the most important participants in this activity appear to have had their internal development stimulated by the demands or the attractions of external trade possibilities. The pattern would be much less intriguing if the observation was merely that trading states became wealthier and more complex as a consequence of participating in trade. But the argument goes beyond this truism. The pattern appears to be one of external trade playing some sort of role in stimulating or contributing to the very ability of a state or prestate formation to participate in trade. Various scholars have noted this sort of dynamic in the

Ubaid-Uruk sequence, the unification of the Egyptian state, the Proto-Elamites, the hazy emergence of the Indus complex, the Cretan Minoans, Old Assyria, possibly the Hittites, and trading states such as Mari. In addition, there are various sorts of knock-on and knock-down effects of trade reported in terms of development in Syria-Palestine (in each millennium between the 4th and the 1st), Central Eurasia, and the Iranian plateau, southeast Arabia and Nubia. If we push the analysis further into the 1st millennium BC, it is also difficult to overlook trade-driven activity on the part of the Phoenicians/Carthaginians and the Greeks and its impacts on the Mediterranean basin.[19]

One explanation for this recurring phenomena is suggested by Stein (1994b:40) based on Earle's (e.g. 1997) ideas on the political economy of prehistoric chiefdoms. He suggests that chiefs have two fundamental strategies for creating an economic base for developing and extending political power. One can extract some proportion of agrarian production to underwrite a political elite. One can utilize the redistribution of valued commodities as rewards for loyal followers. Or, ambitious chiefs can make use of both strategies. External trade enters this picture by introducing exotic or luxury items that can be useful for creating and reinforcing economic stratification and elite status. The control of trade, then, is a political prize of some value to developing political power, more complex political organizations, and, for that matter, more economic surplus.

But Stein also argues that the two basic strategies have different costs and benefits. Extracting economic surplus is both simple and direct but its scale is limited by storage, transportation and control costs. Increases in scale for the purposes of political expansion may well require sustained coercion. Redistributing prestige goods can be less costly and work more quickly but is also more vulnerable to boom and bust cycles, depending on the persistent availability of exchange possibilities.

Both strategies appear to have been important to the emergence of the two ancient growth poles, Sumer and Egypt. In the southern Mesopotamian case, Stein (1994b:39–40, 43) argues that there is little or no evidence of violence, fortifications, chiefs, exotic (i.e. non-local) goods, or interest in controlling trade until the very end of the 5th millennium, almost immediately before the emergence of the Urukian era.[20] The simultaneous development of these indicators and their timing hint that the origins of Uruk were stimulated to some extent by a newfound interest in long-distance trade control.

Maisels (1999:57, 63) disagrees about the early absence of evidence for Ubaid stratification but accepts the argument that trade was important for elite differentiation in southern Mesopotamia (on this score, see also Oates 1993:408). Thus, we lack suitable information at this time to be able to say anything more than that trade may have played some facilitative role in the initial emergence of Urukian Sumeria. After its emergence, there is virtually no disagreement that the Urukian expansion in the 4th millennium was predicated at least in part on developing a trade network for the acquisition of highland resources in Iran, Syria, Anatolia and beyond.[21]

If the origins of Uruk Mesopotamia remain hazy, the Egyptian case seems a bit more solid. The rival centers for political power in Upper Egypt (Naqada, Hierakonopolis, Abydos) were situated so as to control access to Eastern Desert raw materials—for instance, Naqada translates to The Golden Town (Trigger 1983:39), just as precocious Çatal Höyük may have had a monopoly on Anatolian obsidian several millennia earlier. Such situations could easily have enabled local chiefs to combine Stein's two basic strategies (surplus extraction and redistribution) to enhance their power. That this process may have been operating in several southern Egyptian sites adds an element of rivalry and competition between expanding chiefs hundreds of years before any Egyptian state emerged (Trigger 1983:40; Moorey 1987:41–2; Mayer 1992:230–1; Wilkinson 1996:89–90). If we also add the undisputed injection of Mesopotamian ideas, commodities and trade demands immediately prior to southern Egypt's expansion and perhaps earlier (Frankfort 1951:110; Mark 1998:21; Joffe 2000: 116, 119), and maybe as well a desire to eliminate Lower Egyptian interference in trade with the non-Egyptian world (Trigger 1983:49), control over trade routes has to be counted as a factor in the emergence of the Egyptian state. There is no need to argue that trade concerns were the primary driver if we conclude only that trade probably played a significant role in the emergence of the western growth pole.

The Urukian retrenchment towards the end of the 4th millennium created incentives for northeastern Syrian towns and to the east, the Proto-Elamites, to step in and create their own trade monopolies (Kelly-Buccellati 1990:123; Potts 1994:81; Algaze 1995:96). Refugees from the Urukian colonial settlements are credited with stimulating early Palestinian urbanization (Surenhagen 1986; Portugali and Gophna 1993; Maisels 1999). Rattenagar (1981:240) speculates that the emergence of the Harappan phenomenon was predicated on Indus chiefdoms exploiting the Mesopotamian demand for lapis lazuli after the Sumerians were cut off from their usual sources of supply. Just how much of a role Mesopotamian demand played is unknown and perhaps unknowable, but the Gulf linkage to Oman, Arabia and Mesopotamia must have played a contributing role to Indus political and economic expansion.[22] The Dilmun role as Gulf intermediary between Mesopotamia and Indus obviously was a trade-driven process, even though it may also have been structured by Akkadian military coercion (Edens 1992:132; Eiden and Hojilund 1993:446). Southeast Arabian development in the 3rd millennium was also strongly influenced by the demand for copper (Edens 1993:354). The increasing maritime traffic through the Gulf may have contributed to the decay of development in Central Eurasia, Afghanistan, and Turkmenistan (Dales 1976; Frank 1993:392–3 but see as well Kohl 1987a:18). Watrous (1998:20–1) suggests that the Minoans were drawn to the Near East in search of raw materials before they had begun to develop Cretan economic power. As the Gulf trade withered away, trade and power within Mesopotamia shifted north to Assur and Assyria (Muhly 1969:603). The Assyrian metals trade and tin monopoly with Anatolia was highly successful until the Assyrian traders were evicted by the Hittites whose power, in turn, may have been stimulated by Mesopotamian trade (Larsen 1987:55). Mari emerged as an important node on land and river trade routes and became the main supplier of tin to Crete (Kuhrt 1995:100–1). Extensive trade relations and an entrepot status appears to have been important in the metamorphosis of Cyprus from a set of poorly connected villages/economic backwater to a major power in the Eastern Mediterranean between 1700 and 1400 (Knapp 1988:151–2).

The above paragraph does not exhaust all of the examples of trade-affected development in ancient Southwest Asia but it hopefully makes the point that trade-stimulated growth and expansion (as well as destruction) was a continuous process in ancient international political economy. One could say that trade helped begat socioeconomic and political development and, in the process, more trading partners. The process was initially gradual and slow-paced but picked up speed midway through the 3rd and into the 2nd millennia. At the same time, and not coincidentally, processes of diffusion were supplanting production concentration processes. It would be difficult to pinpoint with any degree of precision exactly when in the 3rd millennium this transition took place but the date should be approximately mid-millennium. The date 2350 seems close enough as a working approximation.

The Crisis Reorientation Hypothesis

The second hypothesis assumes recurring system-wide crises involving environmental, center-hinterland, and regime survival problems. Were they also trading network crises? Were these crises used to reorient or reconfigure the shape of the Near Eastern trading network? Do these reorientations also contribute to the concentration-diffusion process in some way?

It stands to reason that system-wide crises should impact trading networks. If they did not, one would have to question the genuine scope of the crises being labeled as system-wide. The real question is whether for every system-wide crisis, there is a corresponding trade crisis and whether there is an absence of trade crises at other times? Table 5 summarizes the outcome.

Table 5. Systemic crises and changes in trade in the ancient Near East.

Systemic Crisis	Trade Changes
Late 4th Millennium (3500–3000)	Uruk retrenchment; Egyptian links to Near Eastern trade network severed
Mid-3rd Milliennium (2600–2400)	Eastern orientation of Near Eastern trade network develops
Late 3rd Millennium (2200–2000)	Indus decline, Mesopotamian decline, Gulf trade decline, Egyptian links to Near Eastern trade network reduced
	Near Eastern trade network develops a greater western bias
Mid-2nd Millennium (1800–1500)	Egyptian trade links to Levant and Eastern Mediterranean strengthened; Mesopotamian circumstances hazy
	Western orientation of Near Eastern trade network stronger
Late 2nd Millennium (1200–900)	Near Eastern trade collapse
(1st Millennium)	Near Eastern/Mediterranean trade network expands with even stronger western orientation

Towards the end of the 4th millennium, the first system crisis led to a major reorganization of the Uruk trading network. The colonial outposts in the east, the north, and the northwest were withdrawn and abandoned. What had become the customary access routes to highland raw materials were blocked or reduced. The western Mesopotamian-Egyptian link also was broken. An eastern link to the Gulf, Magan/Oman and Meluhha/Indus was forged to substitute for the Zagros/Taurus problems.

Chernykh's second crisis again fails to correspond very well to southwest Asian history. Yet the crisis that did develop toward the end of the 3rd millennium led to, or at least was associated with, considerable political-military turmoil in Syria/ the Levant/ Palestine that isolated Egypt temporarily from the rest of the southwest Asian trading network.[23] Mesopotamian aggression was also registered in all directions, including the Gulf and what appears to be the beginning of decay in the Mesopotamian-Gulf trade linkage. Indus decline appears to have begun around this time as well, indicating either an independent or interdependent atrophy of the eastern wing of the Near Eastern trade network. The trading network began to swing decisively back toward the west.

The third crisis deviated from the strong impact pattern. The roughly mid-2nd millennium crisis had less impact on Egyptian trade patterns because the Hyksos were apparently already integrated into the Levantine trading subsystem. Their movement into Egypt did not sever relations with the outside world and may even have intensified those relations. We know less about Mesopotamian affairs after the rise to power of the Kassites but one has the impression that any interruptions in the presumably already diminished Mesopotamian trade were fairly temporary. The Kassites remained in power in Mesopotamia for some time and appear to have attempted to re-establish many of the traditional sources of trade, although at a lower volume than had been the case in earlier eras.

The fourth crisis, traditionally commemorated as the end of the Bronze Age toward the end of the 2nd millennium, reverted to the earlier pattern with a major breakdown in trade that could hardly be avoided given the mass movements of displaced people, the destruction of cities and the general system-wide turmoil. That Mesopotamia was less affected by this turmoil only indicates that the center of the system had moved west. The fourth crisis was centered in and around the eastern Mediterranean littoral, which is precisely the direction of movement of the trading network in the centuries that immediately preceded the 1200 BC breakdown.

No other trade crises are discernible in the record. Thus, three of the four system-wide crises entailed major disruptions of the trading network. Only one of the four crises did not lead to significant trade disruption, and that exception appears to be traceable to the idiosyncratic nature of the Hyksos hinterland incursion into Egypt. The Hyksos, unlike the majority of hinterland intruders, were already integrated into the trading system before the incursions began. It also can be traced to the fact that the system had become less centered in the eastern part of the Near East by the mid-2nd millennium. The Mesopotamian growth pole had declined in significance while the Egyptian pole and Aegean actors had become more significant. [24]

So, with one exception, the system wide crises in center-hinterland relations, and regime transitions also involved major trading disruptions. Again, with the same exception, they all involved subsequent shifts in the geographical orientation of the trading network—first to the east, then to the near west, and then even farther west. Do these tendencies suggest a linkage to the production-diffusion pattern? The answer is yes but the linkages are multiple, not singular.

The first clue is the timing of the crises. The 3400–2350 period experienced one crisis that was clearly traumatic in the short run. Nevertheless, the system responded to the crisis (limited access to raw materials) by developing or extending the network in an entirely different direction. In a pattern that is replicated in subsequent production phases, developing new routes circumvented access blockages to desired commodities. Developing new routes as substitutes for old ones is a form of innovation and we should anticipate this sort of behavior in production concentration phases.

In contrast, the 2350–1200 diffusion period experienced three crises. An increase in the frequency of crises should be a warning sign of bigger problems to come. An increasing frequency of crises suggests that human agents are experiencing increasing difficulty in resolving their policy problems, which may also be increasing in intensity. Both aspects seem likely given the transformations of the ancient world. Major innovations do not occur at a constant rate. Sumerian and Egyptian innovations had been produced in one era and were diffusing in another. But diffusion, like innovation, is neither constant nor finite and reaches limits. A waning diffusion process needs renewed innovation as a stimulus. Presumably 1200 BC demarcates a point in time at which the momentum of diffusionary processes had reached some kind of limitation. That does not mean that another round of innovation was inevitable. But it does mean that considerable stagnation and contraction would have been the outcome in the absence of another round of innovation.

The limits to diffusion merely create opportunities for somebody to begin developing new ways of doing things (innovating). One of the reasons the ancient world was experiencing more crises was that its traditional productivity base had been transformed. One of its pillars or growth poles had declined significantly. This transformation was all the more critical because, perhaps unlike more contemporary processes, the growth poles of the ancient system, Mesopotamia and Egypt, were more geared to act as demand poles—as opposed to supply poles—for commodities at least.[25] The trading network was more biased to supplying their needs for raw materials than it was in finding markets for their export products. One of the corollaries of this facet of ancient international political economy, at least after the 4th millennium, is that the main agents of trade tended to be neither Mesopotamian nor Egyptian. Indus traders came to Mesopotamia and not the other way around. Entrepots (Dilmun, Byblos, Ugarit, Mari) flourished as long as the supply and demand connections could be maintained. They floundered when the connections broke down. If demand was weakening in general, short-term crises in demand brought on by lack of water, crop failures, increased violence and governmental collapse could be increasingly devastating, as demonstrated in 1200 BC.

Then, too, there is probably a role for rigidities *à la* Mancur Olson's (1982) argument. Systems build up rigidities in elite stratification and interest groups wedded to traditional ways of doing things over time. To break down these rigidities, some type of revolutionary turmoil may be required to weaken traditional forces of conservatism. Again, the argument is not that the build up of rigidities implies that transformational disorder is inevitable. Rather, the argument is only that the possibilities for transformation are greater to the extent that disorder weakens resistance to change.

What sort of rigidities characterized the ancient world toward the end of the 2nd millennium? Empires were one. Egypt became imperial early on but southern Mesopotamia had been able to avoid that prior to the rise of Akkad. Much of the Near East had become imperial territory long prior to 1200 BC. The problem is that established empires, as a rule, are not known for their innovations. Established empires simply do not encourage experimentation and change. For example, the Levantine/Phoenician traders were most successful when they enjoyed some autonomy from their imperial neighbors. That autonomy was only possible in portions of the first halves of the 2nd and 1st millennia BC. The windows for trading autonomy closed down later in the second halves of those millennia as trading states were subordinated and absorbed by adjacent land empires.

In addition, attention is often drawn to the ancient world's tendency to conduct trade through first temple, and then state, agencies. Only these institutions initially had the resources to fund large-scale trading efforts. Temple and palace monopolies on trade, although perhaps never quite as absolute as is sometimes portrayed, should be counted as another rigidity of the ancient world. It is also one that seems to have been swept aside, in favor of greater private participation in trading enterprises, in the 1st millennium BC. Here, the presumption is that private traders were more likely to be experimental and innovative in responding to trading problems than bureaucratic agents. And that should encourage, in turn, a greater expansion of the network than might be the case otherwise.[26]

Finally, the role of metal for making tools and weapons was clearly a dominant factor in the development of the ancient trade networks. Initially focused on obsidian, copper and tin (to make bronze), gradually became one of the central foci of ancient world trade. 1200 BC is called the end of the Bronze Age because iron had begun supplanting bronze toward the end of the 2nd and into the 1st millennium. That implied that an acquisition infrastructure geared to delivering copper and tin to make bronze was in the gradual process of becoming less valued—perhaps not unlike the switch in emphasis from Indonesian spices to Chinese tea in 18th century AD commerce. Agents successful in the old emphasis frequently are not in a good position to make the shift. Their skills, investments, and contacts are not easily transferred to an entirely different enterprise. Other agents, less committed to the old emphasis, are less handicapped in this respect. [27]

Equally important is the fact that iron innovations were taking place outside of Mesopotamia and Egypt. The center for economic innovations and new sources of productivity was moving west of the Euphrates. Shifting centers of new innovation is a proclivity that will characterize the emerging world economy for millennia to follow the 1200 BC crisis. Once again, no new center of production innovation has to emerge following a period of diffusion. But, when the diffusionary process has reached its effective limits, opportunity space for a new round of innovation opens. Moreover, the westward adrift of the Near Eastern trading network, by facilitating development in Crete, Cyprus, and Greece, made it more likely that any new centers of innovation would have a western location or orientation. This observation applies as well to the Phoenicians, despite their eastern location, whose opportunity space opened for a while as a consequence of the relaxation of imperial constraints in the Levant and who were then able to devote considerable resources to opening the western Mediterranean to further development.

Conclusion

Two general hypotheses have been examined in this analysis. The first one argues that world system development has advanced over time in an alternating pattern. An initial period of production innovation on a relatively narrow scale is followed by a period of diffusion over a broader scale. Trade diffusion then gives way to a new round of production innovation and, subsequently, another phase of trade diffusion. The broader argument is that this long-term alternation has been repeated three times, with an ancient, a classical, and a modern set of phases. In this analysis only the ancient phases are scrutinized. Earlier work (for example, Modelski and Thompson 2001) focused primarily but not exclusively on the timing of ancient and classical innovation and found that innovation tended to take place in the production concentration phase. The current analysis asks whether trade in 2350–1200 BC was more diffused than in 3400–2350 BC. The outcome is positive. An initial emphasis on Urukian and Egyptian pioneering production, including colonial expansion, gave way to an increasingly complex system with a good number of actors ranging, at various times, from Indus to Greece and western Italy.

One of the reasons this seems to be the case is that the trade process itself can create ever more sophisticated trading networks by facilitating the development of new participants. It does not have to work this way. Nor does it always work this way. In the ancient world, however, attempts to find raw materials contributed to the development of a number of the places controlling those same raw materials. Even the emergence of the two growth poles of the ancient world, Sumer and Egypt, seem to have been facilitated by this 'trade yeast' process. But, so too, were the Harappans, the Proto-Elamites, the Dilmunites, the Minoans, the Cypriots, and a number of actors in the Fertile Crescent area (Syria, the Levant and Palestine) in repeated waves.

The second general hypothesis concerned whether trade collapses were closely linked to crises in other spheres of activity (center-hinterland conflict and regime transitions). Each of the trade collapses was linked to one of a series of system-wide crises. Only one system crisis did not appear to be linked to a trade collapse. Yet these crises were also opportunities to do something differently. Each trade collapse led to a reorientation of the trading network, first to the east and then farther and farther to the west. Through this reorientation process, the 'trade yeast' process contributed to the probability of first trade diffusion and then renewed production innovation in the west.

Joseph Schumpeter is rightfully well known for his argument that innovation brings about intermittent but creative destruction in modern capitalism. Or, as a number of observers emphasize, this is the way an economy periodically transforms itself. Innovations have played this role for thousands of years before Schumpeter developed his appreciation for innovation as the prime mover in economics. But in the ancient world economy, as contended here, it was a combination of innovation and serial system-wide crises that, in some respects, were both exogenous and endogenous to the economic system that helped transform the ancient world into the classical world. The point to be stressed here is that periodical transformations are the norm in history—they are hardly novel phenomena.

Whether the combination of innovation and system-wide crises played exactly the same role in the next iteration of world system development remains to be explored. It need not have worked exactly the same in subsequent eras. The production innovation phases certainly have not proceeded identically in each iteration. The numbers of innovative centers increased from two relatively close areas in ancient southwest Asia, to several distant Eurasian foci in the classical period, to a string of successive lead economies on the far eastern and western fringes of Eurasia in modern times. If the innovation phases have not played themselves out exactly identically, there is little reason to assume that the diffusion phases have proceeded in exactly the same way. For instance, where vulnerabilities to environmental crisis have been less than in the ancient Near East, disease may have emerged as a functionally equivalent problem in contributing to system-wide crises. Most recently (in the past 500 years), global war has emerged as one of the defining stimuli in provoking system-wide crisis.

There is also the question of the geographical scope of these alternations. China appears to have remained outside the reach of trade diffusion and some of the early Chernykh crises in the ancient world, even if it was not immune to the transfer of western technology and ideas. Indus was certainly co-opted (or welcomed) into the southwest Asia system as long as the Harappans flourished. The Indus decline corresponds closely to Chernykh's third crisis period. Europe, also, seems to have been linked fairly closely to Near Eastern rhythms. A. Sherratt (1997:502–3), for instance, argues that during 3500–2500 BC Near Eastern innovations spread into Europe and encouraged the development and expansion of cultural units. In the next millennium (2500–1500 BC), the European emphasis was placed on elaborating trade routes and the homogenization of bronze-oriented economies. This period was followed in turn by a 1500–500 BC era characterized by an initial collapse of the urban world and a shift to iron before the regional system returned to an expansive mode and increased north-south interaction. Since we have already observed the southwest Asian system transforming itself into a Mediterranean-southwest Asian system, some correlation in adjacent European fluctuations is hardly surprising. Still, Sherratt's dates come very close to those stipulated by the production-diffusion argument. The real question is how much of Europe approximated these alternating phases. Was southern Europe more closely attuned to southwest Asian rhythms than northern or eastern Europe? Were European areas that did not trade directly with southwest Asia as affected as those that did trade directly? Were various parts of Europe also impacted by Chernykh's Pan-Eurasian crises as much, if not more, than southwest Asia seems to have been? Whatever the specific answers to these questions are, there is once again a strong hint that at least some of the Eurasian sub-regions were less autonomous in ancient times than is frequently assumed.

Nonetheless, the more fundamental question remains one of whether the (or a ?) long-term beat of world system development is one of simple alternation—a period of production innovation is followed by a period of diffusion, punctuated by intermittent crises. The evidence examined here and elsewhere suggests that this punctuated binary pattern fits the ancient world and the serial if occasional transformations in its trading networks. That is encouraging for the study of the very *longue durée*; it should also help us in deciphering the ancient world—and the worlds that have come into being in the wake of the first iteration.

Notes

1. See, for instance, Freeman and Perez (1988) or Modelski and Thompson (1996) for analyses predicated on this assumption.
2. This interpretation problem cannot be pursued here. See, among others, McNeill (1982) and Modelski and Thompson (1996) for further discussion of this problem.
3. See Marfoe 1987:35; Kohl 1975a, 1975b, 1978, 1979, 1987a, 1987b, 1997a; Algaze 1993; Lupton 1996; Sherratt and Sherratt 1998:337; Stein 1999.
4. See Frank 1993; Gills and Frank 1993; Wilkinson 1993; Cioffi-Revilla 2000; Buzan and Little 2000. But, of course, this question depends on what types of interaction are thought to be most important. Trading patterns, assuredly, will cast one of the widest nets, with only ideas having a longer reach. Military conflict patterns may do the opposite—that is, construct the most limited interaction nets.
5. See, for instance, the extensive literature cited by Niemeier (1998:20–3) on the disputed location of Ahhiyawa.
6. Hiebert (1994) argues for an Indus connection to the Bactrian oases, but it is far from clear how strong the trade connections might have been.
7. The assumption is not that all innovations emerge in one place—only that the generation of important innovations tends to be concentrated in time and space. Metallurgical innovations, in particular, appear less likely to correspond to this generalization. See, for instance, Chernykh (1992) and Yemer (2000).
8. No assumption need be made that trading relationships cannot also be the object of innovation.
9. The modern string have been examined theoretically and empirically in Modelski and Thompson (1996).
10. Doumas (1998:129–30) briefly summarizes the Renfrewian orthodoxy as one of system breakdowns are rarely caused by external agents, natural or human ...[they are] the outcome of internal processes, which societies are unable to reverse, prevent or influence.
11. This work is in essential agreement with S. Sherratt's point that we should avoid relying on migrations/invasions as complete explanations unto themselves. Hinterland incursions can be deadly and can certainly facilitate the termination of regimes, but the timing of hinterland behavior does not appear to be random. It is influenced by regime weakness, external pressures from other groups and environmental deterioration. Thompson (2000) found these periods of Near Eastern crisis to be associated with aridity and water shortages which presumably exacerbated the conflicts between center and hinterland and the probability of regime transition. Still, more work needs to be done on the climate data before the evidentiary base is adequate.
12. In the subsequent classical period, an eastern reorientation reemerged in the first millennium BC reaching ultimately , if indirectly, to China at a time when China was aggressively seeking western connections. The Chinese had been influenced in various ways, including most definitely the idea of chariots, a millennium and a half earlier. However, it is not clear that

anything resembling trading relationships were established between the Shang and western/Indo-European residents of central Eurasia. See Barber (1999) and Mallory and Mair (2000) for informed speculation on the nature of these early contacts.

13. In this spirit, Dever (1992:107) argues that the failures of multiple subsystems at the time sets in motion a downward spiral that feeds upon itself and increases in momentum. Although Butzer (1997) chooses to privilege Egyptian militarism as the First Intermediate Period culprit, his argument is similar.

14. Frank (1993) is one noteworthy exception.

15. Unfortunately, the 'what' has been sacrificed in the interest of space considerations. Somewhat more detail is provided in Thompson (2001).

16. Lamberg-Karlovsky's (1993) observation that the Sumerians, the Elamites, the Harappans, and the Turanians, and one could add the Egyptians to this list, all experimented with colonial efforts very roughly in the same time period. Perhaps such efforts are more probable early in a production concentration phase that precedes a trade diffusion phase in which trading partnerships are more developed and more easily developed. Colonialism seems to reappear when old trading networks have broken down, as in the Greek expansion in the classical age, or when new territories are encountered, as in the European subordination of the Americas. How much and how effective the resistance is probably also matters.

17. Production concentration phases have startup periods that precede the period of strong innovation and productivity. Roughly speaking, one might divide each production concentration period into two sub-periods. The first sub-period is the startup period, with peak growth occurring in the second sub-period. Thus, it does make some difference when one starts the clock so to speak on the Sumerians. If the dating of their activities is to begin earlier in the 4th millennium, the question then is whether their most impressive innovations in production are also pushed forward in time.

18. See Marcus (1998) for a useful argument that envisions ancient state formations as a cycle of centralization and decentralization over time, measured in terms of the varying sizes of the state. My argument is only that the first expansion may be more significant than the subsequent ones, regardless of the comparative sizes of imperial territory.

19. Rice (1994:144) suggests that the Phoenicians claimed Dilmun ancestry but Culican (1966: 72), among others, has also stressed the likelihood of a Sea Peoples' infusion into the coastal Canaanite population toward the end of the 2nd millennium. The idea that the Dilmun entrepot was transferred to the Mediterranean is quite attractive and it does not seem all that incredible. If Indus traders were resident in Mesopotamian ports in the 3rd millennium and Dilmun traders were running land caravans into the Levantine areas in the early 2nd millennium, it seems possible that some Dilmun traders may have remained in the areas as the Gulf trade declined.

20. Stein (1994b:39–40) argues against the idea that the Ubaids had developed a wide acquisition network until the very end of the Ubaid era.

21. One exception is that some Urukian colonists may have been refugees from problems associated with shifting coastlines in southern Mesopotamia. But even if that applied to every Urukian highland outpost, it would not necessarily negate their subsequent role as agents in a widespread acquisition network. Urukian expansion was also too long-run an affair to be traced to a single source of motivation.

22. There are of course more conservative interpretations of the role of trade in the Indus phenomena that would give much less weight to trade's role (see, for example, Kenoyer 1998).

23. As noted earlier, Butzer (1997) argues that the turmoil was primarily due to Egyptian attacks, or at least Egyptian attempts to maintain their control in Palestine and Syria.

24. In point of fact we do not seem to know much about Mesopotamia in the mid-2nd millennium. There is some evidence for deurbanization and abandonment of cities (Ur, Uruk, Larsa, Girsu, Lagas, Isin, Nippur, Sippar) possibly due to water scarcities from low river levels (Gache *et al.* 1998:7–8).

25. This statement is not meant to suggest that Mesopotamia and Egypt were unsuccessful in exporting various products that were based on agricultural and manufacturing innovations (e.g. plows and irrigation generated grain, weaving looms produced linens, and pottery wheels created pots).

26. On this argument, see Liverani 1987:72; Muhly 1992:19; Sherrat and Sherratt 1993:361–2, 1998:339–40).

27. What remains unclear are the details concerning the shift from bronze to iron and just how critical the shift was in ushering in a new metal orientation. For instance, Waldbaum (1978) argued that the 1200 BC troubles could have disrupted the supply of tin on the Mari-Ugarit route, thereby forcing people to use more iron. However, Muhly (1998:323–4) contends that there was no shortage of copper and tin in the Aegean between 1200 and 700 BC. As a consequence, he is doubtful that Phoenicians sailed west in search of either silver or tin.

References

Adams, W. (1977) *Nubia: Corridor to Africa*. London: Allen Lane.

Algaze, G. (1986) Kurban Hoyuk and the late Chalcolithic Period in the Northwest Mesopotamian periphery: a preliminary assessment. In *Gamdat Nasr: Period or Regional Style?*, edited by Uwe Finkbeiner and Wolfgang Rollig. Weisbaden: Dr. Ludwig Reichert Verlag, pp. 274–315.

Algaze, G. (1992) Dynamics of trade in the ancient Mesopotamian world system. *American Anthropologist* 94:118–39.

Algaze, G. (1993) *The Uruk World System: The Dynamics of Expansion of Early Mesopotamian Civilization*. Chicago, IL: University of Chicago Press.

Algaze, G. (1995) A fourth millennium BC trade in Greater Mesopotamia: did it include wine? In *The Origins and Ancient History of Wine*, edited by P. E. McGovern, S. J. Fleming, S. H. Katz. Amsterdam: Gordon and Breach.

Barber, E. (1999) *The Mummies of Urumichi*. New York: W.W. Norton.

Buccellati, M. (1990) Trade in metals in the third millennium: northeastern Syria and eastern Anatolia . In *Resurrecting the Past*, edited by P. Matthiee, M. Van Loon and H. Weiss. Leiden: Nederlands Institut voor het Nabije Oosten, pp. 17–40.

Butzer, K. (1997) A sociopolitical discontinuity in the Near East c. 2200 BCE: scenarios from Palestine and Egypt. In *Third Millennium BC Climate Change and Old World Collapse*, edited by H. Nuzhet Dalfes, George Kukla, and Harvey Weiss. Berlin: Springer, pp. 245–96.

Buzan, B. and Little, R. (2000) *International Systems in World History*. Oxford: Oxford University Press.

Castells, M. (2000) *The Rise of the Network Society: The Information Age: Economy, Society and Culture* 1. 3 vols. 2nd edn. Malden, MA: Blackwell Publishers.

Chavalas, M. (1992) Ancient Syria: a historical sketch. In *New Horizons in the Study of Ancient Syria*, edited by M. W. Chavalas and J. L. Hayes. Malibu, CA: Udena Publications, pp. 1–22.

Chernykh, E.N. (1992) *Ancient Metallurgy in the USSR: The Early Metal Age*. Cambridge: Cambridge University Press.

Cioffi-Revilla, C. (2000) War and warfare: scales of conflict in long-range analysis. In *World System History: The Social Science of Long-term Change*, edited by R. A. Denemark, J. Friedman, B. K. Gills, and G. Modelski. London: Routledge, pp. 253–72.

Cline, E. (1994) *Sailing the Wine Dark Sea: International Trade and the Late Bronze Age Aegean*. Oxford: British Archaeological Reports.

Crawford, H. (1992) An Early Dynastic trading network in North Mesopotamia? In *La Circulation Des Biens, Des Personnes et Des Idees Dans Le Proche Orient Ancien*, edited by D. Charpin and F. Joannes. Paris: Editions Recherche sur les Civilisations.

Culican, W. (1966) *The First Merchant Venturers: The Ancient Levant in History and Commerce*. London: Thames and Hudson.

Dales, G. (1976) Shifting trade patterns between the Iranian plateau and the Indus Valley in the third millennium BC . In *Le Plateau Iranien et l'Asie Centrale des origines au la Conquete Islamique*, edited by J. Deshayes. Paris: Collogue Internationaux de CNRS.

Dever, W. (1992) The Late Bronze–Early Iron I Horizon in Syria-Palestine: Egyptians, Canaanites, Sea Peoples and Proto-Isrealites. In *The Crisis Years: The 12th Century BC, from beyond the Danube to the Tigris*, edited by W. A. Ward and M. S. Joukowsky. Dubuque, Io: Kendall/Hunt, pp. 99–110.

Doumas, C. (1998) Aegeans in the Levant: myth and reality. In *Mediterranean Peoples in Transition: Thirteenth to Early Tenth Centuries BCE*, edited by S. Gitin, A. Mazar and E. Stern. Jerusalem: Israel Exploration Society, pp. 114–28.

Earle, T. (1997) *How Chiefs Came to Power: The Political Economy in Prehistory*. Stanford: Stanford University Press.

Edens, C. (1993) Indus-Arabian Interaction during the Bronze Age: a review of evidence. In *Harappan Civilization: A Recent Perspective*, edited by G. L. Possehl. 2nd rev. edn. New Delhi: Oxford University Press, pp. 335–64.

Eiden, J. and Hojlund, F. (1993) Trade or Diplomacy: Assyria and Dilmun in the eighteenth century BC. *World Archaeology* 24:441–48.

Frank, A. (1993) Bronze Age world system cycles. *Current Anthropology* 34:383–405.

Frankfort, H. (1951) *The Birth of Civilization in the Near East*. Bloomington: Indiana University Press.

Freeman, C. and Perez, C. (1988) Structural crises of adjustment: business cycles and investment behavior. In *Technical Change and Economic Theory*, edited by G. Dosi, C. Freeman, R. Nelson, G. Silverberg, and L. Soete. London: Pinter, pp. 38–66.

Gasche, H., Armstrong, J., Cole, S. and Gurzadyan V. (1998) *Dating the Fall of Babylon: A Reappraisal of*

Second-Millennium Chronology. Ghent, Bel./Chicago, IL.: University of Ghent and the Oriental Institute of the University of Chicago.

Gills, B. and Frank, J. (eds) (1993) *The World System: Five Hundred Years or Five Thousand*. London: Routledge.

Hiebert, F. (1994) *Origins of the Bronze Age Oasis Civilization in Central Asia*. Cambridge, MA: Peabody Museum of Archaeology and Ethnology.

Hole, F. (1994) Environmental instabilities and urban origins. In *Chiefdoms and Early States in the Near East: The Organizational Dynamics of Complexity*, edited by Gil Stein and Mitchell S. Rothman. Madison, WI: Prehistory Press.

Joffe, A. (2000) Egypt and Syro-Mesopotamia in the 4th millennium: implications of the new chronology. *Current Anthropology* 41:113–23.

Kantor, H. (1992) The relative chronology of Egypt and its foreign correlations before the First Intermediate Period. In *Chronologies in Old World Archaeology*, vol. 1, edited by G. Stein and M. S. Rothman. 3rd edn. Chicago, IL: University of Chicago Press, pp. 3–21.

Kemp, B. (1983) Old Kingdom, Middle Kingdom and Second Intermediate Period, c. 2686–1152 BC. In *Ancient Egypt: A Social History*, edited by B.G. Trigger, B.J. Kemp, D. O'Connor and A.B. Lloyd. Cambridge: Cambridge University Press, pp. 71–182.

Kenoyer, J. (1998) *Ancient Cities of the Indus Valley Civilization*. Karachi: Oxford University Press.

Klengl, H. (1992) *Syria, 3000 to 300 BC: A Handbook of Political History*. Berlin: Akademie Verlag.

Knapp, B. (1988) Copper production and Eastern Mediterranean trade: the rise of complex society on Cyprus. In *State and Society: The Emergence and Development of Social Hierarchy and Political Centralization*, edited by J. Gledhill, B. Bender and M. T. Larsen. London: Unwin Hyman, pp. 149–72.

Knapp, B. and Cherry, J. (1994) *Provenience Studies and Bronze Age Cyprus: Production, Exchange and Politico-economic Change*. Madison, WI: Prehistory Press.

Kohl, P. (1975a) The archaeology of trade. *Dialectical Anthropology* 1:43–50.

Kohl, P. (1975b) Carved chlorite vessels: a trade in finished commodities in the mid-third millennium. *Expedition* 18:18–31.

Kohl, P. (1978) The balance of trade in Southwestern Asia in the third millennium BC. *Current Anthropology* 19:463–92.

Kohl, P. (1979) The world economy of West Asia in the third millennium BC. In *South Asian Archaeology*, edited by M. Tardei.

Kohl, P. (1987a) The ancient economy, transferable technology and the Bronze Age world-system: a view from the northeastern frontier of the ancient Near East. In *Centre and Periphery in the Ancient World*, edited by M. Rowlands, M. Larsen and K. Kristiansen. Cambridge: Cambridge University Press, pp. 13–24.

Kohl, P. (1987b) The use and abuse of world systems theory: the case of the pristine west Asian state. *Advances in Archaeological Method and Theory* 11:1–36.

Kuhrt, A. (1995) *The Ancient Near East, c. 3000–330 BC*, vol. 1. London: Routledge.

Lamberg-Karlovsky, C. C. (1993) Sumer, Elam and the Indus: three urban processes equal one structure? In *Harappan Civilization: A Recent Perspective*, edited by G. L. Possehl, 2nd rev. edn. New Dehli: Oxford University Press, pp. 61–8.

Larsen, M. (1987) Commercial networks in the ancient Near East. In *Centre and Periphery in the Ancient World*, edited by M. Rowlands, M. Larsen and K. Kristiansen. Cambridge: Cambridge University Press, pp. 47–56.

Leemans, W.F. (1960) *Foreign Trade in the Old Babylonian Period*. Leiden: E.J. Brill.

Liverani, M. (1987) The collapse of the Near Eastern regional system at the end of the Bronze Age: the case of Syria. In *Centre and Periphery in the Ancient World*, edited by M. Rowlands, M. Larsen and K. Kristiansen. Cambridge: Cambridge University Press, pp. 66–73.

Lupton, A. (1996) *Stability and Change: Socio-political Development in North Mesopotamia and Southeast Anatolia, 4000–2700 BC*. Oxford: British Archaeological Reports.

Maisels, C. (1999) *Early Civilizations of the Old World: The Formative Histories of Egypt, the Levant, Mesopotamia, Indus and China*. New York: Routledge.

Mallory, J.P. and Mair, V. (2000) *The Tarim Mummies: Ancient China and the Mystery of the Earliest Peoples from the West*. London: Thames and Hudson.

Marcus, J. (1998) The peaks and valleys of ancient states: an extension of the dynamic model. In *Archaic States*, edited by G. M. Feinman and J. Marcus. Santa Fe, NM: School of American Research.

Marfoe, L. (1987) Cedar Forest to Silver Mountain: social change and the development of long-distance trade in early Near Eastern societies. In *Centre and Periphery in the Ancient World*, edited by M. Rowlands, M. Larsen and K. Kristiansen. Cambridge: Cambridge University Press, pp. 25–33.

Mark, S. (1998) *From Egypt to Mesopotamia: A Study of Predynastic Trade Routes*. College Station, TX: A and M University Press.

Mayer, J. (1992) The Eastern Desert and Egyptian Prehistory. In *The Followers of Horus: Studies Dedicated to Michael Allen Hoffman*, edited by R. Friedman and B. Adams. Oxford: Oxbow Books.

McNeill, W. (1982) *The Pursuit of Power: Technology, Armed Force and Society Since AD 1000*. Chicago, IL: University of Chicago Press.

Merrillees, R. (1998) Egypt and the Aegean . In *The Aegean and the Orient in the Second Millennium*, edited by E. H. Cline and D. Harris-Cline. Liege, Belgium: Annales d'archeologie Egeenne de l'Universite de Liege et UT-PASP.

Modelski, G. (1999) Ancient world cities, 4000–1000 BC: center/hinterland in the world system. *Global Society* 13 (October).

Modelski, G. (2000) World system evolution. In *World System History: The Social Science of Long Term Change*, edited by R. Denemark, J. Friedman, B. Gills and G. Modelski. London: Routledge, pp. 24–53.

Modelski, G. and Thompson, W. (1996) *Leading Sectors and World Powers: The Coevolution of Global Economics and Politics*. Columbia: University of South Carolina Press.

Modelski, G. and Thompson, W. (2002) Evolutionary pulsations in the world system . In *Structure, Culture, and History: Recent Issues in Social Theory*, edited by D. Knottnerus and S. Chew. Boulder, CO: Rowman and Littlefield, pp. 177–96.

Moorey, P.R.S. (1987) On tracking cultural transfers in prehistory: the case of Egypt and Lower Mesopotamia in the fourth millennium BC. In *Centre and Periphery in the Ancient World*, edited by M. Rowlands, M. Larsen and K. Kristiansen. Cambridge: Cambridge University Press, pp. 36–46.

Moorey, P.R.S. (1994) *Ancient Mesopotamian Materials and Industries: The Archaeological Evidence*. Oxford: Clarendon Press, pp. 36–46.

Muhly, J. (1969) Copper and Tin: The Distribution of Mineral Resources and the Nature of the Metals Trade in the Bronze Age. PhD dissertation: Yale University.

Muhly, J. (1992) The crisis years in the Mediterranean world: transition or cultural disintegration? In *The Crisis Years: The 12th Century BC: From Beyond the Danube to the Tigris*, edited by W. A. Ward and M. S. Joukowsky. Dubuque, IO: Kendall/Hunt, pp. 10–26.

Muhly, J. (1995) Mining and metalworking in ancient Western Asia . In *Civilizations of the Ancient Near East*, vol. 3, edited by J. M. Sasson. New York: Simon and Schuster, pp. 501–22.

Niemeier, W. (1998) The Mycenaeans in Western Anatolia and the problem of the origins of the Sea Peoples. In *Mediterranean Peoples in Transition: Thirteenth to Early Tenth Centuries BCE*, edited by S. Gitin, A. Mazar and E. Stern. Jerusalem: Israel Exploration Society, pp. 17–65.

O'Connor, D. (1983) New Kingdom and Third Intermediate period, 1552–664 BC. In *Ancient Egypt: A Social History*, edited by B.G. Trigger, B.J. Kemp, D. O'Connor and A.B. Lloyd. Cambridge: Cambridge University Press, pp. 183–228.

Oates, J. (1993) Trade and power in the fifth and fourth millennium BC: new evidence from Northern Mesopotamia. *World Archaeology* 24 (3):403–22.

Olson, M. (1982) *The Rise and Decline of Nations: Economic Growth, Stagflation, and Social Rigidities*. New Haven, CT: Yale University Press.

Piesinger, C. (1983) Legacy of Dilmun: The Roots of Ancient Maritime Trade in Eastern Coastal Arabia in the 4th/3rd Millennium BC. PhD dissertation, Madison, WI: University of Wisconsin.

Porada, E., Hansen, D. Dunham, S. and Babcock, S. (1992) The Chronology of Mesopotamia, ca. 7000–1600 BC. In *Chronologies in Old World Archaeology*, vol. 1, edited by R. W. Ehrlich. 3rd edn. Chicago, IL: University of Chicago Press, pp. 77–121.

Portugali, J. and Gophna, R. (1993) Crisis, progress and urbanization: the transition from Early Bronze I to Early Bronze II in Palestine. *Tel Aviv* 20(2):164–86.

Postgate, N. (1986) The transition from Uruk to Early Dynastic: continuities and discontinuities in the record of settlement. In *Gamdat Nasr: Period or Regional Style?*, edited by U. Finkbeiner and W. Rollig. Weisbaden: Dr. Ludwig Reichert Verlag, pp. 90–106.

Potts, D. T. (1990) *The Arabian Gulf in Antiquity: From Prehistory to the Fall of the Achaemenid Empire*. Oxford: Clarendon Press.

Potts, T. (1994) *Mesopotamia and the East: An Archaeological and Historical Study of Foreign Relations, ca. 3400–2000* BC. Oxford: Oxbow Books.

Rattenagar, S. (1981) *Encounters: The Westerly Trade of the Harappa Civilization*. Delhi: Oxford University Press.

Redford, D. (1992) *Egypt, Canaan, and Israel in Ancient Times*. Princeton, NJ: Princeton University Press.

Renfrew, C. (1978) Trajectory discontinuity and morphogenesis: the implications of catastrophe theory for archaeology. *American Antiquity* 43:203–22.

Renfrew, C. (1987) *Archaeology and Language*. New York: Cambridge University Press.

Rice, M. (1994) *The Archaeology of the Arabian Gulf, c. 5000–323* BC. London: Routledge.

Roaf, M. and Galbraith, J. (1994) Pottery and P-values: seafaring merchants of Ur? Re-examined. *Antiquity* 68:770–83.

Schneider, J. (1977) Was there a pre-capitalist world-system? *Peasant Studies* 6:20–9.

Shaffer, J. (1992) The Indus Valley, Baluchistan, and Helmand traditions: Neolithic through Bronze Age. In *Chronologies in Old World Archaeology*, vol. 1, edited by R. W. Ehrlich. 3rd edn. Chicago, IL: University of Chicago Press, pp. 441–64.

Sherratt, A. (1997) *Economy and Society in Prehistoric Europe: Changing Perspectives*. Princeton, NJ: Princeton University Press.

Sherratt, A. (2000) Envisioning global change: a long-term perspective . In *World System History: The Social Science of Long-term Change*, edited by R. A. Denemark, J. Friedman, B. K. Gills and G. Modelski. London: Routledge, pp. 115–32.

Sherratt, A. and Sherratt, S. (1998) Small worlds: interaction and identity in the Ancient Mediterranean. In *The Aegean and the Orient in the Second Millennium*, edited by E. H. Cline and and D. Harris-Cline. Liege, Belgium: Annales d'archeologie Egeenne de l'Universite de Liege et UT-PASP, pp. 292–313.

Sherratt, S. (1998) Sea Peoples and the economic structure of the late second millennium in the eastern Mediterranean. In *Mediterranean Peoples in Transition: Thirteenth to Early Tenth Centuries* BCE, edited by S. Gitin, A. Mazar and E. Stern. Jerusalem: Israel Exploration Society.

Sherratt, S. and Sherratt, A. (1993) The Growth of the Mediterranean Economy in the Early First Millennium BC. *World Archaeology* 24(3):361–78.

Stager, L. (1992) The periodization of Palestine from Neolithic through early Bronze times . In *Chronologies in Old World Archaeology*, vol. 1, edited by R. W. Ehrlich. 3rd edn. Chicago, IL: University of Chicago Press, pp. 22–41.

Stein, G. (1994a) The organizational dynamics of complexity in Greater Mesopotamia. In *Chiefdoms and Early States in the Near East: The Organizational Dynamics of Complexity*, edited by G. Stein and M. S. Rothman. Madison, WI: Prehistory Press.

Stein, G. (1994b) Economy, Ritual and Power in Ubaid Mesopotamia. In *Chiefdoms and Early States in the Near East: The Organizational Dynamics of Complexity*, edited by G. Stein and M. S. Rothman. Madison, WI: Prehistory Press.

Stein, G. (1999) *Rethinking World-Systems: Diasporas, Colonies and Interaction in Uruk Mesopotamia*. Tucson: University of Arizona Press.

Steinkeller, P. (1993) Early political development in Mesopotamia and the origins of the Sargonic Empire. In *Akkad, The First World Empire: Structure, Ideology, Traditions*, edited by M. Liverani. Padua, Italy: Sargon.

Surenhagen, D. (1986) The dry farming belt: the Uruk period and subsequent developments . In *The Origin of Cities in Dry-Farming Syria and Mesopotamia in the Third Millennium* BC, edited by H. Weiss. Guilford, CT: Four Quarters Publishing Co.

Thompson, W. (2000) Environmental crises, regime transitions, and center-hinterland conflict. Paper presented at the annual meeting of the International Studies Association, Los Angeles, CA, March.

Thompson, W. (2001) Trade, diffusion and collapse. Paper presented at the annual meeting of the International Studies Association, Los Angeles, California, February.

Thompson, W. (2002) Testing a cyclical instability theory in the ancient Near East. *Comparative Civilizations Review* 46:34–78.

Tosi, M. (1993) The Harappan civilization beyond the Indian Subcontinent. In *Harappan Civilization: A Recent Perspective*, edited by G. L. Possehl. 2nd rev. edn. New Delhi: Oxford University Press, pp. 365–80.

Trigger, B. G. (1983) The rise of Egyptian civilization. In *Ancient Egypt: A Social History*, edited by B.G. Trigger, B. J. Kemp, D. O'Connor and A. B. Lloyd. Cambridge: Cambridge University Press, pp. 1–70.

Waldbaum, J. (1978) *From Bronze to Iron: The Transition from the Bronze Age to the Iron Age in the Eastern Mediterranean*. Göteborg: Paul Ästroms Forlag.

Ward, W. (1971) *Egypt and the East Mediterannean World, 2200–1900* BC. Beirut, Lebanon: Heidelberg Press.

Warren, P. (1995) Minoan Crete and Pharaonic Egypt. In *Egypt, the Aegean and the Levant: Interconnections in the Second Millennium* BC, edited by W. Vivian Davies and L. Schofield. London: British Museum Press.

Watrous, L. (1998) Egypt and Crete in the Early Middle Bronze Age: a case of trade and cultural diffusion. In *The Aegean and the Orient in the Second Millennium*, edited by E. H. Cline and D. Harris-Cline. Liège, Belgium: Annales d'Archeologie Egéenne de l'Université de Liège et UT-PASP.

Watson, P. (1983) The Halafian Culture: a review and synthesis. In *The Hilly Flanks and Beyond: Essays on the Prehistory of Southwestern Asia*, edited by T. Cuyler Young, Jr., P. E.L. Smith and P. Mortensen. Chicago, IL: University of Chicago Oriental Institute, pp. 231–50.

Weinstein, J. M. (1998) Egyptian relations with the eastern Mediterranean world at the end of the second millennium BCE. In *Mediterranean Peoples in Transition: Thirteenth to Early Tenth Centuries* BCE, edited by S. Gitin, A. Mazar and E. Stern. Jerusalem: Israel Exploration Society, pp. 188–96.

Wilkinson, T. (1996) *State Formation in Egypt: Chronology and Society*. Oxford: British Archaeological Reports.

Wright, G. (1968) Obsidian Analyses and Early Trade in the Near East: 7500 to 3500 BC. PhD dissertation, University of Michigan.

Wright, H. (1987) The Susiana hinterlands during the era of primary state formation. In *The Archaeology of Western Iran: Settlement and Society from Prehistory to the Islamic Conquest*, edited by F. Hole. Washington, D.C. Smithsonian Institute Press, pp. 141–56.

Wright, H. (1998) Uruk states in Southwestern Iran. In *Archaic States*, edited by G. Feinman and J. Marcus. Santa Fe, NM: School of American Research Press, pp. 173–98.

Yemer, K. (2000) *The Domestication of Metals: The Rise of Complex Metal Industries in Anatolia*. Leiden: E.J. Brill.

Yoffee, N. (1988) Orienting collapse. In *The Collapse of Ancient States and Civilizations*, edited by N. Yoffee and G. L. Cowgill. Tucson: University of Arizona Press.

Yoffee, N. (1995) The economy of ancient Western Asia. In *Civilizations of the Ancient Near East*, vol. 3, edited by J. M. Sasson. New York: Simon and Schuster, pp. 1387–1400.

Young, T. (1986) Godin Tepe Period VI/V and Central Western Iran at the end of the fourth millennium. In *Gamdat Nasr: Period or Regional Style?*, edited by U. Finkbeiner and W. Rollig. Weisbaden: Dr. Ludwig Reichert Verlag, pp. 212–28.

Zarins, J. (1989) Ancient Egypt and the Red Sea trade: the case for obsidian in the Predynastic and Archaic Periods. In *Essays in Ancient Civilization Presented to Helene J. Kantor*, edited by A. Leonard, Jr. and B. B. Williams. Chicago, IL: University of Chicago Oriental Institute, pp. 339–68.

Zettler, R. (1992) 12th century BC Babylonia: continuity and change. In *The Crisis Years: The 12th Century* BC, *from beyond the Danube to the Tigris*, edited by W. A. Ward and M. S. Joukowsky. Dubuque, IA: Kendall/Hunt, pp. 174–81.

Zettler, R. and Miller, N. (1995) Searching for wine in the archaeological record of ancient Mesopotamia of the third and second millennium BC. In *The Origins and Ancient History of Wine*, edited by P. E. McGovern, S. J. Fleming, and S. H. Katz. Amsterdam: Gordon and Breach.

Section Two: Cognitive Globalization in History

Introduction to Section Two: Cognitive Globalization in History

All of the authors featured in this section address globalization both old and new. Traditional archaeologists prefer to materialize largely imaginary places by calling them sites and obsessing on their pottery styles rather than by imagining, on the basis of the remains, what the real place was like and what the meaning of its artifacts were. The part of that meaning which we archaeologists are disadvantaged in discerning is dealt with in the discussions in this section. Both Paul Ray and Bethany Walker are archaeologists who look at the non-material aspects of culture—language, aspirations, goals and ideology. Ray uses spatial analysis to achieve this end, while Walker turns to texts to augment the material culture. Walker's historical overview suggests another incarnation of the globalizing net—this time in the form of the pan-national obligatory religious journey that the Hajj represents.

Figure 6.1 Sign in Shanghai (which says 'country's best yoghurt').

Gosline has devised a model for looking at state formation that differs somewhat from Castells' in that he views modern multi-national corporations as pseudo-societies undergoing the same pressures of globalization and socialization as other societies. He concludes that the processes of technology and communication leading to 'globalization' have always brought about the historical effects of change, as different cultures cope with the pressures of that change over time and that without the constant flux of globalization, 'history' could not exist, as we perceive it in human society. Ray gives us a regional approach to the phenomenon of globalization in the ancient world, showing those effects in an area that witnessed a succession of empires in addition to the rise of its own tribal kingdoms. With the historical perspectives offered by Walker and Ray and the philosophical approach offered by Gosline, the papers in this section all complement the detailed materialist and regional approaches of the previous section to demonstrate the cognitive bases of global systems.

The Globalizing Effects of 'Hajj' in the Medieval and Modern Eras

Bethany J. Walker

In medieval society, travel functioned as an important agent of 'connectivity', reinforcing communications links and creating new identities that transcended those of blood and nation. Before the creation of the states of the modern Middle East, travel helped to define for Muslims the dimensions of the *Dar al-Salaam* (the Islamic world as the 'world of peace') and reinforced a global Muslim identity. The injunction for Muslims to travel has its origins in the *hadith* (sayings of the Prophet Muhammad); pilgrimage to Mecca is required of all Muslims in the Qur'an. Islamic travel takes many forms: migration (or *hijra*), travel for learning (*talab al-'ilm*), travel for blessing, or *baraka*, and religious pilgrimage, specifically the annual *hajj* to Mecca and Medina (Walker 2000:1).

Of these, the most important is the *hajj*. Pilgrimage to Mecca at least once during one's lifetime is the fifth pillar of Islam and, as such, is a canonical duty and expression of Islamic identity. As the five daily prayers mark the passing of the day, the *hajj* is the highlight of the year, taking place on the 8th–10th days of the last month of the Muslim calendar, Dhu al-Hijja. On the individual level, *hajj* is often described as a life-changing experience that makes the believer aware of the worldwide *umma* (the Islamic community, generally understood to be based on an orthodox understanding of Islam) and allows the pilgrim to tap into a shared value system. It certainly transformed the life of Malcolm X, who wrote home after his own pilgrimage in 1964:

> There were tens of thousands of pilgrims from all over the world. They were of all colors, from blue-eyed blonds to black-skinned Africans. But we were all participating in the same ritual, displaying a spirit of unity and brotherhood that my experiences in America had led me to believe could never exist between the white and non-white (Haley 1999:346–7).[1]

Hajj, however, does not always succeed in convincing the pilgrim of the unity of the Islamic world. Tension between *umma* (the global Islamic community) and *'asabiyya* (nationalism) has always been part of the pilgrim's experience. In their monograph on Muslim travel, Eickelman and Piscatori remind us that travel actually creates boundaries (Eickelman and Piscatori 1990b:5). By meeting Muslims from other parts of the globe whose practices may differ from his own, the pilgrim is challenged to define who he is and in what ways he is truly Muslim. This encounter with 'the Muslim "other"' plays an important role in self-discovery (Eickelman and Piscatori 1990a:xv).

Depending on the circumstances, *hajj* can reinforce either a global or a particularist identity. As such, the *hajj* is an ideal testing ground for Castells' model of globalization, which, he claims, operates in a dialectic relationship with 'identity formation' in the modern world. In this model, institutions legitimize their political and ideological control of society by means of a 'legitimizing identity' that defines what should be universal values and common points of reference, all Western. On the local level, members of society may respond in defiance by redefining their group values and reference points, or formulating 'resistance identities'. In the second of his three volumes collectively entitled *The Rise of the Network Society*, Castells argues that in the last quarter of the 20th century there have been 'powerful expressions of collective identity that challenge globalization...

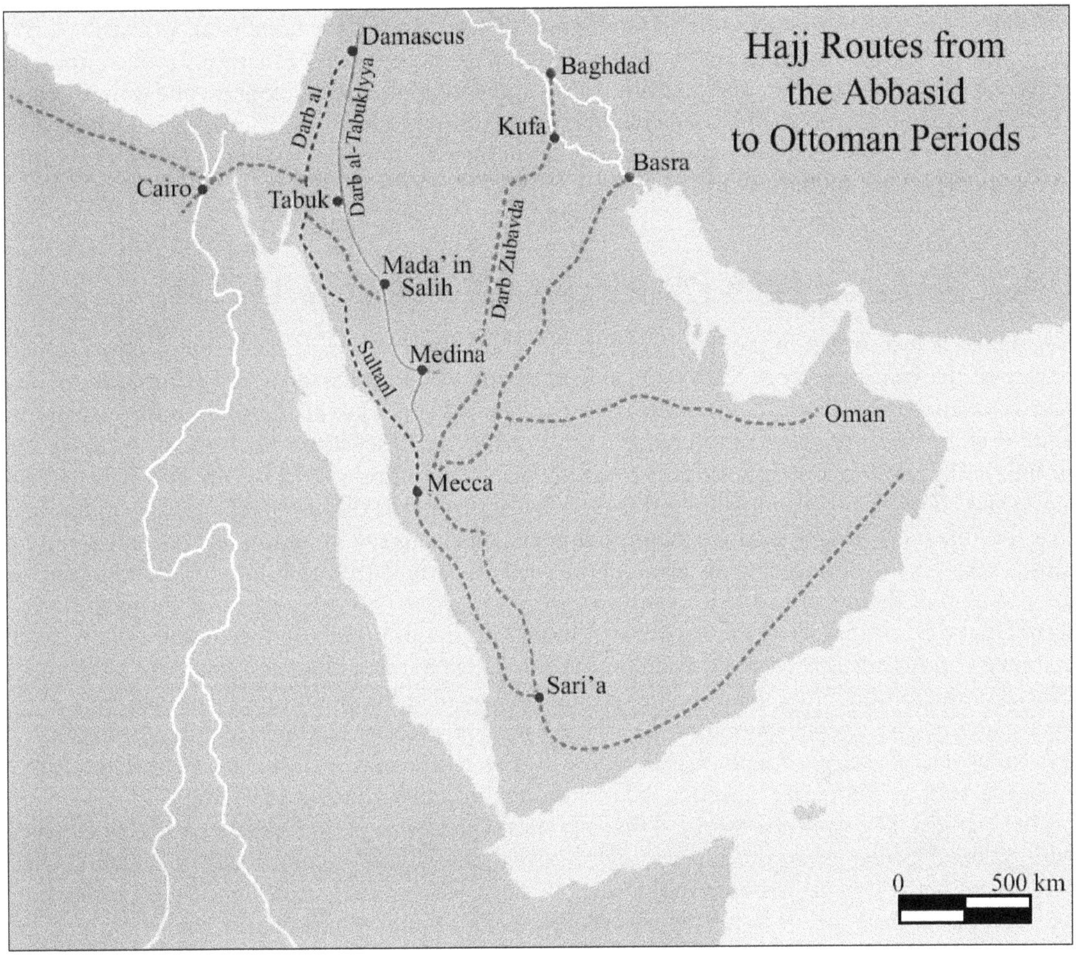

Figure 7.1 Hajj routes from the Abbasid to Ottoman Periods. (Map courtesy of Ernest Cowles, Oklahoma State University.)

on behalf of cultural singularity and people's control over their lives and environment' (1997:3). With regard to Islamic identity, he claims that the concept of *umma* has today superseded that of *watan*, or homeland (1997:14). It remains to be proven, however, that religious identity was antithetical to alternative forms of identity before this past century. Moreover, it is not certain that a single, unified vision of Islam is the normative response to international challenges on the political and economic fronts. Political manipulation of international Islamic networks will engender a multiplicity of responses on the local and personal levels. An analysis of *hajj*, in this regard, is particularly illuminating.

In its structure, process and function, Muslim pilgrimage certainly qualifies as a form of network. In its structure, the *hajj* route has 'nodes' (pilgrim stops and saints' shrines) in a network of routes that takes the pilgrim from his or her earthly residence to the spiritual home of Mecca. The process of pilgrimage transforms notions of 'locality' by creating a new global center, which is the destination of the pilgrim. As for function, the *hajj* not only facilitates face-to-face contact of Muslims across the globe, but also reinforces a global culture defined by religious identity and practice.

It is the purpose of this paper to trace the history of *hajj* as a factor in creating international networks in the Islamic world. To this end, the study will illustrate ways in which state control of the Muslim pilgrimage has created both a global Islamic identity (based on the concept of *umma*) and particularist identities (manifested in religious sectarianism and nationalism). In order to highlight the ambiguities of identity induced by the pilgrimage experience, I will use a variety of sources: archaeological (inscriptions and architecture), anthropological (travelogues and tombstones), historical (medieval geographies, administrative guides and chronicles), and technical (today's Internet). The study concludes with an assessment of the effectiveness of *hajj* as a globalizing factor in the medieval and modern worlds.

Hajj in the Early Islamic Period—the Abbasids (750–1250 CE)

Regular state investment in the *hajj* began in the Abbasid period, with the leveling, clearing, and paving of the *hajj* route from Kufa to Mecca; the provision of milestones (*amyal*) for identifying rest stops along the way; the construction of fortified posts (*qusur*) to protect pilgrims from bandits; and the endowment of water installations (such as cisterns and settling tanks, reservoirs, dams and troughs). Our written sources for this period emphasize the central role of the Abbasid state in regulating and controlling the annual pilgrimage. It is clear from the distances recorded on milestones that the mile (*mil*) and postal stage (*barid*, one of which equals twelve miles) had become standard units of the state for measuring distance on the road (al-Rashid 1992:140). Several of the Muslim geographers of the ninth and tenth centuries were Ministers of State Posts and, in this capacity, were able to record in detail the network of roads, stops and installations that were the Abbasid communications infrastructure (al-Rashid 1980:2). While most of these constructions were under official state sponsorship, some were the result of endowment (*waqf*) by pious Muslims. One of the most generous sponsors in this regard was Umm Zubayda, the wife of Harun al-Rashid, after whom the Kufa-Mecca road was named. According to the tenth-century historian al-Mas'udi, Umm Zubayda built caravanseries, cisterns and wells along this route (Peters 1994:69).

In a pattern that was to be repeated throughout the medieval period, the Abbasids, when faced with political challenges to their hegemony, responded with intense patronage of religion. Their investment in the Iraqi *hajj* route should, then, be understood as a form of political legitimization. Milestones, for instance, occasionally record renovations done by a particular caliph. By marking the pilgrimage roads in this way, Abbasid caliphs both laid claim to the territory through which the roads passed as well as fulfilled their role as protectors of the *umma* and Holy Places, two of the responsibilities of the caliph according to contemporary Islamic political theory. In this way the globalizing concept of *umma* was manipulated by the state for state purposes. Such politicization of Muslim pilgrimage would be part of the official programs of both the Mamluks and Ottomans who followed.

If the state's manipulation of the annual pilgrimage is clear from the written and archaeological sources, the impressions and attitudes of individual pilgrims are more difficult to assess. Miscellaneous prayers inscribed on boulders along the *hajj* route, the tombstones of the pilgrims who died on the way, and occasional travellers' accounts give some indication that the personal experience of the *hajj* was an ambiguous one. Prayers for pardon characterize Abbasid-period graffiti, such as one on a hillside north of al-Suwarqiyya in the Hijaz, which reads: 'O God, pardon Habab, the son of 'Ubayd, his terrible sin' (al-Rashid 1980:241–2). To make the *hajj* for absolution of a sin is a common enough theme in pilgrims' accounts from all periods, thus an inscription such as this is in keeping with universal, orthodox attitudes towards the pilgrimage. Many of these pilgrims died *en route* to Mecca. Tombstones of the Abbasid period reused in mosque walls or found in nearby cemeteries carry Quranic verses that attest to the inevitability of death. One grave marker from the same village of al-Suwarqiyya carried the following epitaph: 'I, Sulayman ibn Muhammad ibn Har Malah, testify that there is no god but Allah and Muhammad is His Messenger, that death is a reality and so is the Day of Resurrection' (paraphrased from al-Rashid 1980:245).

While these inscriptions appear to reflect a unified and orthodox image of Islamic identity and expectations, pilgrims' accounts of the later Abbasid period present us with a picture of cultural and religious alienation in a world divided by factionalism. 'Disillusionment', 'alienation', 'suspicion', and 'sectarian squabbles' are words that I. R. Netton uses to describe the *hajj* as experienced by Ibn Jubayr, the famous 12th-century Andalusian traveler. In his encounter with the Muslim 'other', Ibn Jubayr is deeply disappointed by disunity and heresies within the *umma* and is convinced more than before of his distinct identity as a *Maghribi* Muslim and Malikite scholar. His disappointment is most acute when he reaches the Holy Places of the Hijaz, where he finds that:

> most of [the people of] these Hijazi regions and other areas are sectarians and Shi'ites who have no religion and have split into diverse schools of thought... [They] most deserve to be cleansed by the sword and have their filth and uncleanness purged in blood shed in Holy War... (Netton 1993:63–4).

Al-Jubayr and Malcolm X experienced the *hajj* in very different ways. Clearly, the unifying ideal of *umma* was not always accomplished by pilgrimage. In the case of Ibn Jubayr, making the *hajj* actually reinforced a local, as opposed to a global, identity. The tension between *umma* and *'asabiyya* became even more marked during the Middle Islamic period.

Hajj in the Middle Islamic Period—The Mamluks (1250–1517 CE)

The collapse of the Abbasid state in the 10th century created political and cultural fragmentation in the Islamic world. Partial unification on both levels was made possible in the 13th century by the emergence of the Mamluk state in Egypt. This military dynasty of slave origin imposed a postal (*barid*) system in Greater Syria for security purposes. By the 14th century it mushroomed into a comprehensive communications network of postal centers (*marakiz*), pigeon and fire towers, and caravan stops that served multiple functions: military and economic.[2]

Pilgrimage was part of this system. Many *hajj* stops, such as Hasa and 'Aqaba in Jordan, were provided with structures that housed customs officials (*qusur*, *jusur*), sheltered travelling merchants and their goods (*khanat*), and provided services (such as water) for pilgrims (Ghawanmeh 1987: 324–5).[3] At the larger pilgrimage rest stops were seasonal markets (*aswaq mawsimiyya*) from which pilgrims could purchase supplies for the remainder of their journey or even sell some of their own merchandise and turn a profit (Ghawanmeh 1997:324–5).[4] Many pilgrimage accounts of the period included market guides that described how best to do business at these stops (El Moudden 1990:75). In his analysis of Transjordan in the Middle Islamic period, Jum'a Kareem suggests that *hajj* was only one part of the Mamluks' larger plan for economic investment in the region (Kareem 1987; Kareem 2000:11–17). While it is true that the *hajj* had always been tied up with business, it was the Mamluks who formalized this relationship by combining pilgrimage routes with market institutions.

The Mamluk state not only made use of the pilgrimage for its own security and economic purposes, but it also militarized the structure of the *hajj*. For instance, the *Amir al-Hajj* (a commander of a thousand) was both policeman and judge of the caravan and could depose the Sharifs of Mecca and Medina on behalf of the Sultan ('Ankawi 1974:157–8). This, of course, played a political purpose: all aspects of the pilgrimage, from its internal security to international relations, would fall under the control of Cairo, the capital.[5] The Mamluks could now rightfully claim the title of the 'protectors of the *hajj*'. The political potential of the *hajj* was further exploited by sending a *mahmal* (empty camel litter) with the *kiswa* (Kaaba cover) to Mecca with the annual Egyptian caravan, a practice begun by Sultan Baybars in 1266 and brought to an end long after the Mamluk period by Wahhabi reformers in 1926 (Peters 1994: 165, 167). Because the *kiswa* was inscribed with the Sultan's name and titles, it became a powerful symbol of authority over the Holy Places and, by

Figure 7.2 Mamluk caravanserai at 'Aqaba. Under the orders of Sultan Qansuh al-Ghuri, Amir Khayrbey al-'Ala'i built this caravanserai in 'Aqaba, Jordan's port on the Red Sea, to shelter, feed and provide security for Egyptian and Syrian travellers. The foundation inscription is unclear and states that the building was erected in either 1504 or 1514.

extension, over the entire *Dar al-Salaam*. Patronage of the Holy Places in Mecca through the building and restoration projects of Sultan Qaytbay in the fifteenth century continued this political process.[6]

In spite of its rigid control of the *hajj*, the Mamluk state was not entirely successful at using it to foster political allegiance or religious solidarity based on a universal Muslim identity. As with the Abbasid period, the official image of the annual pilgrimage often contrasted significantly from the personal experience of it. Education and Sufism were important incentives for many pilgrims as contemporary accounts would lead us to believe. For example, Ibn Battuta, the great Moroccan 'globetrotter' of the fourteenth century, made a practice of stopping at each major academic center *en route* to Mecca for extended study there (Gibb 1958:x). Centers of learning, such as Cairo, Damascus, Jerusalem and Zabid, attracted (and distracted) would-be pilgrims in this period. In fact, the security of pilgrimage routes under the Mamluks facilitated travel from one university to another, making these cities practical 'nodes' in the pilgrimage network ('Ankawi 1974:149). For many pilgrims, making the pilgrimage *was* a search for knowledge, or in Arabic terms, *hajj* became *talab al-'ilm*.

While academic pursuits did little to create particularist identities (if anything, the university network helped consolidate an 'orthodox' Islamic identity), Sufism, or mystical Islam, helped to foster religious and political allegiances on a new level, that of the multiplicity of Sufi brotherhoods (or *tariqas*). Through official sponsorship of Sufi brotherhoods in the fourteenth century, the stigma attached to this 'heterodox' expression of Islam disappeared. It now became possible, and even common practice, for the Muslim faithful to travel from one end of the Islamic world to another to visit the burial places of Sufi saints. *Ziyara*, or voluntary travel to these 'saints' shrines', became a

Figure 7.3 Bayn al-Qasrayan—a Street of Schools in Mamluk Cairo. The madrasas of Mamluk Cairo were among the most renowned in the Islamic world. Students came from as far as Spain and Central Asia, often combining their study of *fiqh* (Islamic jurisprudence) with pilgrimage. The Bayn al-Qasrayn, the 'main street' of Mamluk Cairo, is framed by the façades of several adjoining madrasa complexes. Visible in this photograph are those of Sultans al-Nasir Muhammad (built over the years 1295–1304) and Barquq (1384–86).

kind of 'little pilgrimage' and was often combined with the obligatory and canonical *hajj* to Mecca (Tapper 1990:241). For the most celebrated traveler of the Mamluk period, Ibn Battuta, travel to saints' shrines for the purpose of acquiring blessing (*baraka*) was more important on a personal level than the *hajj* itself. While his description of Mecca is brief (and quite possibly lifted from an earlier traveler's account), he goes to great lengths to detail what he sees, does and hears at popular local shrines (Walker 2000:9–10). Ibn Battuta was a Sunni scholar of the Maliki school of jurisprudence; he was, therefore, an orthodox, mainstream Muslim. His attitude towards pilgrimages of all levels, then, was more or less representative of his time.

Travel also functioned to highlight another cleavage in the *umma*: that between Sunni and Shi'i. Like Ibn Jubayr before him, it is during the *hajj* that Ibn Battuta was confronted for the first time with what were in his mind the glaring differences between Sunni and Shi'i Islam.[7] In fact, it becomes a common theme of pilgrimage accounts from this point on to condemn the Shi'ite 'heresies' of Syria and Persia, encountered on one's travels. Through such passages the pilgrim personalizes his accounts and defines for himself a Muslim identity that is distinct from other believers. The result is a diary-like account that emphasizes sectarianism and reflects a 'sense of local consciousness' (El Moudden 1990:69). Sectarianism takes on a regional flavor in these accounts. For Ibn Battuta, being Moroccan meant being Sunni and, therefore, a 'legitimate' Muslim, whereas some Syrians and most Persians, as Shi'is, were heretics.

Together the Mamluk-period chronicles, administrative manuals, and travelers' accounts indicate that local and sectarian identities grew stronger as state control over the *hajj* was intensified and systematized. The globalizing ideal of the *umma* was in many ways at odds with the actual practice of *hajj*. Local identity-creation at the expense of Muslim unity progressed further under the Ottomans, who conquered the Mamluks in 1517.

Hajj in the Late Islamic Period—The Ottomans (1517–1918 CE) and the Post-Ottoman Period (1920s)

While the conquest of neighboring Muslim states is not technically sanctioned by Islam, the Ottoman sultans were able to legitimize their expansionism, in part, through political rhetoric and official titles. One royal title is particularly illustrative for this study: 'Servant of the Two Sanctuaries'. As the defender of Mecca and Medina, the Sultan was able to claim authority over all Muslims internationally. Control over the Hijaz, then, played an important role in regional politics and the later diplomatic confrontations with Europe.

The Ottomans invested in the *hajj* on a greater scale than any of their predecessors. Soon after coming to power in Syria, the Ottoman state embarked on an ambitious campaign to defend the Damascus–Mecca route. The old Mamluk route, the Darb al-Sultani (otherwise known as the 'King's Highway'), was replaced with a new route that ran further east, through the interior deserts of Jordan—the Darb al-Tabukiyya (see Figure 7.1).[8] Sultan Selim I [r. 1512–1520] and Suleiman

Figure 7.4 Mosque-mausoleum of Mursi Abu al-'Abbas, Alexandria. The Spanish spiritual leader Sidi Shihab al-Din Abu al-Khazragi is buried at the medieval mosque he built in Alexandria, Egypt. Today it is the largest and most popular mosque in the city and continues to be a focus of pilgrimage and Sufi festivals.

'the Magnificent' [r. 1520–1566] built several forts (*qala'at*) in Transjordan, which garrisoned troops and protected cisterns from the predations of Bedouin (see Petersen 1989 and 1995 for architectural analyses of these constructions).The route north of Damascus was equipped with large caravansaries, many of which included marketplaces, shops, bathhouses and mosques (Sauvaget 1937; Petersen 1995:300).

The Ottomans invested in *hajj* security in other ways. They regulated the guild of guides, a self-regulating body of transportation agents in Mecca and Jedda (the *muqawwims* who provided pilgrims with camels for transport and other supplies); established guidelines for merchants accompanying the pilgrim caravans; and created supervisory organizations to oversee preparations for the caravans each year, such as the Bureau of Pilgrimage in Cairo (for details on these developments see Peters 1994:144–83). This structure has remained more or less intact today under Saudi supervision (see Figure 7.2).

The nineteenth century witnessed new regulations in the operation of the *hajj* machinery, many of which reflected tensions between the Ottoman state and Europe. The spread of cholera worldwide between 1831 and 1912 made the annual pilgrimage to Mecca an international issue, as Muslims from all over the world (including Europe) now traveled to the Hijaz. Technological improvements in pilgrim transport (the use of steamships on the Red Sea in the 1830s and in the Persian Gulf from 1865, the opening of the Suez Canal in 1869, and the construction of the Hijaz Railway as far as Medina in 1908) brought ever larger numbers of pilgrims to the shores of the peninsula, increasing the risks of contagious diseases (Peters 1994:298). In an effort to supervise health inspections, look after the safety of their own nationals, and maintain espionage missions against the Ottoman state, several European countries opened consulates in Jedda, Mecca's port (Roff 1982). Under European pressure, the Ottomans organized their own health program for pilgrims (administered through quarantine centers, health certificates, and an expanded network of hospitals and clinics) and introduced an immigration system (by requiring passports and visas from foreign pilgrims for the first time in the 1880s—Peters 1994:273).

Such regulations had mixed effects on the way pilgrims experienced the *hajj*. On one level, Ottoman, and then Saudi, control impacted identity formation worldwide by standardizing Islamic practice. It was the annual pilgrimage that made possible the spread of Wahhabism to areas outside the Arabian peninsula over the course of the nineteenth century. This strictly orthodox, revivalist movement of the Hanbali school of Islamic jurisprudence attempted to eliminate such 'innovations' in Islam as Sufism. When the Saudi family gained control of the Hijaz in 1926, Wahhabism became the official version of Islam in the Holy Places; Sufi and Shi'i pilgrims, in particular, became targets of abuses during the *hajj* season (for eyewitness accounts of the first pilgrimages under Wahhabi supervision, see Peters 1994:352–62).

Wahhabism was also a driving force behind Islamic reform movements in places as far from the Hijaz as West and East Africa, Central Asia, and South and Southeast Asia. Pilgrims from these regions, the so-called 'periphery' of the Islamic world, were by and large practicing Sufis back home. For many of them, it was on the *hajj* to Mecca that they first encountered 'orthodox' Islam. Wahhabi missionaries and reformers actively networked during the *hajj* season to reach such pilgrims in an effort to wipe out Sufism worldwide and create a uniform vision of Islam. Their efforts had some noticeable success in West Africa and Southeast Asia to where Wahhabism was exported (for Indonesia, see Lapidus 1988:757–1; for Morocco, see El Moudden 1990:70; for Malaysia consult McDonnell 1990:116–18). These reform movements did much to create a sense of religious solidarity worldwide, a symbolic *umma* that transcended ethnic, linguistic and political boundaries.

State control over the pilgrimage, however, did not always reinforce the *umma*. In the nineteenth century it often had the opposite effect, laying the foundations for nascent nationalism and fueling separatist movements as far afield as Central Asia and Indonesia. At the same time that Wahhabi

Figure 7.5 Ottoman caravanserai at Qatrana. Qatrana is located on the Desert Highway, the primary *hajj* route for Syrian pilgrims traveling through Jordon under the Ottomans. While the date of the original construction of this caravanserai has been disputed, it serviced large numbers of pilgrims in the 16th century.

reformers tried to stamp out Sufism at home, the *tariqas* (Sufi brotherhoods) were equally active during the pilgrimage season, establishing new ties across borders and reinforcing old ones. Contact between members of the same brotherhood, renewed during *hajj*, helped create the dissident networks behind the uprisings against Russian occupation in Central Asia, British and French colonialism in West Africa, and foreign rule in East Africa (Lapidus 1988:784–817, 823–78). In this way, *hajj* fed early expressions of nationalism (*'asabiyya* or *wataniyya*).

Hajj Today

The annual pilgrimage today continues the parallel and contradictory trends in identity-making that characterized the Ottoman *hajj*. Rigid state control over who can make the pilgrimage each year, where and when they can travel, and what practices will be allowed at the Holy Places has helped Muslims realize the idea of Islamic unity, by recreating Mecca as the geo-spiritual center of the Islamic world, while at the same time it has reinforced political, ethnic and cultural dividing lines within the *umma*.

In 1998, because of the unprecedented increase in the number of pilgrims coming from abroad, the Saudi state imposed a quota system on every foreign nation, one that is supposed to be based on that country's population.[9] Although the decision on how to apportion the annual pilgrimage certificates is left up to the authorities of each country, the Saudis, through their consulates and embassies abroad, have maintained strict control over the immigration process, from issuing Pilgrimage

Visas to organizing the local transportation agents, called *mutawwifs*, who accompany every group of 5000 nationals.

In every foreign country, authorized travel agencies, often under the direction of an Islamic association, help pilgrims obtain their visas and ID cards and make sure they comply with Saudi requirements for the pilgrimage, such as proof of immunization for meningitis and writing a will. American Muslims, in addition, are still required to render proof of their conversion or understanding of Islam.[10] Travel agencies also facilitate this and have names of scholars in the US who are authorized by the Saudi state to approve the pilgrim's application. Pilgrimage has now become a 'package deal' in most countries, where travel, food, lodging, and even pre-*hajj* video tapes, books, and classes on Arabic and *hajj* rituals are included in one price. Many aspects of Saudi immigration law are actually an extension of Ottoman pilgrimage regulations. Most of the modern *hajj*-related restrictions, such as the obligation to carry an identity card and to remain with your own national group at all times have the effect of consolidating ethnic or political identities. Pilgrims from one country often note that they have had little contact with fellow believers from other nations. In an analysis of travel journals written by South Asian pilgrims in the late nineteenth and early twentieth century, Barbara Metcalf has discovered that the pilgrim almost always describes himself as an 'Indian Muslim' and that his frame of reference is his own people (Metcalf 1990:90). The separation of national groups of pilgrims from one another may have also had an impact on modern Malaysian identity-making, by creating a newly moneyed and respectable 'middle class' at home (McDonnell 1990). The experience of *hajj* today is as ambiguous as it was hundreds of years ago.

Figure 7.6 Reservoir of Qatrana caravanserai. To provide water for the public is one of the highest forms of almsgiving in Islam, bringing the donor *barakhat* (blessings). The caravanserai at Qatrana was provided with a large reservoir to serve the needs of pilgrims, merchants and their transport animals. The Ottomans regularly stationed small garrisons at these *khans* to guard the water supplies.

Conclusions

The practice of making a pilgrimage to Mecca once in one's lifetime has as its objective the ritual creation of a symbolic geo-spiritual center. The rituals associated with *hajj* and, indeed, the entire language used to describe it emphasize the ideal of community and equality. In this sense, *hajj* has always been a globalizing force.

Muslim pilgrimage has at the same time been a factor in realizing divisions in the *umma* and in creating multiple identities based on local images of what it means to be Muslim. This double process of unification and division in identity-making may be, in part, a response to the ways states have controlled the Holy Places. As a symbol of both sovereignty and community, the *hajj* has historically been the object of political manipulation. In terms of today's discourse on Islamic dissidence, globalization has itself been the process of setting the concept of *umma*, or the worldwide community of believers, against that of *watan*, or nation (Kamal Pasha and Samatar 1996). Failed modernization and nationalism, the theorists hold, have created the conditions in which alternative identities have emerged. One form of identity is a reaction to the other. So, too, do regional expressions of Islam resist the standardization of a politicized pilgrimage.

The ritual of making pilgrimage to Mecca annually recreates a global identity, which in this case is universal Islam. That it has also inadvertently sown the seeds, at one time or another, of political dissidence and nationalism illustrates one way that this historical 'network instrumentality', under political control, has created 'resistance identities', to use the terms coined by Manuel Castells. However, unlike his definition of *umma* as a resistance identity to economic and cultural globalization in the twentieth century, both *umma* and particularist Islamic identities (as 'legitimizing' and 'resistance' identities, respectively) have historically been products of Muslim pilgrimage. *Hajj* is, therefore, a complex, but at the same time very modern, agent for globalization.

Notes

1. Malcolm X's pilgrimage was a turning point in the development of American Islam.
2. Moreover, many of the buildings associated with *barid* stops were eventually converted into caravansaries. Because caravan rest houses (caravansaries) and their services were maintained with *waqf* monies from private endowments, the financial burden to the state was reduced (Sauvaget 1941: 54 and 63, n. 261).
3. To this may also be added several small, fortified sites with accompanying water installations, identified by archaeological survey: al-Tuwana (Fiema 1993 and 1997; MacDonald 1999) and Zarqa and Jiza (Petersen 1991). For an excellent theoretical analysis of archaeological evidence for pilgrimage sites, see Insoll 1999: 109–14.
4. According to Ghawanmeh, two of the most important markets in Transjordan that catered to the needs of pilgrims were 'Aqaba (a seasonal market) and 'Ajlun (the town's permanent *suq*). For a description of water facilities, see Petersen 1994.
5. Walker 2004 explores the political agenda of Mamluk investment in one particular pilgrimage site, the Great Mosque of Damascus. This was accomplished through a combination of endowments, renovations, and architectural inscriptions.
6. For an art historical analysis of Qaytbay's building projects in Mecca and Medina, see Newhall 1987.
7. In his words, the Shi'ites were 'abominable people who hate the Ten Companions and every person whose name is "Omar"' (Gibb 1969:61).
8. This route was also called the *Tariq al-Bint* ('The Daughter's Route'), named after Sultan Selim's daughter who complained of the banditry and difficulty of travel along the King's Highway (Petersen 1995:300; Schick 1998:570).
9. For current statistics on pilgrimage in recent years, see the internet site: islam.about.com/library/weekly/aa022701.htm
10. An excellent description of this process in the 1960s can be found in Malcolm X's autobiography, where he explains how he was required to obtain a letter from a Dr Shawarbi in order to make the *hajj* (Haley 1999:326–7).

References

'Ankawi, A. (1974) The pilgrimage to Mecca in Mamluk times. *Arabian Studies* 1:146–70.

Burgoyne, M. (1987) *Mamluk Jerusalem: An Architectural Study*. London: World of Islam Festival Trust.

Castells, M. (1997) *The Power of Identity: The Information Age: Economy, Society and Culture* 2. 3 vols. Cambridge, MA: Blackwell Publishers.

Eickelman, D. and Piscatori, J. (eds) (1990a) *Muslim Travellers: Pilgrimage, Migration and the Religious Imagination*. Berkeley: University of California Press.

Eickelman, D. and Piscatori, J. (1990b) Social theory in the study of Muslim societies. In *Muslim Travellers: Pilgrimage, Migration and the Religious Imagination*, edited by D. Eickelman and J. Piscatori. Berkeley: University of California Press, pp. 3–25.

Fiema, Z. T. (1993) Tuwaneh and the *Via Nova Traiana* in southern Jordan. A short note on the season. *Annual of the Department of Antiquities of Jordan* 37:549–50.

Fiema, Z. T. (1997) At-Tuwana – the development and decline of a classical town in southern Jordan (with a note on the site preservation). In *Studies in the History and Archaeology of Jordan* 6:313–16.

Ghawanmeh, Y. (1987) al-Tijara al-Dawliyya fi al-Urdunn fi al-'Asr al-Mamluki. *Studies in the History and Archaeology of Jordan* 3: 323–31.

Gibb, H. A. R. (1958) *The Travels of Ibn Battuta, AD 1325–1354*, vol. I. Cambridge: Hakluyt Society.

Gibb, H. A. R. (1969) *Ibn Battuta: Travels in Asia and Africa, 1325–1354*. New York: Augustus M. Kelley.

Haley, A. (1999) *The Autobiography of Malcolm X*. New York: The Ballantine Publishing Group.

Insoll, T. (1999) *The Archaeology of Islam*. Malden, MA: Blackwell Publications.

Kamal Pasha, M. and Samatar, A. I. (1996) The resurgence of Islam. In *Globalization: Critical Perspectives*, edited by J. Mittelman. Boulder, CO: Lynne Rienner, pp. 187–201.

Kareem, J. (1987) Evidence of the Umayyad Occupation in the Jordan Valley as seen in the Jisr Hussein Region. MA thesis, Yarmouk University.

Kareem, J. M. H. (2000) *The Settlement Patterns in the Jordan Valley in the Mid- to Late Islamic Period*. BAR Int Series 877. Oxford: British Archaeological Reports.

Lapidus, I. M. (1988) *A History of Islamic Societies*. Cambridge: Cambridge University Press.

Long, D. E. (1979) *The Hajj Today: A Survey of the Contemporary Makkah Pilgrimage*. Albany, NY: State University of New York Press.

MacDonald, B. (1999) Tafila-Busayra Survey. *ACOR Newsletter* 11.1: 4–5.

McDonnell, M. B. (1990) Patterns of Muslim pilgrimage from Malaysia, 1885–1985. In *Muslim Travellers: Pilgrimage, Migration, and the Religious Imagination*, edited by D. F. Eickelman and J. Piscatori. Berkeley: University of California Press, pp. 111–30.

Metcalf, B. D. (1990) The pilgrimage remembered: South Asian accounts of the *Hajj*. In *Muslim Travellers: Pilgrimage, Migration, and the Religious Imagination*, edited by D. F. Eickelman and J. Piscatori. Berkeley: University of California Press, pp. 85–107.

el Moudden, A. (1990) The ambivalence of *Rihla*: community integration and self-definition in Moroccan travel accounts, 1300–1800. In *Muslim Travellers: Pilgrimage, Migration, and the Religious Imagination*, edited by D. F. Eickelman and J. Piscatori. Berkeley: University of California Press, pp. 69–84.

Netton, I. R. (1993) Basic structures and signs of alienation in the *Rihla* of Ibn Jubary. In *Golden Roads: Migration, Pilgrimage and Travel in Medieval and Modern Islam*, edited by I. R. Netton. Surrey, UK: Curzon Press, pp. 57–74.

Newhall, A. (1987) The Patronage of the Mamluk Sultan Qa'it Bay, 872-901/1468-1496. Unpublished PhD dissertation, Harvard University.

Peters, F. E. (1994) *The Hajj: The Muslim Pilgrimage to Mecca and the Holy Places*. Princeton: Princeton University Press.

Petersen, A. (1989) Early Ottoman forts on the Darb al-Hajj. *Levant* 21:97–119.

Petersen, A. (1991) Two forts on the medieval Hajj route in Jordan. *Annual of the Department of Antiquities of Jordan* 35:347–60.

Petersen, A. (1994) The archaeology of the Syrian and Iraqi Hajj routes. *World Archaeology* 26:47–56.

Petersen, A. (1995) The fortification of the pilgrimage route during the first three centuries of Ottoman rule (1516–1757). *Studies in the History and Archaeology of Jordan* 5:299–305.

al-Rashid, S. (1980) *Darb Zubayda: The Pilgrim Route from Kufa to Mecca*. Riyadh: Riyadh University Libraries.

al-Rashid, S. (1992) A new Abbasid milestone from al-Rabada in Saudi Arabia. *Arabian Archaeology and Epigraphy* 3:138–43.

Roff, W. (1982) Sanitation and security: the imperial powers and the nineteenth century and the Hajj. *Arabian Studies* 6:143–60.

Sauvaget, J. (1937) Les caravanserais Syriens du Hadj de Constantinople. *Ars Islamica* 4:98–121.

Sauvaget, J. (1941) *La Poste aux Chevaux dans l'Empire des Mamelouks*. Paris: Librairie D'Amèrique et d'Orient.

Schick, R. (1998) The archaeology of Palestine/Jordan in the Early Ottoman period. *ARAM* 10:563–75.

Tapper, N. (1990) *Ziyaret*: gender, movement, and exchange in a Turkish community. In *Muslim Travellers: Pilgrimage, Migration, and the Religious Imagination*, edited by D. F. Eickelman and J. Piscatori. Berkeley: University of California Press, pp. 236–55.

Walker, B. (2000) Muslim Images of the Holy Land: Ibn Battuta's *Rihla* in Bilad al-Sham. Unpublished conference paper, Annual Meeting of the American School of Oriental Research, panel entitled 'Accounts of Travelers to the Holy Land', Nov 15–18.

Walker, B. (2004) Commemorating the sacred spaces of the past: the Mamluks and the Umayyad mosque at Damascus. *Near Eastern Archaeology* 67.1:27–39.

Connectivity: Transjordan during the Persian Period

Paul J. Ray, Jr.

Introduction

Post-processual archaeology has stressed theory-building and synthesis. Based on a dialectic which holds that the interpretation of data (including history and literary sources) mediates as an analogy between past and present as distant and recent sources of experience and understanding, Hodder (1992:178–9) has suggested that this process involves both observation and theoretical reconstruction in creative tension contributing to both past and present.

One way that archaeologists have contributed to theory-building is to borrow concepts from the social sciences and the humanities. One of the more recent theories within the social sciences is based on Manuel Castells' *The Rise of the Network Society* (1996). Yet the same processes (economy, society and culture) by which Castells defines the 'Information Age', were at work throughout history, especially history as conceived in terms of the *longue durée* of Braudel (1972). The *longue durée* focuses on those aspects of everyday life, such as language, trade and routes of travel, which remain relatively unchanged for long periods of time. Using Castells' construct of globalization and taking up David Ludden's (1997) cues for applying it to history as mediated through Braudel's temporality of the *longue durée* we will explore such factors as the strivings of empire, long-term growth in the number and significance of sites, technology, routes of travel, trade and language during the Iron IIC/Persian period in Transjordan in an attempt to assess 'global' connectivity in the distant past.

The Persian period (539–332 BC) was international (or 'global') in scope, with trade connections from as far away as Attic Greece and southwest Arabia; the former mediated by the maritime trade networks of the Phoenicians and the latter with the aid of Arab caravans and middlemen. The Persians built administrative centers connected by a vast road system. The imperial bureaucratic system, facilitated by a standard coinage and Aramaic as the *lingua franca* of the empire, broke down barriers of culture and language, as well as allowing for the long-range exchange of ideas and material culture. These factors make the Persian period an interesting test case as an early globalizing force.

In the following overview, we will focus primarily, but not exclusively, on the Persian province of Ammon since this region of Transjordan is better known archaeologically. Moab and Edom were probably also provinces during the Persian period, but there is as yet no conclusive evidence for this assertion (Stern 2001:369–70).

'Globalization'

According to Ludden (1997:1) globalization is:

> a long term historical process, but it is also a project and a paradigm whose contours have changed dramatically over time. As a process, it can be defined as an on-going increase in the number of

effective interactions among sites around the globe, a deepening and expansion of the power of those influential elements that circulate widely among people and places to effect change in local conditions and experience.

Strivings of Empire

The globe in 'globalization' is a type of human territory, a space marked by human aspirations and power. Historically, globalization has emerged from the expansion of territorial powers over the globe. This imparts to the process a sense of direction, but also a historical geography that can be mapped by locating routes of travel, centers of institutional order and symbols of legitimacy and leadership (Ludden 1997:3). By the end of the reign of Darius I (522–486 BC), the Persian empire stretched from India (Indus River) to Europe (parts of Thrace) in the north and Africa (Libya, with Cyrene and Barca) in the south as well as Cyprus in the Mediterranean Sea, and from the Caucasus Mountains and the Aral Sea in the north to the Persian Gulf and Indian Ocean in the south, reaching the largest extent ever attained by an empire in the Near East (Olmstead 1948:110–16, 135–50; Lyon, Rowen and Hamerow 1969:10; Stern 2001:254) up to the time of Imperial Rome. The main accomplishments of Darius' reign were in the realm of imperial administration, based to a certain extent on the Assyrian model (Roux 1980:377). He organized (or rather expanded) the empire into twenty satrapies (Herodotus *Histories* 3.89), developed a sophisticated road and postal/communication system to maintain control over the most remote areas of the realm, and instituted legal and economic reforms. The latter along with the establishment of a system of tribute and taxation, was based on coinage, adopted from the Lydians, and unified on the gold standard. The coin used in banking (on banking during the Persian period cf. the Murashu documents, Coogan 1974:6–12; Yamauchi 1996:243, 274–5) and trade was the gold *daric*, worth twenty silver *sigloi*, the coin struck by local authorities in the satraps (Olmstead 1948:185–94, 299–301; Roux 1980:377; Betlyon 1992:1082; Yamauchi 1996:174–82; Stern 2001:354, 371). Transjordan, along with Syria, Phoenicia, Palestine and Cyprus (together with Babylon until c. 482 BC), was part of the fifth Persian Satrap (Herodotus *Histories* 3.91) known in Aramaic as *'ăbar năharāh* (Ezra 4:10-11) and in Hebrew as *'ēber hannāhār* (Ezra 8:36; Neh 2:7), derived from *ebir-nari,* the name of the earlier administrative district during the Assyrian and Babylonian periods (Stern 2001:366, 369, 372). Transjordan was further sub-divided into the province of Ammon, and probably also Moab and Edom. These provinces, each headed by a local governor (*peḥāh*) were small courts imitating those of the satraps (Stern 1995a: 432). In terms of Ammon, two provincial seals with one of its officials *Shuba* (šb'), the governor or perhaps the treasurer, from the end of the 6th or early 5th century BC, have recently been found at Tell al-'Umayri (Herr 1992:163–6; 1995a:124; 1997:335–37).

Chronology

As is now known, the Ammonites and probably the other Transjordan cultures of Moab and Edom did not disappear with the arrival of the Babylonians, but continued to flourish throughout the Persian period (Herr 1993:29, 35; 1995b:617–19; 1999:232–4; Sauer 1986:18; 1994:248; Younker 1994:314–15) and, perhaps later. In the Ammonite region, ostraca and seal impressions indicate that although the script used was Aramaic, the language was Ammonite. In addition, pottery typical of the Cisjordan, including such forms as sausage jars and to a certain extent mortaria, is for the most part not found in this region. Instead, there was a continuation of Iron Age II pottery traditions (Herr 1995b:619; 1999:234), including a multiplicity of black ware bowls, in central Transjordan. Apparently, there was no cultural break with the coming of the Persians, hence the term Iron IIC/Persian period for the material culture in this region.

Site Development, Settlement Pattern and the Significance of Sites

Empirically, 'globalization' can be see as long-term growth in the number and significance of sites in which circulatory movements intersect and from which they emanate; and historically, data from ancient times to the present depict circles of rippling influences being broadcast outward along networks of movement, representation and communication to influence the character of locality (Ludden 1997:1–2). Evidence, mostly from survey data, indicates a definite development of sites from earlier in the Iron Age to the Iron Age IIC/Persian period in Transjordan.[1]

The significance of this data might be seen by a closer look at a particular region. On the Ammonite plateau, other than the capital, the largest sites during the Iron IIC/Persian period appear to have been Madaba, Jalul and Umm el-'Amad on the northern end of the Madaba Plains (the Mishor). These sites, located within the bread basket of the region, were probably large towns. In addition, both Madaba and Umm el-'Amad were located along major and secondary north-south roads respectively. The other major town sites include Tell el-'Umeiri, Khirbet el 'Al, and Tell Ikhtanu, also on major road systems. Tell Jawa, as well as the large site of el-Yaduda, were located on a secondary north-south road, and Tell er-Rameh was located on the east-west trunk road. Both of these sites were no doubt important towns. Tell Hesban was strategically located at the crossroads of the main north-south and the east-west trunk road. Other town sites included Umm el-Hanafish on the plateau and Umm el-Qanafid, guarding the spring of 'Ain Rawda on the Wadi Hesban. Khirbet 'Ayun Musa, a relatively small fortress guarded the spring of the same name. In addition, there was Masuh on the plateau and Tell el-Kafrein in the Jordan Valley. Though both are prominent sites, neither seem to have been connected with a road system. The latter may have functioned as yet another barrier to would-be attackers from the west.

The remainder of the sites in the region were probably small villages, farmsteads, and watch-towers. The majority of these were located within the highland plateau region[2] with a smaller, but significant number in the wadis.[3] The large number of sites on the highland plateau would seem to reflect the continued emphasis, in this region, on land-tied cereal production, which was for the most part dependent on ridge soils (silty loam) (Christopherson and Guertin 1995:18–19; Christopherson *et al.* 1996:11, 17, 19, 24). Though there was always the need to protect water sources, most of the sites located in the wadis reflect the utilization of less desirable areas for food production. In addition to a drying of the climate during the Iron Age II/Persian period (Bruins 1994), this type of settlement pattern probably came about as a result of population pressures as well as being a response to a wider diversity of subsistence strategies (Christopherson *et al.* 1996:24). The system of agricultural terraces, already in use since Iron Age I, was evidently expanded considerably at this time (Christopherson and Guertin 1995:17, 19; Christopherson *et al.* 1996:17, 19).

The number and size of Iron Age I and early Iron Age II sites had remained fairly stable in this part of Jordan, but during the Iron IIC/Persian period there seems to have been a mushrooming of sites (Herr 1992:176; McGovern 1992:181), the intensification process finally reaching its climax (LaBianca 1990:156; LaBianca and Younker 1995:409–10). Though most of these sites were rather small, with some of the larger ones such as Tell el-'Umeiri even apparently becoming smaller (Herr 1992:176), the region still appears to have been fairly prosperous, much of it connected with wine production (Herr 1995a:121–5).

Unlike the coastal plain of Cisjordan, where a number of sites reveal typical Persian period architectural elements based on the Hippodamian plan, with streets laid out on a grid and residential quarters consisting of insulae with an open court plan, in Transjordan only a few Phoenician elements, which had already began to appear in late Iron Age II (Stern 1992:303–5), such as the quoin and pier technique of ashlar walls filled with fieldstones (at Tall Jawa) and occasional proto-Aeolic (Ionic) capitals (Amman and Mudaybi'), can be demonstrated at sites with Iron IIC/Persian period remains. In terms of burial customs of the era, there seem to have been two main types: a western

Phoenician-type shaft grave, occasionally with Egyptian inspired anthropoid coffins, along the coastal plain of Cisjordan (Stern 2001:473–4, 77) and an eastern/Achaemenid-type cist grave, sometimes with Mesopotamian-style clay larnax-type coffins such as the one found at Cemetery A at Tell Mazar (Yassine 1984:29; figs 2, 24). The coffin is similar to the one found in the tomb of Adoni-Nur at Amman (Harding and Tufnell 1953:59, pl. 6.47), which is perhaps slightly earlier (c. 650 BC) (Stern 2001:256, 264–5, 341, 474–5). A third type, also found in Transjordan, continues the rock-cut bench-type tombs of the Iron Age. Good representatives of this type are the Tobiad (Tobiah, Neh 2:10, who was probably the governor of Ammon cf. B. Mazar 1957) tombs at 'Iraq el-Emir and the tombs at Khilda and Amman (Stern 2001:477).

Figure 8.1 Jordanian terraces.

Technology

'Global' connectivity is thought to spread in bursts with the coming of new technologies (Ludden 1997:2). Though certainly not to the extent that has pervaded modern society, this concept may still be applicable to various historical periods. During the late Iron Age II/Persian period the main technological industries would have included metallurgy. Though neither bronze or iron technology could be said to be 'new' inventions, there are indications that there were major investments in these technologies at this time, so much so, that one, if not both, appear to have been produced on industrial proportions.

In the Feinan region, sites such as Khirbet Feinan, Khirbet en-Nahas (Hauptmann and Weisgerber 1987:419–35, pls LXVI.1-2, LXVIII, LXIX.1, LXX.2; Khouri 1988:125–6) and Kirbet el-Jariyeh / Glueck Sites 12 (Glueck 1935:20–34) and 22 (Glueck 1939a:270) (Hauptmann and Weisgerber

1987:422; Khouri 1988:125), with mineral concentrations and Iron IIC/Persian period mining activities in other nearby wadis (Dana and Khalid), were being worked from mine shafts sunk 20 m deep (at Wadi Khalid) to exploit ore horizons (or lenses of high-grade ore embedded in the host rocks deep inside the mountains) and in chamber-pillar mines (supported by natural rock pillars left in place as they dug) on an industrial scale. They also recycled old Chalcolithic and Bronze Age slag (crushing it with basalt anvils and hammers, collecting the droplets of ore and resmelting it). Analysis of the slags indicate a firing temperature in the range of 1250–1300 °C. Oak forests east of Fenian in the Tafila district and Al-Hisha between Shaubak (up Wadi Ghuweir / Shobak) and Petra as well as strands of Acacia in the Arava (Al-Eisawi 1985:52, fig. 9, 53, 55–6) would have been needed to fuel the copper kilns. Copper from the mines in this area was produced in quantities unparalleled in the southwestern Mediterranean, with the possible exception of Cyprus, at this time (Hauptmann and Weisgerber 1987:419).

The only iron ore deposits in Jordan are at Abu Thawab and Mugharat al-Warda (Coughenour 1976; Veldhuijzen and van der Steen 1999), the latter having 30 + mines in the area consisting of caves, some with horizontal shafts leading to the mines. Iron production is known to have occurred at the site of Tell el-Hammeh (east, or az-Zarqa = Glueck Site 190 and East Jordan Valley Site 115). This site is located at a point where the Wadi Zarqa opens into the Jordan River and the hot eastern (Sharqiya) winds blow through the majority of the year. Recently, smelting furnaces, tuyères and slag have been excavated at this site, the oldest example of iron production in the region. Mineralogical phases present in the slag definitely point to smelting as opposed to smithing and the fine under-developed dendrites indicate a furnace temperature in excess of 1200 °C. Trace elements in the slag have pointed to Mugharat al-Warda as the source of the iron deposit. Pottery associated with the furnaces indicate that the iron production at this site took place in Iron Age II (Veldhuijzen and van der Steen 1999:195–8). However, since ceramics found by the East Jordan Valley survey (Yassine *et al.* 1988: 190, 198–9) indicate a continuation of site settlement into the Persian period, it is likely the iron production continued that late as well. The oak forests in the Gilead/Ajlun area (Al-Eisawi 1985:52, fig. 9, 53) would have been needed for fuel to fire iron furnaces.

Routes of Travel and Trade

According to Ludden (1997:4) state and business interactions create overlapping frontiers of expansion and conflict. The state has a dual responsibility to facilitate the expansion of its native business interests as well as to protect its own territory, thus determining where the influence of one expansive state ends and another begins. During the Persian period the interest in products of long-distance trade created overlapping frontiers and potential or actual conflicts with other political entities such as Arabia and Greece respectively, the former having exemptions from certain taxes and free passage of trade for keeping peace and security along the trade routes and the latter who had trading colonies within the Persian realm along the coasts of Egypt, Palestine and Phoenicia (Stern 2001:420, 518–9). Phoenicia (with certain privileges extended for maritime aid), as well as Egypt and Cyprus, with their own brand of luxury goods, although usually under direct Persian control, occasionally rebelled creating additional conflict.

Besides completing a canal between the Nile and the Red Sea to facilitate trade from Egypt to the Arabian peninsula and the Persian Gulf, through the Red Sea (Kent 1953:147; Shea 1977:31–8; Yamauchi 1996:152–4), Darius I developed a sophisticated network of roads, upon which royal couriers were able to ride swiftly from the Aegean Sea to the Persian Gulf (Roux 1980:377), changing horses every 20 miles or so (Yamuchi 1996:174–5). Prior to this, with the exception of the area just outside Assyrian cities (Olmstead 1948:299), the primary connections over the Mesopotamian hills and plains were overland routes or tracks (von Soden 1994:119). In Transjordan the main

Figure 8.2 Ajlun region, Jordan.

north-south route was the King's Highway, a route existing already in the Iron Age. It stretched from the Red Sea at Aqaba, riding the watershed of Edom and Moab, passing near Buseirah, then through the Wadi Hesa to Kerak, through the Wadi Mujib to Dibon, then passed Madaba and Hesban before reaching Amman. From there it went through the Beq'ah Valley, through the Wadi Zerqa to Jerash across Gilead, over the Yarmuk River through Bashan to Damascus and farther north to Harran, in Anatolia. It appears to have followed the same basic route, at least in part, as in the Bronze Age, as Redford (1982a, 1982b) has reconstructed an itinerary of Thutmose III (No's 89-101), which went from Damascus over the Yarmuk River through Der'a, likely passing near Jerash before continuing south of the Wadi Zerqa, through the Baq'ah Valley and the Amman and Madaba districts and points farther south such as Dibon, then over the Wadi Mujib to Yarut and Kerak and finally taking an east-west route to the Lisan where he must have crossed the fords to Cisjordan (King *et al.* 1987:444–5, fig. 3).

An alternate route bypassing the deep gorges of the Wadis Hesa and Mujib, known in the Old Testament as *Way of the wilderness of Edom and Moab* (Deut 2:8; 2 Kgs 3:8, 20; Aharoni 1979:58) and currently as the Desert Highway, may also have been in existence at the time. There is also a natural route on the Moabite Plateau that runs between this desert highway and the King's Highway known as the Fajj al-'Usaykir).

From Cisjordan, Leonard (1987:261–6) has suggested two trade routes whereby imported Mycenaean and Cypriot wares were distributed throughout Transjordan. From the Mediterranean coast at Tell Abu Hawam these wares were brought through the Jezreel Valley as far as Beth-shean, then across the Jordan River to Pella. At this point one route went south through the Jordan Valley and then to Amman. The other route went north through the Wadi Ziqlab and/or the Wadi Taiyiba to Irbid and then south through the Baq'ah Valley to Amman, Sahab and Madaba. Although these routes were originally hypothesized for Late Bronze Age times, the fact that Tell Abu Hawam (Stratum V) continued to be a major commercial center and entry point for imports through the Iron Age (Stratum IV and III) and the Persian periods (Stratum II, possibly Akschaph of Pseudo-Scylax) (Balensi *et al.* 1993:7–9) suggests a continuation of the route at later points in time, as newer routes tend to follow earlier ones (Borstad 2000: 14–15, 121–2).

Farther south, another east-west route, the former *Way of Beth-jeshimoth* (Josh 12: 3), which had its origins at the main north-south highway of Cisjordan (sometimes called the Via-Maris) went up to Jerusalem in the central hill country of Cisjordan, and from there went down into the Ghor and came to Jericho. From this point it crossed over the fords of the Jordan River, and went to Hesban, which was at the crossroads of the main N-S (King's Highway) and this E-W road (Ray 2001). Other east-west routes still farther south consisted of the route across the Lisan (mentioned above) and another route which passed from the King's Highway at Ma'an, down into the 'Araba, and across the Negev to Gaza.

The main item of trade from the south was incense from Arabia. The incense bearing kingdoms of southern Arabia were Sheba, which had began to flourish as much earlier (c. 1300 BC) (Sauer 1995:42; Wilkinson 2001:45), and had its capital at Marib, Qataban, with its capital at Timna', the Minaeans, with their capital at Ma'in, and the Hadramaut, with its capital at Shabwa (Sauer 1995:42; van Beek 1997a:384, 1997b:18).

Camel caravans originated at the coast where incense products from India and Somalia (Punt) were brought by ship to Qana and Aden and trans-shipped with local incense products to markets in the north, including Jordan. From the frankincense forests in Dhofar, the material was brought along routes from Moscha and Syagrus to Qana. Along with myrrh from the Aden and Muza areas, these 'spices' were transshipped over the principal overland route to Shabwa with stops at Marib, Timna', and Ma'in to Nejran, and then to Yathrib, and al-'Ula, and farther up into Transjordan along the King's Highway to Damascus or through the Negev route to the Mediterranean Sea at the seaport emporium of Gaza (van Beek 1960; Zayadine 1995:69–70; Stern 2001:415).

Sheba was the earliest of these incense bearing Kingdoms (1 Kgs 10) to dominate the trade, with the northern Arabian kingdom of Dedan, centered at the oasis of al-'Ula, apparently functioning as middlemen Isa 21:13; Eze 27:15-20; Dedan is consistently associated with Sheba cf. Gen 10:7; 25:3; 1 Chr 1:32) along with or in competition to Tema' (Knaf 1992:346; Parr 1997b:160) during the early part of the Persian Period, as it had, it would seem, during the preceding Assyrian and Neo-Babylonian periods (Singer-Avitz 1999:41,47–50; Pritchard 1969:562; Graf 1992:122). One of the governors of Dedan, *Jašm, son of Šahr and 'Abd*, is evidently the Geshem of Neh 2:19; 6:1 (Winnett 1937:50–1; Yamauchi 1996:268–9). The fact that two other inscriptions of Geshem (*Geshem son of Shahar* and *Qainu son of Geshem, the king of Qedar*) were found at Tell el-Maskhuta in Egypt would seem to indicate that Dedanite traders were in charge of a large north Arabian confederacy that controlled an area between northern Arabia and northeastern Egypt, including southern Trans- and Cisjordan (Yamauchi 1996: 269). Another 5th century BC governor of Tema', *Pṣgw Shahru*, confirms that the ruling governors of the Hijaz were Qedarites. Though a powerful figure, Geshem would have been somewhat overseen by the Persian empire, as a satrap and governor of Qedar is known as early as the fifth year of Cyrus (Graf 1992:123).

The Minaeans, along with the kingdoms of Qataban and Hadhramaut, who flourished from the 11th through the 1st centuries BC, began to challenge Sheban supremacy for control of the trade routes around the end of the 5th century BC, with their major period of strength from c. 400 BC through the 2nd century BC (van Beek 1997a: 384). The Minaeans built a trading colony at al-'Ula and held control of the spice trade until the end of the 2nd century BC. The town of Ma'an, in southern Jordan, along the King's Highway, may possibly have been another trading colony of the Minaeans. Al-'Ula was replaced by a new colony at the town of Hegra (Meda'in Saleh) when the

Nabateans, who had formerly been middlemen for the Minaeans, took over the caravan routes in the vacuum that took place when Ma'in fell to Qataban and the subsequent jockeying for power by the southern Arabian kingdoms (Graf 1992:122; Zayadine 1995:70; Parr 1997a:133–4 and van Beek 1997a:384).

Frankincense from the Boswellia trees of the Dhofar forests and Myrrh *(Balsamodendrum myrrha)* from the Aden and Muza areas are fragrant gum-resins. They were used as aromatics (incense); fumigants; in igious rites (ceremonies and liturgy, as well as funerary rituals and mummification or embalming in Egypt); medicine (digestive aids, anointing oils for healing of wounds and infections of eyes and ears, as well as relief of pain); perfumes and cosmetics.

While the Persian Empire was a true state, and from a substantivist or structuralist approach (Dever 1995:113), its 'embedded' economic behavior is reflected in a market economy, the local provinces within Transjordan, as well as various other parts of the 5th Satrap, were for the most part tribal kingdoms (a complex social organization with simpler kin-based structures embedded within it, Younker 1997:242). Hence, long-distance trade is most readily recognized in trade items that are found archaeologically. From Transjordan, Persian period artifactual evidence of the incense trade consists of numerous small four-legged limestone incense altars (Stern 1982:182–95) from various sites (Tell es-Sa' idiyeh, cf. Pritchard 1985:66–8, figs 18.22, 174; and Twailan, cf. Bennett and Bienkowski 1995:85; figs 9.14.1, 9.59). Such altars had already been found during the Assyrian period along the trade route to Gaza in an area held by the Edomites (Singer-Avitz 1999; Stern 2001:513), but these altars became very popular in the Persian period. Another type of incense burner, a bronze caryatid censer was also found at the Umm Udhayna tomb near Amman (Khalil 1986:109). Additional evidence for the importance of the King's Highway trade route may possibly be recognized in artifacts such as Ostracon A5 from Tell Hesban, which has a list of Aramaized Arab traders (Cross and Geraty 1994:173); the cuneiform tablet (business document) from Harran, that was found at the site of Tawilan, in southern Jordan (Dalley 1995:67–8; figs 7.1–7) and the Minaean or proto-Dedanite inscription fragment on a jar from Tell el-Kheleifeh (Glueck 1938:15–16, fig. 5; 1939b:19; 1967:22, fig. 6.1, 24; Divito 1993:62, pl. 80b). In general, the relative prosperity on the Transjordanian provinces had much to do with the revival of international trade and the use of the King's Highway during the early years of the Persian period. This route probably also facilitated copper production at Feinan (Stern 2001:459–60), which as already pointed out, was produced on industrial scale at this time.

The coastal towns of Palestine consisted of a Phoenician population (with some Greeks living in trading colonies cf. Waldbaum 1997:12; Stern 2001:387, 521–2) during the 5th–4th centuries BC. As commercial traders the Phoenicians expanded the geographic scope of obtaining natural commodities (ivory, ebony and precious stones) and exploiting ore sources (gold, silver, tin, copper, iron and lead) by the use of trade routes earlier established by the Mycenaeans. Their trade network stretched from Gibraltar to Persia and from the Caucasus to Nubia. Their craftsmen manufactured small objects such as gold jewelry, engraved metal dishes, colored glass, and ivories, and produced exquisite textiles from purple dye made from the secretions of the *Murex* marine snail. In addition to establishing trading colonies throughout the Mediterranean, where immigrant craftsmen were set up in local workshops, they had a reciprocal trade relationship with Cyprus as well as sometimes acting as a middlemen for Greek goods (Ward 1997:314–15; Markoe 1997:326). Both Greek (Ionian) and Phoenician ships carried cargo on the Mediterranean at this time, being levied from 10% (the Phoenician ships) to 20% (the Ionian ships) customs duties as indicated on a recently published Aramaic text from Elephantine dated to the 11th year of Xerxes (475 BC). The cargo on Ionian ships included gold, silver, oil, wine and empty jars, while that on the Phoenician ships included cedar and other types of wood, iron, wool, copper, tin and Sidonian wine (Yardeni 1994:70–73, Table 3; Waldbaum 1997:12; Stern 2001:521–2). Harbor towns with a number of quays, warehouses and foreign elements (such as the dog cemetery at Ashkelon) and ship wreck evidence attest to the intensity of the maritime trade along the Mediterranean coast (Stern 2001:393; 407–10). Under Achaemenid rule, the Phoenicians were granted a greater degree of autonomy (cf. the well known kings Tabnit I and Eshmun'asar) than under the Assyrians and Babylonians, with Sidon serving as the administrative center of the 5th Satrap (Ward 1997:314–15; Markoe 1997:326). While the hill country of Cisjordan and Transjordan for the most part still remained somewhat local in character along with some eastern (Mesopotamian and Egyptian) influences, the western or coastal culture (Greco-Phoenician) can be observed in the relative abundance of objects of Greek material culture that are found as imports in other parts of the provinces (Stern 1995a:444; 1995b:89–90; 2001: 382). These objects apparently were used without acquiring the significance they had in their native land, being adapted to the local traditions and customs of the Levant. Hence, through free trade, Hellenistic culture seems to have triumphed considerably before the conquest of the land by its producers (Stern 1995a:444; 2001:522). That extensive contact and trade with Greece and Phoenicia is found in Transjordan is evidenced by the Aramaic and Phoenician ostraca, including wine receipts, with Greek loan words, and Arabic and Phonecian names, from Tell el-Kheleifeh (Glueck 1939b:21; 1939c:40–1; 1940a:16; 1940b:3–10; Divito 1993:51, 58–62, figs 81a–c, 83a; Stern 2001:458). That Greek culture was also known and appreciated farther south can be seen from the extensive imitation of Attic coins of the 5th and 4th centuries BC found throughout northern and southern Arabia (Hill 1922:pl. 7.11, cf. Glueck 1940b:3, n. 2a).

Other evidence for long-distance trade items in Transjordan include Greek attic ware found at such sites as 'Umayri (a Kylix, cf. Herr 1991: figs 3.15.31, 4.9.30; 243) the Umm Udhayna tomb at Amman (three lekythoi, cf. Hadidi 1987:101–2; figs 3.105; 4.104, 106; 18.1-3) and Tell el-Kheleifeh (Glueck 1939b:21; 1939c: 40–1; 1940a:16; Stern 2001:453, 458); Phoenician glass (aryballos from Tell Mazar Cemetery A, cf. Yassine 1984:82–3, fig. 52.60 with parallels from the tombs of Adoni-Nur at Amman, cf. Harding and Tufnell 1953:70–1, pl. 7.42 and Meqabelein, cf. Harding 1950: 46.36, pl. 13.3); fish imported from the Mediterranean Sea (see Neh 13:16, cf. stone bass, *Polyprion americanus* fish bones from Tell Hesban, Ray 2001); Mesopotamian bronze bowls, dippers and strainers (at Umm Udhayna, cf. Hadidi 1987:101; figs 3. 162, 165, 167, 174; 10.1–5, 10.8–10, Meqabelein, cf. Harding 1950:45.10, pl. 14.6, Cemetery A at Mazar, cf. Yassine 1984:76–80, figs 7.1–7, 8.1–3, and Tell es-Sa'idiyeh, cf. Pritchard 1985: fig. 172.1); seals (at Mazar cemetery A, cf. Yassine 1984:103–6, figs 9.1–6, 57. 181–6, Adoni-Nur at Amman, cf. Harding and Tufnell 1953:53–4, pl. 6.4, 6, Meqabelein, cf. Harding 1950:46.33 pl. 15.9 and Tawilan, cf. Bennett and Bienkowski 1995:79, 9.1.1; 9.46); horse and rider figurines and their many local imitations (Meqabalein, cf. Harding 1950: 46.37, pls 13.1, 15.12, Jalul); Egyptian alabaster vessels (Umm Udhayna, cf. Hadidi 1987:101, fig. 17.1-2; Meqabelein, cf. Harding 1950:47.39, pl. 15.13, and Tell Mazar Cemetery A, cf. Yassine 1984:82, fig. 52.61–3); faience Bes amulets (Tell Hesban, cf. Ray 2001); bronze mirrors (Umm Udhayna, cf. Hadidi 1987: figs 6.2–5, Meqabelein, cf. Harding 1950:45.12, pl. 14.9, Tell Mazar Cemetery A, cf. Yassine 1984:100, fig. 56.166); Cypriot jewelry including fibulae (usually bronze) (Umm Udhayna, cf. Hadidi 1987:101, fig. 5.1–14; Adoni-Nur at Amman, cf. Harding and Tufnell 1953:55, pl. 7.19–22, 41, Meqabelein, cf. Harding 1950:45.2–9, pl. 14.1–5, Tell Mazar Cemetery A, cf. Yassine 1984:97–100, fig. 55.15–16; Tawilan, cf. Bennett and Bienkowski 1995:80–1; fig. 9.5.1–5, Tell el-Kheleifeh, cf. Pratico 1993a:66, pl. 73.16, 18, 20) and occasionally gold or electrum (Adoni-Nur at Amman, cf. Harding and Tufnell 1953: 56, pl. 7.41) as well as silver earrings, finger rings and bangles (Umm Udhayna, cf. Hadidi 1987: fig. 11.1-21, Adoni-Nur at Amman, cf. Harding and Tufnell 1953:55, pl. 7.12. 14–18, and Meqabelein, cf. Harding 1950:45.24–6, pl. 15.4–6) have been found. In terms of media of exchange, at least one gold *daric* has been found in Transjordan (Stern 2001:557) with silver coins found at a number of sites including an Athenian *tetradrachma* at Tell al-'Umayri (Herr *et al.* 2000:37).

In terms of ceramics, Persian period vessels found in Transjordan based on foreign prototypes include: 1) a sack-shaped, pointed-based jar with loop handles found at Umm Udayna (Hadidi

1987:120, fig. 16.5) which is typical of Stern's type H6 and subtypes H7-9 (1982:108–10) originally from the Greek island of Rhodes; 2) cylindrical (torpedo) jars with one handle, originally from Syria (type G.2, Stern 1982:107) with examples found at Umm Udayna (Hadidi 1987:120, fig. 16.1–4), Adoni Nur (Harding and Tufnell 1953:58, fig. 23.113) and Meqabelein (Harding 1950:-47.43, pl. 16.1); 3) alabastra, which are imitations of alabaster vessles from Egypt (Stern 1982:125), were found at Umm Udayna (Hadidi 1987:120, fig. 17.1-4), Adoni Nur (Harding and Tufnell 1953:68, fig. 23, 126–8), Meqabelein (Harding 1950:47.52–6, pl. 16.13–16) and Tell Mazar (Yassine 1984:69–70, figs 3.11–17; 46.9–11, 47.12–15); 4) carrot-shaped bottles, which apparently derive from Assyrian bottles, found at Adoni Nur (Harding and Tufnell 1953:67, fig. 22.94–9A, pl. 6.97), Meqabelein (Harding 1950:48.57–8, pl. 16.17–18) and Tell Mazar (Yassine 1984: figs 4.12; 49.41); as well as pointed jars with handles from Umm Udayna (Hadidi 1987:120, fig. 16.6–7) and those more commonly, without handles from Adoni Nur (Harding and Tufnell 1953:67, fig. 22.89–90), Meqabelein (Harding 1950:47.44–6, pl. 16.2–5); and Tell Mazar (Yassine 1984:74–5, figs 3.11–17; 49.35–40); and 5) beakers such as those found at Tell Mazar (Yassine 1984:67–8, figs 3.6–7; 46.6–7). Both the pointed jars and beakers seem to be derived from Assyrian ware or Mesopotamian forms (Yassine 1984:68, 75).

Language

The spread of language is another important force for global connectivity as nation-states form territories of linguistic homogenization (Ludden 1997:8–10). In Persian times, although many languages persisted on a local level throughout the empire, the official language or *lingua franca* was Aramaic. It was used in administration, law and literature from the 6th through the 3rd centuries BC. Old Aramaic had gradually been adapted as the international language of diplomacy in the latter days of the Assyrian Empire (cf. 2 Kgs 18:26), but with the vast new territories under the Neo-Babylon and Persia Empires, it spread far beyond its native boundaries. They adopted the efficient alphabetic script of Aramaic over the cumbersome cuneiform of Akkadian and standardized it into the highly developed Official (or Imperial) Aramaic of the Persian period (Olmstead 1948:57, 78, 116; Rosenthal 1974:6; Kaufman 1992:173-7; Yamauchi 1996:244; Cook 1997: 178,182). This homogeneity of language was not only important for official communication and consolidation of the Empire, but no doubt also facilited trade relationships as indicated by the Aramaic text from Elephantine (Yardeni 1994) and the Ostracon A5 from Hesban (discussed above).

Global Systems and Territoriality

Theorists have tended to see national and international (or global) territory as being formed simultaneously. These territories both support and contradict (or compete) with each other for resources. They each are composed of institutions, activities, a complex mix of symbolism, power relations, centers and networks nested in clusters that form their constituent sub-territories. Globalization is thus, territoriality on a world scale and global institution-building has been traditionally led by economically and militarily dominant states (Ludden 1997:6). Global territory includes a huge number of interconnected constituent national and local territories and thus global institutions sustain credibility and viability only if these constituent territories provide home space for the enterprising interests of the global community (whether voluntarily or by force). The expansive activities of the local and national constituent territories integrate the economy of the global territory which in turn feeds the wealth of the national and local territories (Ludden 1997:7).

Taking up these observations one might suggest, in terms of the parameters of this paper, and within a systems model (Portugali 1994:211), that during the Persian period, the Empire of Persia represented the 'global' territory or system, with the 5th Persian Satrap as one of its regional territories or subsystems and that the Transjordanian provinces of Ammon, Moab and Edom were local territories or subsystems.

Notes

1. In central Transjordan, surveys have so far indicated sparsely settled conditions during early Iron Age II, (McGovern 1992:181; Sauer and Herr 1997:234; Herr 1997:146 (box), 148; 1999:222). Only 16 sites (1, 26, 29, 39, 95, 96, 97, 102, 108, 110, 135, 143, 146, 149, 151, and 153) out of the 63 Iron Age II sites from the Hesban Survey were settled at this time. Of these, ten (1, 26, 102, 110, 135, 143, 146, 149, 151, and 153) were located on the plateau; three (29, 39, 108) in the wadis and three (95, 96, and 97) in the Jordan Valley. All but four (96, 110, 151, and 153) of these sites were occupied in Iron Age I, with three of the new ones (110, 151, and 153) only inhabited during this sub-division of the Iron Age.

However, during the Iron IIC/Persian period the number of sites in the Hesban region increased to 58 (1, 2, 3, 4, 5, 6, 7, 8, 9, 10, 21, 26, 29, 36, 40, 41, 42, 44, 47, 59, 72, 74, 80, 82, 91, 92, 94, 95, 96, 97, 98, 99, 100, 101, 102, 103, 104, 105, 108, 127, 128, 129, 131, 132, 133, 136, 138, 139, 140, 141, 143, 144, 145, 146, 147, 148, 149, and 150). Of these sites, 33 (2, 3, 4, 5, 8, 9, 10, 21, 36, 41, 42, 59, 74, 80, 82, 92, 94, 98, 99, 100, 104, 127, 128, 131, 132, 133, 136, 138, 139, 140, 144, 145, and 148), were settled for the first time during the Iron Age. Among them were five major sites, six large sites, 11 medium sites, 21 small sites and 15 very small sites (fig. 25; Ibach 1987:164–8, Table 3.11). In addition, Madaba also seems to have been inhabited at this time (Harrison 1996:7; Herr 1997:170) with tomb evidence (Thompson 1986:334–45) even earlier (Iron Age IIA–B).

The 'Umeiri Survey located only six sites with ceramic features typical of Persian period Cisjordan (sites 6, 29, 36, 38, 69 and 126). However, Herr (1995a:121–5; 1999:232–4) has pointed out that the Iron IIC/Persian administrative complex in Field A Tell el-'Umeiri, which was constructed c. 580 BC, and 'Umeiri Survey Site 84, excavated in 1994, were contemporaneous and further that this farmstead with three winepresses was similar in architecture and ceramic repertoire to numerous other farmstead sites with winepresses in the region. Hence, there are actually up to 52 Iron Age IIC/Persian sites (4, 6, 8, 9, 10, 13, 14, 17, 18, 19, 21, 22, 23, 25, 26, 27, 28, 29, 30, 31, 33, 34/Rujm Selim, 35, 36, 37, 38, 43, 45, 46, 49, 51, 52, 54, 55, 64, 68, 69, 74, 83, 84, 85, 100, 101, 116B, 116D, 118, 122, 125, 126, 128, 129, and 133) within a 5 km radius of Tell el-'Umeiri (Boling 1989: 99, fig. 8.1; 188; fig. 8.117; Younker 1991:270, fig. 12.2; Christopherson 1997:291–302; Christopherson *et al.* 1997:36–42). In addition, 23 of the 38 random squares visited in the 1984 season produced Iron II/Persian pottery (Cole 1989:54–5, figs 7.3 and 4) as well.

Both the Hesban and 'Umeiri regions were no doubt part of the Persian province of Ammon at this time. Very little of the Iron Age II/Persian period capital of Rabbath-Ammon, at the headwaters of the Wadi Zerqa (biblical Jabbok), has been excavated. However, walls of a residential (or palace ?) area on the lower terrace (Zayadine 1973:28–9, 31–5; Bennett 1975: 141; Zayadine *et al.* 1989:360, fig. 3, 362) and part of the (casemate) fortification system (Dornemann 1983:90–3) have been found on the citadel. Otherwise evidence comes from tombs (Adoni Nur, and Umm Udhayna cf. Harding and Tufnell 1953 and Hadidi 1987).

In addition, the Survey of Greater Amman (Abu Dayyah *et al.* 1991) located 14 sites (53-39.8, 55-36.10, 56-38.1 (= Glueck Site 240), 54-33.2, 54.39.7/1. 55-35.2, 55-35.4, 55.39.7/2, 56-30.1 (Qasr Khilda/Glueck Site 230; Glueck 1939a: 164-65), 57-31.1, 58-33.1, 58.34.1 (= Glueck Site 248), 58-34.2, and 59.33.1) with Persian period sherds. Thirty-eight (53-39.1, 53-39.3, 53-39.8, 54-36.7, 54-36.9, 54-39.6, 54-41.3, 55-38.2, 56-41.1, 48-37.1, 48-37.3, 48-37.4, 48-37.5, 48-37.6, 54-33.1, 54-33.3, 54-46.1, 55-29.1, 55-30.1, 55-30.2, 55-32.1, 55-35.1, 55-35.4, 56-29.5, 56-29.11, 56-30.1, 56-30.3, 56-30.4, 56-30.5, 56-30.6, 56-30.8, 56-30.10, 56-30.11, 56-34.1, 56-34.2, 57-30.1, 57-30.2, and 58-35.1) of the 222 sites from this survey were either towers or had towers on them. As these sites were for the most part on the plateau, they probably served agricultural functions as well as maintaining good visual contact with the main sites in the area. Since Christopherson and Guertin (1996:9) have suggested that a number of sites designated as farmsteads from the 'Umeiri Survey could also have functioned as watchtowers, one could make a similar case for related sites in the Amman and Hesban regions (Younker 1989:196–7). Kletter (1991:39–41) has also suggested that the towers or Rujm el-Malfuf buildings throughout the region served more than one function. That most of the towers in the Ammonite region that have been excavated so far (Rujm el-Malfuf South, Khirbet el-Hajjar, Rujm el-Mekheizin, and Rujm el-Henu West) have dated to the Iron IIC/Persian period (Thompson 1972:63; 1973:49; 1984:31, 38; and McGovern 1983:112, 127, 134–6) would seem to strengthen the case. Indeed, some of the towers, formerly interpreted as 'forts', were found in the Hesban (132/Fohrer Site C; 135 (al-Dreijat) /Fohrer Site D; and 'Umeiri (Site 46/ Fohrer Site E) regions (Kletter 1991:39–42, fig. 10, Table 1).

Other Iron Age II/Persian sites in the Amman region include Safut (Wimmer 1987a:166–72; 1987b:281; 1989:513–14); Rujm al-Henu West (Site 2), Khirbet Umm ad-Dananir (Site 3/Field V), and Rujm al-Hawayah (Site 4) (McGovern

1986:8, Table 1, 9) in the Baq'ah Valley. The er-Rumman Survey, farther to the north, found 14 (2/3, 2/4, 3/3, 4, 6/1, 6/2, 15/3, 21, 23/Glueck Site 300; 26, 27, 28, 34 and 40) Iron Age II/Persian sites (Gordon and Knauf 1987:290, fig. 1;294–7). Other sites to the north of Amman include Tell 'Alla (Site 8) of the Telul edh-Dhahab and environs survey (Gordon and Villiers 1983:279 Fig. 1; 286, Table 1), and Glueck (1939a) Sites 267 and 316. The East Jordan Valley Survey also located seven sites (151, 182/Tell Nimrin, 185/Tell el-Kafrein, Hesban Survey Site 96; 189/Glueck Site 213; 191/Tell Iktanu; 195/Tell er-Rama, Hesban Survey Site 95 and Glueck Site 214; 199/Glueck Site 203 south of the Wadi Zerqa (Yassine *et al.* 1988:191–3, 198–9). According to Ji (1998) 'Iraq el-Emir and 14 other sites found on the survey in its immediate vicinity had Iron II/Persian sherds.

Farther north in the Gilead region, Mittmann (1970) located 53 Iron II sites with only one possible site (81) with Persian period ceramics. However, this survey was completed before much was known about the continuation of the Iron II pottery traditions into the Persian period. It is therefore probable that a number of these sites actually go much later. Site 1 from the King Talal Reservoir Area (Yassine *et al.* 1978:225) yielded Persian period sherds as did 11 sites (19, 20, 25, 45, 56, 61, 103/Tell Mazar; 104, 115/Tell el-Hammed (East)/Glueck Site 190, 119/Deir 'Alla and 135) from the East Jordan Valley Survey north of Wadi Zerqa (Ibrahim *et al.* 1976:48–50; 56; and Yassine *et al.* 1988:190–1, 198–9). Excavated sites with Iron II/Persian material in this region include Tell Mazar, Strata II-I, (Yassine 1983:498–503; 1984), Tell es-Sa'idiyeh, Stratum III (Pritchard 1985) and Deir 'Alla, Phases VI–II (Ibrahim and van der Kooij 1983:577–85; van der Kooij 1993:341–2).

South of the Amman was the site of Sahab (Ibrahim 1975:70–4; 1987:78–9). Other Iron Age II/Persian period sites in immediate proximity to Amman include Meqabelein (Harding 1950). There are a number of sites with undifferentiated Iron II sherds south of the Madaba Plains to the Wadi Mujib. Some of these must have been inhabited in the Iron II/Persian. Those known for sure include Jalul, Umm el-'Amad, Khirbet el-Heri (Herr 1997:169–70; Daviau 1997:226–7), and Khirbet Medeiniyeh on the Wadi eth-Themed (Daviau 1997:223–4; 1998:2, 4). Ji and Lee (1998) have reported eight sites from the Dhiban Plateau survey (including sites 20/Glueck Site 93, 143, 149 and 172/Glueck Site 174) with Iron II/Persian period sherds.

South of the Wadi Mujib the Karak Plateau Survey (Miller 1991) located 20 (15, 35/Balu', 63, 64, 90, 108, 193, 197, 198, 204, 207, 211, 233, 238, 262, 264, 307, 363, 399 and 400) Iron II/Persian sites. Farther to the south below the Wadi Hesa, the Wadi Hesa (MacDonald 1988) and Southern Ghors Northeast 'Araba surveys (MacDonald *et al.* 1987:391–418; MacDonald *et al.* 1988); have reported undifferentiated Iron Age II sherds. Some of these sites no doubt were occupied during the Iron II/Persian period. In Edom, seven sites (Khirbet al-Megheitah and Khirbet Ishra (Hart 1987:287–90); Feinan (Hauptmann and Weisgerber 1987:419–35, pls LXVI.1–2, LXVII, LXIX.1, LXX.2; Khouri 1988:125–6) Khirbet el-Jariyeh/Glueck Sites 12 (Glueck 1935:20–34) and 22 (Glueck 1939a:270) (Hauptmann and Weisgerber 1987:422; Khouri 1988:125), Buseirah Phase 4 (Bienkowski 1992: 104), Tawilan Stages 1-5 (Bennett and Bienkowski 1995:102–3) and Tell el-Kheleifeh post-fortified settlement/Glueck's Period 5 (Pratico 1993a:71; 1993b: 870), possibly a Persian garrison perhaps with Greek and/or Phoenician troops (Stern 2001:372, 420, 446, 458), have yielded sherds from this period.

2. Hesban Sites 1, 2, 3, 4, 5, 6, 8, 9, 10, 72, 98, 99, 101, 127, 128, 129, 131, 132, 133, 136, 138, 139, 140, 141, 144, 145, 146, 147, 148 and 150.

3. Hesban Sites 21, 36, 40, 41, 42, 44, 47, 59, 74, 80, 82, 91, 92, 94, 104 and 105.

References

Abu Dayyah, A. S., Green, J. A., Hassan, I. H. and Suleiman, E. (1991) Archaeological survey of Greater Amman, Phase 1: Final Report. *Annual of the Department of Antiquities of Jordan* 35:361–95.

Aharoni, Y. (1979) *The Land of the Bible: A Historical Geography*. 2nd edn. Philadelphia: Westminster.

Al-Eisawi, D. M. (1985) Vegetation in Jordan. In *Studies in the History and Archaeology of Jordan II*, edited by A. Hadidi. Amman: Department of Antiquities, pp. 45–57.

Balensi, J., Herrera, M. D. and Artzy. M. (1993) Abu Hawam, Tell. In *The New Encyclopedia of Archaeological Excavations in the Holy Land*, vol. 1, edited by E. Stern. Jerusalem: Israel Exploration Society, pp. 7–14.

Betlyon, J. W. (1992) Coinage. In *The Anchor Bible Dictionary*, vol. 1, edited by D. N. Freedman. New York: Doubleday, pp. 1076–89.

Bennett, C. M. (1975) Excavations at the Citadel, Amman, 1975. *Annual of the Department of Antiquities of Jordan* 20:131–42.

Bienkowski, P. (1992) The Beginning of the Iron Age in southern Jordan: a framework. In *Early Edom and Moab: The Beginning of the Iron Age in Southern Jordan*, edited by P. Bienkowski. Sheffield Archaeological Monographs 7. Sheffield: J. R. Collis, pp. 1–12.

Bennett, C. and Bienkowski, P. (eds) (1995) *Excavations at Tawilan in Southern Jordan*. British Academy Monographs in Archaeology 8. British Institute at Amman for Archaeology and History: Oxford University.

Boling, R. G. (1989) Site survey in the el-'Umeiri region. In *Madaba Plains Project 1: The 1984 Season at Tell el-'Umeiri and Vicinity and Subsequent Studies*, edited by L. T. Geraty, L. G. Herr, Ø. S. Labianca and R. W. Younker. Berrien Springs, MI: Andrews University/Institute of Archaeology, pp. 98–188.

Borstad, K. A. (2000) Ancient Roads in the Madaba Plains of Transjordan: Research from a Geographic Perspective. Unpublished Dissertation. University of Arizona.

Braudel, F. (1972) *The Mediterranean and the Mediterranean World in the Age of Phillip II*, vol. 1 (trans. Siân Reynolds). New York: Harper and Row.

Bruins, H. J. (1994) Comparative chronology of climate and human history in the southern Levant from the Late Chalcolithic to the Early Arab Period. In *Late Quaternary Chronology and Paleoclimates of the Eastern Mediterranean*, edited by O. Bar-Yosef and R. S. Kra. Tucson, AZ: Radiocarbon, Dept. of Geosciences, University of Arizona, pp. 301–14.

Castells, M. (1996) *The Rise of the Network Society: The Information Age: Economy, Society and Culture* 1. 3 vols. Cambridge, MA: Blackwell Publishers.

Christopherson, G. L. (1997) Madaba Plains Project: Regional Survey Sites, 1989. In *Madaba Plains Project 3: The 1989 Season at Tell el-'Umeiri and Vicinity and Subsequent Studies*, edited by L. T. Geraty, L. G. Herr, Ø. S. Labianca and R. W. Younker. Berrien Springs, MI: Andrews University/Institute of Archaeology, pp. 291–302.

Christopherson, G. L. and Guertin, D. P. (1995) Soil erosion, Agriculture Intensification, and Iron Age Settlement in the Region of Tall al-Umayri, Jordan. Paper Presented at the Annual Meeting of the American Schools of Oriental Research. November 1995, Philadelphia.

Christopherson, G. L. and Guertin, D. P. (1996) Visibility Analysis and Ancient Settlement Strategies in the Region of Tall al-Umayri, Jordan. Paper Presented at the Annual Meeting of the American Schools of Oriental Research. November 1996, New Orleans.

Christopherson, G. L., Guertin, D. P. and Borstad, K. A. (1996) GIS and Archaeology: Using Arc/Info to Increase our Understanding of Ancient Jordan. Paper Presented at the Annual Meeting of the American Schools of Oriental Research. November 1996, New Orleans.

Christopherson, G. L., Boling, R. G., Cole, J. A., Hopkins, D. C., Mattingly, G. L., Schnurrenberger, D. W. and Younker, R. W. (1997) Summary Descriptions of Archaeological Sites from the Survey at Tall al-'Umayri, Jordan. http://www.casa.arizona.edu/MPP/umsites/umsitesintro.html

Cole, J. A. (1989) Random square survey in the el-'Umeiri Region. In *Madaba Plains Project 1: The 1984 Season at Tell el-'Umeiri and Vicinity and Subsequent Studies*, edited by L. T. Geraty *et al.* Berrien Springs, MI: Andrews University/Institute of Archaeology. Andrews University/Institute of Archaeology, pp. 51–97.

Coogan, M. D. (1974) Life in the Diaspora: Jew at Nippur in the fifth century BC. *Biblical Archaeologist* 37.1:6–12.

Cook, E. M. (1997)Aramaic language and literature. In *The Oxford Encyclopedia of Archaeology in the Near East*, vol. 1, edited by E. M. Meyers. Oxford: Oxford University, pp. 178–84.

Coughenour, R. A. (1976) Preliminary report on the exploration and excavation of Mugharet el Warda and Abu Thawab. *Annual of the Department of Antiquities of Jordan* 21:71–6.

Cross, F. M. and Geraty, L. T. (1994) The Ammonite Ostraca from Tell Hesban. In *Hesban after 25 Years*, edited by D. Merling and L. T. Geraty. Berrien Springs, MI: Institute of Archaeology/ Horn Archaeological Museum, pp. 169–74.

Dalley, S. (1995) The cuneiform tablet. In *Excavations at Tawilan in Southern Jordan*, edited by C. M. Bennet and P. Bienkowski. British Academy Monographs in Archaeology 8. British Institute at Amman for Archaeology and History: Oxford University, pp. 67–8, 272–4.

Daviau, M. (1997) Moab's northern border: Khirbat al-Mudayna on the Wadi ath-Thamad. *Biblical Archaeologist* 60:222–8.

Daviau, M. (1998) Canadian Team Finishes First Season of Excavations at Khirbat al-Mudayna. Http: //info.wlu.ca/~wwwarch/jordan/stairway.html.

Dever, W. G. (1995) Orienting the study of trade in the Near East archaeology. In *Recent Excavations in Israel: A View to the West*, edited by S. Gitin. Dubuque, IA: Kendall/Hunt, pp. 111–10.

Divito, R. A. (1993) The Tell el-Kheleifeh inscriptions. In *Nelson Glueck's 1938–1940 Excavations at Tell el Kheleifeh: A Reappraisal*, edited by G. D. Practico. Atlanta: Scholars, pp. 51–63.

Dornemann, R. H. (1983) *The Archaeology of the Transjordan in the Bronze and Iron Ages*. Milwaukee: Milwaukee Public Museum.
Glueck, N. (1935) Explorations in eastern Palestine, II. *Annual of the American Schools of Oriental Research* 15. New Haven: American Schools of Oriental Research.
Glueck, N. (1938) The first campaign at Tell el-Kheleifeh (Ezion-Geber). *Bulletin of the American Schools of Orientral Research* 71:3–17.
Glueck, N. (1939a) Explorations in eastern Palestine, III. *Annual of the American Schools of Oriental Research* 18–19. New Haven: American Schools of Oriental Research.
Glueck, N. (1939b) The second campaign at Tell el-Kheleifeh (Ezion-Geber: Elath). *Bulletin of the American Schools of Orientral Research* 75:8–22.
Glueck, N. (1939c) Ezion-Geber: Elath, the gateway to Arabia. *Biblical Archaeologist* 2:37–41.
Glueck, N. (1940a) The third season of excavation at Tell el-Kheleifeh. *Bulletin of the American Schools of Oriental Research* 79:2–18.
Glueck, N. (1940b) Ostraca from Elath. *Bulletin of the American Schools of Oriental Research* 80:3–10.
Glueck, N. (1967) Some Edomite Pottery from Tell el-Kheleifeh, Parts I and II. *Bulletin of the American Schools of Oriental Research* 188:8–38.
Gordon, R. L. and Knauf, E. A. (1987) Er-Rumman Survey 1985. *Annual of the Department of Antiquities of Jordan* 31:289–98.
Gordon, R. L. and Villiers, L. E. (1983) Telul Edh Dhahab and its environs surveys of 1980 and 1982: A preliminary report. *Annual of the Department of Antiquities of Jordan* 22:275–89.
Graf, D. F. (1992) Dedan. In *The Anchor Bible Dictionary*, vol. 2, edited by D. N. Freedman. New York: Doubleday, pp. 121–3.
Hadidi, A. (1987) An Ammonite tomb at Amman. *Levant* 19:101–20.
Harding, G. L. (1950) An Iron-Age tomb at Meqabelein. *The Quarterly of the Department of Antiquities in Palestine* 14:44–8.
Harding, G. L. and Tufnell, O. (1953)The Tomb of Adoni Nur in Amman. In *Four Tomb Groups from Jordan*. Palestine Exploration Fund Annual VI, by G. L. Harding. London: Palestine Exploration Fund, pp. 121–3.
Harrison, T. P. (1996) Tell Madaba Archaeological Project. Paper Presented at the Annual Meeting of the American Schools of Oriental Research. November 1996, New Orleans.
Hart, S. (1987) The Edom Survey Project 1984–85: The Iron Age. In *Studies in the History and Archaeology of Jordan III*, edited by A. Hadidi. Amman: Department of Antiquities, pp. 287–90.
Hauptmann, A. and Weisgerber, G. (1987) Archaeometallurgical and mining–archaeological investigations in the area of Feinan, Wadi 'Arabah (Jordan). *Annual of the Department of Antiquities of Jordan* 31:419–37.
Herr, L. G. (1991) Pottery typology and chronology. In *Madaba Plains Project 2: The 1987 Season at Tell el-'Umeiri and Vicinity and Subsequent Studies*, edited by L. G. Herr, L. T. Geraty, Ø. S. Labianca and R. W. Younker. Berrien Springs, MI: Andrews University/Institute of Archaeology, pp. 232–45.
Herr, L. G. (1992) Shifts in settlement patterns of Late Bronze and Iron Age Ammon. In *Studies in the History and Archaeology of Jordan IV*, edited by S. Tell, G. Bisheh, F. Zayddine, K. 'Amr and M. Zaghloul. Amman: Department of Antiquities, pp. 175–7.
Herr, L. G. (1993) Whatever happened to the Ammonites? *Biblical Archaeology Review* 19.6:26–35, 68.
Herr, L. G. (1995a) Wine production in the hills of southern Ammon and the founding of Tall al-'Umayri in the sixth century BC. *Annual of the Department of Antiquities of Jordan* 39:121–25.
Herr, L. G. (1995b) The Late Iron II-Persian ceramic horizon at Tall al-'Umayri. In *Studies in the History and Archaeology of Jordan V*, edited by K. 'Amr, F. Zayadine and M. Zaghloul. Amman: Department of Antiquities, pp. 617–19.
Herr, L. G. (1997) The Iron Age II period: emerging nations. *Biblical Archaeologist* 60:114–83.
Herr, L. G. (1999) The Ammonites in the Late Iron Age and Persian Period. In *Ancient Ammon*, edited by B. MacDonald and R. W. Younker. Leiden: E.J. Brill, pp. 219–37.
Herr, L. G., Clark, D. R., Geraty, L. T. and LaBianca, Ø. S. (2000) Madaba Plains Project: Tall al-'Umayri, 1998. *Andrews University Seminary Studies* 38:29–44.
Hill, G. F. (1922) *Catalogue of the Greek Coins in the British Museum: Arabia, Mesopotamia and Persia*. London: British Museum.
Hodder, I. (1992) *Theory and Practice in Archaeology*. London: Routledge.

Ibach, R. (1987) *Archaeological Survey of the Hesban Region. Hesban 5*. Berrien Springs, MI: Andrews University.

Ibrahim, M. M. (1975) Third season of excavation at Sahab, 1975. *Annual of the Department of Antiquities of Jordan* 20:69–82.

Ibrahim, M. M. (1987) Sahab and its foreign relations. In *Studies in the History and Archaeology of Jordan III*, edited by A. Hadidi, pp. 219–37. Amman: Department of Antiquities.

Ibrahim, M. and van der Kooij, G. (1983) Excavations at Tell Deir ʻAlla, season 1982. *Annual of the Department of Antiquities of Jordan* 27:577–85.

Ibrahim, M., Sauer, J.A. and Yassine, K. (1976) The East Jordan Valley Survey, 1975. *Bulletin of the American Schools of Oriental Research* 222:41–66.

Ji, C. C. (1998) Archaeological survey and settlement patterns in the region of ʻIraq al-ʻAmir, 1996: a preliminary report. *Annual of the Department of Antiquities of Jordan* 42:587–608.

Ji, C. C. and Lee, J.-K. (1998) Preliminary report on the survey of the Dhiban Plateau, 1997. *Annual of the Department of Antiquities of Jordan* 42:549–71.

Kaufman, S. A. (1992) Languages (Aramaic). In *The Anchor Bible Dictionary*, vol. 4, edited by D. N. Freedman. New York: Doubleday, pp. 173–8.

Kent, R. G. (1953) *Old Persian*. New Haven: American Oriental Society.

Khalil, L. A. (1986) A bronze caryatid censer from Amman. *Levant* 18:103–10.

King, G. R. D., Lenzen, C. J., Newhall, A., King, J. L. and Deemer, J. D. (1987) Survey of Byzantine and Islamic sites in Jordan: third season preliminary report (1982) The southern Ghor. *Annual of the Department of Antiquities of Jordan* 31:439–59.

Kletter, R. (1991) The Rujm El-Malfuf buildings and the Assyrian vassal state of Amman. *Bulletin of the American Schools of Oriental Research* 284:33–50.

Knaf, E. A. (1992) Tema. In *The Anchor Bible Dictionary*, vol. 6, edited by D. N. Freedman. New York: Doubleday, pp. 346–7.

Khouri, R. G. (1988) *The Antiquities of the Jordan Rift Valley*. Amman: Al Kutba.

LaBianca, Ø. S. (1990) *Sedentarization and Nomadization: Food System Cycles at Hesban and Vicinity in Transjordan. Hesban 1*. Berrien Springs, MI: Andrews University.

LaBianca, Ø. S. and Younker, R. W. (1995) The kingdoms of Ammon, Moab and Edom: The archaeology of society in Late Bronze/Iron Age Transjordan (c. 1400–500 BCE). In *The Archaeology of Society in the Holy Land*, edited by T. E. Levy. London: Leicester University Press, pp. 399–415, 590–4.

Ludden, D. (1997) The Newness of Globalization: A Schematic View of the Historical Zones of Territoriality. Http: //www.sas.upenn.edu/~dludden/global2.htm.

Leonard, A. (1987) The significance of the Mycenaean pottery found east of the Jordan River. In *Studies in the History and Archaeology of Jordan III*, edited by A. Hadidi. Amman: Department of Antiquities, pp. 261–6.

Lyon, B., Rowen, H. H. and Hamerow, T. S. (1969) *A History of the Western World*, vol. 1. Chicago: Rand McNally.

MacDonald, B. (1988) *The Wadi el Hasa Archaeological Survey 1979–1983, West-Central Jordan*. Waterloo, Ontario: Wilfrid Laurier University Press.

MacDonald, B., Clark, G.A., Neeley, M., Adams, R. and Gregory, M. (1987) Southern Ghors and Northwest ʻAraba Archaeological Survey 1986, Jordan: a preliminary report. *Annual of the Department of Antiquities of Jordan* 31:391–418.

MacDonald, B., Clark, G.A. and Neeley, M. (1988) Southern Ghors and Northwest ʻAraba Archaeological Survey 1985 and 1986, Jordan: a preliminary report. *Bulletin of the American Schools of Oriental Research* 272:23–45.

Markoe, G. (1997) Phoenicians. In *The Oxford Encyclopedia of Archaeology in the Near East*, vol. 4, edited by E. M. Meyers. Oxford: Oxford University, pp. 325–31.

Mazar, B. (1957) The Tobiads. *Israel Exploration Journal* 7:137–45, 229–38.

McGovern, P. E. (1983) Test soundings of archaeological and resistivity survey results at Rujm Al-Henu. *Annual of the Department of Antiquities of Jordan* 27:105–41.

McGovern, P. E. (1986) *The Late Bronze and Early Iron Ages of Central Transjordan: The Baqʻah Valley Project, 1977–1981*. University Museum Monograph. Philadelphia: University Museum.

McGovern, P. E. (1992) Settlement pattern of the Late Bronze and Iron Ages in the Greater Amman Area. In *Studies in the History and Archaeology of Jordan IV*, edited by S. Tell *et al.* Amman: Department of Antiquities, pp. 179–83.

Mittman, S. (1970) *Beiträge zur Siedlungs- und Territorialgeschichte des nördlichen Ostjordanlandes*. Wiesbaden: Otto Harrassowitz.

Miller, J. M. (ed.) (1991) *Archaeological Survey of the Kerak Plateau*. Atlanta: Scholars.

Olmstead, A. T. (1948) *History of the Persian Empire*. Chicago: University of Chicago.

Parr, P. J. (1997a) Dedan. In *The Oxford Encyclopedia of Archaeology in the Near East*, vol. 2, edited by E. M. Meyers. Oxford: Oxford University Press, pp. 133–4.

Parr, P. J. (1997b) Tayma'. In *The Oxford Encyclopedia of Archaeology in the Near East*, vol. 5, edited by E. M. Meyers. Oxford: Oxford University Press, pp. 160–1.

Portugali, J. (1994) Theoretical speculations on the transition from nomadism to monarchy. In *From Nomadism to Monarchy: Archaeological and Historical Aspects of Early Israel*, edited by I. Finkelstein and N. Na'aman. Jerusalem: Israel Exploration Society, pp. 203–17.

Pratico, G. D. (1993a) *Nelson Glueck's 1938–1940 Excavations at Tell el Kheleifeh: A Reappraisal*. Atlanta: Scholars.

Pratico, G. D. (1993b) Kheleifeh, Tell el-. In *The New Encyclopedia of Archaeological Excavations in the Holy Land*, vol. 3, edited by E. Stern. Jerusalem: Israel Exploration Society, pp. 867–70.

Pritchard, J. B. (1969) *Ancient Near Eastern Texts Relating to the Old Testament*. 3rd ed. Princeton: Princeton University.

Pritchard, J. (1985) *Tell Es-Sa'idiyeh: Excavations on the Tell, 1964–1966*. Philadelphia: University of Pennsylvania.

Ray, P. J. (2001)*Tell Hesban and Vicinity in the Iron Age*. Berrien Springs, MI: Andrews University.

Redford, D. B. (1982a) Contact between Egypt and Jordan in the New Kingdom: some comments on sources. In *Studies in the History and Archaeology of Jordan I*, edited by A. Hadidi. Amman: Department of Antiquities, pp. 115–19.

Redford, D. B. (1982b) A Bronze Age Itinerary in Transjordan. *Journal for the Society for the Study of Egyptian Antiquities* 12: 55-74.

Rosenthal, F. (1974) *A Grammar of Biblical Aramaic*. Wiesbaden: Oto Harrassowitz.

Roux, G. (1980) *Ancient Iraq*. Suffolk: Pelican.

Sauer, J. A. (1986) Transjordan in the Bronze and Iron Ages: a critique of Glueck's synthesis. *Bulletin of the American Schools of Oriental Research* 263:1–26.

Sauer, J. A. (1995) Artistic and faunal evidence for the influence of the domestication of donkeys and camels on the archaeological history of Jordan and Arabia. In *Studies in the History and Archaeology of Jordan* V, edited by K. 'Amr, F. Zayadine and M. Zaghloul. Amman: Department of Antiquities, pp. 39–48.

Sauer, J. A. and Herr, L. G. (1997) Transjordan: Transjordan in the Bronze and Iron Ages. In *The Oxford Encyclopedia of Archaeology in the Near East*, vol. 5, edited by E. M. Meyers. Oxford: Oxford University, pp. 231–5.

Shea, W. H. (1977) A date for the recently discovered eastern canal of Egypt. *Bulletin of the American Schools of Oriental Research* 226:31–8.

Singer-Avitz, L. (1999) Beersheba: A Gateway Community in Southern Arabian long-distance trade in the eight century BCE. *Tel Aviv* 26:3–74.

Stern, E. (1982) *Material Culture of the Land of the Bible in the Persian Period 538–332* BC. Warminster: Aris and Phillips.

Stern, E. (1992) The Phoenician architectural elements in Palestine during the Late Iron Age and the Persian Period. In *The Architecture of Ancient Israel: From Prehistoric to the Persian Periods*, edited by A. Kempinski and R. Reich. Jerusalem: Israel Exploration Society, pp. 302–9.

Stern, E. (1995a) Between Persia and Greece: trade, administration and warfare in the Persian and Hellenistic Periods (539–63 BCE). In *The Archaeology of Society in the Holy Land*, edited by T. E. Levy. London: Leicester University Press, pp. 432–45.

Stern, E. (1995b) Tel Dor: A Phoenician-Israelite trading center. In *Recent Excavations in Israel: A View to the West*, edited by S. Gitin. Dubuque, IA: Kendall/Hunt, pp. 81–93.

Stern, E. (2001) *Archaeology of the Land of the Bible: The Assyrian, Babylonian and Persian Periods 732–332 BCE*, vol. 2. New York: Doubleday.
Thompson, H. O. (1972) The 1972 Excavation of Khirbet al-Hajjar. *Annual of the Department of Antiquities of Jordan* 17:47–72.
Thompson, H. O. (1973) Rujm al-Malfuf South. *Annual of the Department of Antiquities of Jordan* 18:47–50, 117–19.
Thompson, H. O. (1984) The Excavation of Rujm el-Mekheizin. *Annual of the Department of Antiquities of Jordan* 28:31–38.
Thompson, H. O. (1986) An Iron Age Tomb at Madaba. In *The Archaeology of Jordan and Other Studies*, edited by L. T. Geraty and L. G. Herr. Berrien Springs, MI: Andrews University, pp. 331–63.
van Beek, G. W. (1960) Frankincense and Myrrh. *Biblical Archaeologist* 23:69–95.
van Beek, G. W. (1997a) Qataban. In *The Oxford Encyclopedia of Archaeology in the Near East*, vol. 4, edited by E. M. Meyers. Oxford: Oxford University Press, pp. 383–4.
van Beek, G. W. (1997b) Sheba. In *The Oxford Encyclopedia of Archaeology in the Near East*, vol. 5, edited by E. M. Meyers. Oxford: Oxford University Press, pp. 18–19.
van der Kooij, G. (1993) Deir 'Alla, Tell. In *The New Encyclopedia of Archaeological Excavations in the Holy Land*, vol. 1, edited by E. Stern. Jerusalem: Israel Exploration Society, pp. 338–42.
Veldhuijzen, X. and van der Steen, E. (1999) Iron production center found in the Jordan Valley. *Near Eastern Archaeology* 62.3:195–9.
von Soden, W. (1994) *The Ancient Orient: An Introduction to the Study of the Ancient Near East*. Grand Rapids, MI: Eerdmans.
Waldbaum, J. (1997) Greeks *in* the East or Greeks *and* the East? *Bulletin of the American Schools of Oriental Research* 305:1–17.
Ward, W. A. (1997) Phoenicia. In *The Oxford Encyclopedia of Archaeology in the Near East*, vol. 4, edited by E. M. Meyers. Oxford: Oxford University, pp. 313–17.
Wilkinson, T. J. (2001) Excavating the Land of Sheba. *Archaeological Odyssey* 4.6:44–51; 57–8.
Wimmer, D. H. (1987a) Tell Safut Excavations, 1982–1985 Preliminary Report. *Annual of the Department of Antiquities of Jordan* 31:159–74.
Wimmer, D. H. (1987b) The Excavations at Safut. In *Studies . In the History and Archaeology of Jordan III*, edited by A. Hadidi. Amman: Department of Antiquities, pp. 179–282.
Wimmer, D. H. (1989) Safut (Tell). In *Archaeology of Jordan: Field Reports, Surveys and Sites L-Z*, edited by D. Homes-Fredericq and J. B. Hennessy. Leuven: Peeters, pp. 512–15.
Winnett, F. V. (1937) A Study of the Lihyanite and Thamudic Inscriptions. Toronto: University of Toronto.
Yamauchi, E. (1996) *Persia and the Bible*. Grand Rapids, MI: Baker.
Yardeni, A. (1994) Maritime trade and royal accountancy in erased customs account from 475 BCE on the Ahiqar Scroll from Elephantine. *Bulletin of the American Schools of Oriental Research* 293:67–78.
Yassine, K. (1983) Tell El Mazar, Field I preliminary report of Area G, H, L and M: the summit. *Annual of the Department of Antiquities of Jordan* 17:495–513.
Yassine, K. (1984) *Tell el Mazar*, Vol. I*: Cemetery A*. Amman: The University of Jordan.
Yassine, K., Ibrahim, M. and Sauer, J. A. (1988) The East Jordan Valley Survey, 1976. In *Archaeology of Jordan: Essays and Reports*, edited by K. Yassine. Amman: University of Jordan, pp. 189–207.
Yassine, K. *et al.* (1978) An archaeological survey of three reservoir areas in northern Jordan, 1978. *Annual of the Department of Antiquities of Jordan* 22:108–35.
Younker, R.W. (1989) 'Towers' in the region surrounding Tell el-'Umeiri. In *Madaba Plains Project 1: The 1984 Season at Tell el-'Umeiri and Vicinity and Subsequent Studies*, edited by L. T. Geraty *et al.* Berrien Springs, MI: Andrews University/Institute of Archaeology, pp. 195–8.
Younker, R.W. (1991) The judgment survey. In *Madaba Plains Project 2: The 1987 Season at Tell el-'Umeiri and Vicinity and Subsequent Studies*, edited by L. G. Herr *et al.*. Berrien Springs, MI: Andrews University/ Institute of Archaeology, pp. 269–334.
Younker, R.W. (1994) Ammonites. In *Peoples of the Old Testament World*, edited by A. J. Hoerth, G. L. Mattingly and E. M. Yamauchi. Grand Rapids: Baker, pp. 293–316.
Younker, R.W. (1997) Moabite Social Structure. *Biblical Archaeologist* 60:237–48.

Zayadine, F. (1973) Recent excavations on the Upper Citadel of Amman (a preliminary report). *Annual of the Department of Antiquities of Jordan* 18:17–35, 99–114.
Zayadine, F. (1995) Cosmetic techniques: a historical and botanical approach. In *Studies in the History and Archaeology of Jordan V*, edited by K. 'Amr, F. Zayadine and M. Zaghloul. Amman: Department of Antiquities, pp. 67–75.
Zayadine, F., Humbert, J. B. and Najjar, M. (1989) The 1988 excavations on the Citadel of Amman Lower Terrace, Area A. *Annual of the Department of Antiquities of Jordan* 33:357–63.

Organic Globalization and Socialization

Sheldon Lee Gosline

> No thing great is created suddenly, any more than a bunch of grapes or a fig. If you tell me that you desire a fig, I answer you that there must be time. Let it first blossom, then bear fruit, then ripen.
>
> Epictetus, *The Discourses*, I, 15

In his key note address abstract for the 2000 International Conference on Software Engineering (ICSC) in Limerick, Ireland, Manuel Castells, professor of sociology and planning at the University of California, Berkeley, and author of the acclaimed trilogy on *The Information Age: Economy, Society and Culture*, made a point on which I wish to elaborate in my paper. The subject happens to lie near to the core of my own current research interests. Castells observed that the speed of technological innovation requires a parallel development of institutional and cultural innovation, away from bureaucracy but closer to people, to ensure the sustainability of the new economy, and to spur the new wave of technological creativity. I would argue that this parallel development of institutional and cultural innovation is a societal process that has been around at least since the dawn of human civilization and may be identified as *socialization*. This is the nominal form of the verb 'to socialize', which simply means to make social, or to make fit for life in companionship with others. It is a means by which a group identifies itself as both unique from other groups and united for a common purpose, not a process in socialism.

Throughout the course of known history, group leaders have found it necessary to humanize institutions and develop cultural innovations based on core values, away from pure bureaucracy and closer to the people's ideological values. Often the leaders have called upon their populations to engage in major projects, some of which have left impressive archaeological remains. An excellent example is the wave of pyramid building of Old Kingdom Egypt, and its subsequent revival in the Middle Kingdom. The first pyramid was part of a massive effort to solidify the ruler's supremacy over each aspect of society. By the time of King *Djoser*, Egypt had been politically unified for several generations, however in terms of *socialization*, there were still strong religious/political centers throughout the land. The religious structure of phyles appeared during the governmental *socialization* of the Old Kingdom, but emerged from a more ancient organic institution of clans with totemic emblems, with its roots preceding the First Dynasty (Roth 1991). To show the king's authority over various districts, a complex system of royal visitations had been devised, where the king would visit regional shrines to do homage to the local gods. Thereby, he demonstrated supremacy over the entire land. King *Djoser*'s genius was in bringing facsimiles of every major shrine to the capital itself, where he would symbolically do homage to all the gods at once. Instead, the gods came to him. Furthermore, his master architect, *Imhotep*, took the plan further by producing, or reproducing, the entire pageant backdrop as the stage for the ruler's own funerary monument at Saqqara.

A similar concept was carried out by King Louis XIV of France, who brought the entire French court to Versailles; a site that had previously only been a royal hunting lodge. In both instances, the ruler was consolidating his power base. However, the success of Djoser's scheme was far greater than Louis XIV's. *Djoser*'s vision led to massive pyramidal building projects that fueled a divine kingship for several centuries, while Versailles became the last French palace. Indeed, the French Revolution is an excellent example from history of the ruling class becoming too remote and isolated from the needs and concerns of the population they governed. It was a direct result of the French aristocracy becoming out of touch with its own society. In such cases, instability soon followed until a new leadership arose to ensure stability, and a return to the sustainability of the other force at work, *globalization*. On the surface, the two monumental building projects look the same. Price would see each as 'a large chunk of fossilized energy permanently removed from general circulation' (Price 1978), but it is better to think of this type of building project as a *socialization* investment. The investment will pay well if it is closely linked to broadly based traditional social values. However, even a successful system has its limitations. Near the center of the Egyptian kingdom, the royal mortuary cults were staffed by a complex system of periodic service, which drew cult functionaries from the civil bureaucracy and contributed to a stable integration of the religious and political establishments of the state, thereby enforcing the *socialization* process. However, in a small provincial cult, relatively distant from the capital and controlling a much smaller amount of endowment land, a more traditional patrimonial system existed, akin to the family-centered temple organizations found in Mesopotamia (Roth 1987). The pyramid age did end eventually. The agricultural support system needed to sustain massive labor forces and religious establishments became over extended and the ever-increasing bureaucracy of the temple complexes became top heavy and inefficient. By the end of the Old Kingdom, the Egyptian kings could only dream of constructing shabby pyramids that were pale reflections of the 4th Dynasty's massive monuments to royal ego. Still, rulers from the Middle Kingdom revived the idea of pyramids, and again much later in the Kushite Kingdom of the Sudan. The pyramid proved to be a great tool of *socialization* that even was exportable and adapted to other social environments (Lehner 1997).

Finding a Link between Socialization and Globalization

There is a small but growing tendency to link the term *socialization* with that of *globalization*. A quick internet search reveals currently 19 'hits' for '*socialization* and *globalization*' and just eight for '*globalization* and *socialization*'. I would not venture to say why the former order is currently more than twice as popular, but perhaps it reflects a desire to put society first. The subjects concerned with linking these two concepts range from sublime literary criticism to ridiculous studies of punk sub-culture. The phase is used positively by at least one city government think-tank in China to express their development projects, while several religious groups in America used this phrase to express numerous evils of a 'New World Order'. I suspect that in both cases we are seeing kneejerk reactions. In nearly post-Communist China, *socialization* still sounds like a positive thing, with a semblance to socialism. For Americans, such an association is negative. The phrase '*globalization* and *socialization*' dominates economic and political discussions. Nowhere, in any of these citations, is there a clear discussion of how the two forces interact.

So what exactly is *globalization*? According to Maria Livanos Cattaui, *globalization* is 'the flow of information, technology, ideas, goods, services, capital and people across borders, with rules-based agreements particularly for flows of trade and investment'. Her position, with which I would agree, is that *globalization* is a process with a long history. David Held also expressed the idea that *globalization* is not new. He elaborates, 'If you think of the spread of world religions, the huge development of empires in the 18th and 19th centuries, the stretch of the British Empire: global cultural and economic phenomena are not new. But there have been different historical forms of *globalization*, and the contemporary conjuncture is new'. We know, for instance, that from the 1870s to 1914 there was a more open flow of capital than in today's markets. But today, we are seeing many more participants, with communications as the engine of cross-border flows. The extent and intensity of communications is far greater than telegraph, steamship or railroad. Perhaps the most important aspect of our modern *globalization*, is that it is rules-based. It has broken free from the *socialization* force of territorial empires, mostly with the aid of private corporations that rely on agreements with and among countries in small, regional, and above all multilateral, groupings. This multilateral corporate rules-based *globalization* is perhaps the least coercive, and the most unique form of cross-border flows in the history, but it still retains political ties. I would argue that the new element is the rate and volume of *globalization*, which is now completely overwhelming the *socialization* process. Furthermore, what is new is that the forces of *globalization* are far greater than *socialization* for the first time in world history. This not only threatens all existing nation states, but also threatens human social patterns as they have developed for at least the past six thousand years.

To some extent, Karl Marx foresaw our current *globalization* development, which he refers to as the 'bourgeoisie'. In his *Manifesto* he wrote, 'The bourgeoisie [*globalization*], by the rapid improvement of all instruments of production, by the immensely facilitated means of communication, draws all, even the most barbarian, nations into civilization. The cheap prices of its commodities are the heavy artillery with which it batters down all Chinese walls, with which it forces the barbarians' intensely obstinate hatred of foreigners to capitulate. It compels all nations, on pain of extinction, to adopt the bourgeois mode of production; it compels them to introduce what it calls civilization into their midst, i.e., to become bourgeois themselves. In one word, it creates a world after its own image' (Marx and Engels 1888). Of course, Marx not only observes, he also values and his assessment of the *globalization* process is far from favorable. That fact should not distract from his ability to observe how it functions.

For this and other reasons, on which I will elaborate further, I see the primary tension in all human systems to be a delicate interplay between the forces of *socialization* and *globalization*. For much of human history, *socialization* has dominated. There have been punctuated episodes or flourishes of *globalization*, when ideas and products exchanged more freely. Perhaps the earliest recorded event of this nature was the Amarna Period in ancient Egypt. Another example is the Italian Renaissance. Certain aspects of the Tang Dynasty of China could be added to the list of *globalization* eras, along with the Periclean Age of ancient Greece. Despite these bursts of connective energy, certain socio-political forces always held control. That long-standing delicate balance was finally tipped in the favor of *globalization* by the final decades of the 20th century, in large part due to a rapid growth of information technology. What this will mean in the decades to come is yet to be determined, but there are crucial patterns we can see in history from periods following similarly intense globalization.

These two forces function somewhat in a way that resembles magnetic polarity. But they both repel and attract one another in ways that defy magnetism. By its nature, *socialization* attracts together what it identifies as being the same. Primarily, this sameness is defined as language, cultural habits, foods, living patterns, dwelling styles into positively charged nuclei. As these social groups expand, they encounter other groups. If there is sufficient association between the two, they may unite into a single larger group, or they may repel, just as two similarly charged ends of a magnet will repel. The larger and more established the groups in question are, the more likely they will repel despite their similarities, or indeed, because of their similarities. The force of *globalization*, which has now come to dominate human experience, functions both within the structure of individual social groups and dominates extra-group interactions. *Globalization* is essentially characterized by a key role of knowledge and information exchange within and between groups. As a force, it spurs productivity and enhances competitiveness. By its global reach and by its network form of business organization, it breaks down all borders established by the process of *socialization*, including the borders established by the core group from which that particular *globalization* force originally sprang. It is both the product of successful *socialization* and potentially harmful to it.

Perhaps the best scientific model to explain what I mean by this interplay between *globalization* and *socialization* is that of basic atomic structures. Elements of *socialization* are akin to the core of a given atom, while *globalization* is a force like the electrons racing around the atomic core. Larger atoms have more electrons. In the same way, a larger and more defined social group is more likely to originate and sustain more *globalization* forces. Two centuries ago, this played itself out as colonization. Now it functions as market or corporate imperialism. Also, a more unstable atom is likely to lose electrons. Likewise, a group that is poorly held together by a common *socialization* is more likely to lose *globalization* strength to another group. We will explore this analogy further, but first I wish to point out examples of how an overly developed force of *socialization* can stifle, rather than foster, *globalization*. Atomically speaking, this would be parallel to the nucleus of an atom being so dense that the electrons collapse into the core of protons and neutrons.

There are instances in which *globalization* has been forcibly repressed by existing social structures. A well-known children's story ('The Flying Machine' by Ray Bradbury, *Children's Digest*, March 1973) illustrates this point remarkably well:

> In the year A.D. 400, the Emperor Yuan held his throne by the Great Wall of China, and the land was green with rain, readying itself toward the harvest, at peace, the people in his domain neither too happy nor too sad. Early in the morning of the first day of the first week of the second month of the new year, the Emperor Yuan was sipping tea and fanning himself against a warm breeze when a servant ran across the scarlet blue garden tiles, calling, 'Oh, Emperor, Emperor, a miracle!' ... The miracle was that a man was flying...
>
> The Emperor looked into the sky. And in the sky, laughing so high that you could hardly hear him laugh, was a man; and the man was clothed in bright papers and reeds to make wings and a beautiful yellow tail, and he was soaring all above like the largest bird in a universe of birds, like a new dragon in a land of ancient dragons. The man called down to them from high in the cool winds of morning, 'I fly, I fly!'
>
> The servant waved to him. 'Yes, yes!' The Emperor Yuan did not move. Instead, he looked at the Great Wall of China now taking shape out of the farthest mist in the green hills, that splendid snake of stones that writhed with majesty across the entire land. That wonderful wall which had protected them for a timeless time from enemy hordes and preserved peace for years without number...' After learning that no one else had seen the flying man, the Emperor had him called down. The man was instantly seized by royal guards and the executioner was ready. The man pleaded for his life and told the Emperor of the beauty of flying.
>
> 'Yes', said the Emperor sadly, 'I know it must be true. For I felt my heart move with you in the air and I wondered: What is it like? How does it feel? How do the distant pools look from so high? And how my houses and servants? Like ants? And how the distant towns not yet awake?'
>
> 'Then spare me!'
>
> 'But there are times', said the Emperor, more sadly still, 'when one must lose the beauty if one is to keep what little beauty one already has. I do not fear you, yourself, but I fear another man.'
>
> 'What man?'
>
> 'Some other man who, seeing you, will build a thing of bright papers and bamboo like this. But the other man will have an evil face and an evil heart, and the beauty will be gone. It is this man I fear.'
>
> So the Emperor had the man immediately executed, the flying machine destroyed, and the servants sworn to secrecy.

I have pondered that story many years. After the tragic events of September 11th, and their aftermath, we in the West are beginning to understand the Emperor's position concerning the dangers of technology in the wrong hands. Are we learning the wrong lessons? Maria Cattaui said, 'We should be harnessing the unique atmosphere of international co-operation it has created. Rather than being timid and retreating into our respective national shells, now is the time for us to be even more bold and further open the flows of trade and investment around the world' (Cattaui 2001). Is this what is happening? Are our leaders attempting to stifle globalization, as the emperor did, or are they attempting to stifle competing forces of socialization? Most importantly, is either approach a means to solving the current crisis?

Figure 9.1 Emperor's tomb, Xian.

The Emperor's response stifled Chinese technological developments. Seemingly, all the factors had been present in China for the industrial revolution, but it did not happen there. Instead, it happened in the backwater of civilization, northern Europe. Why? It was the late sinologist Joseph Needham who first eloquently stated this conundrum. The answer is far simpler than anyone could imagine. China has historically had a socialization system that is so oppressively strong that there is little room for the kind of creative forces associated with globalization to flourish. Even the complex system of Chinese writing presents a daunting social pattern, intended to control thought patterns into predetermined paths. Only the rare individual can break out of such a system, or dare to question it, and the result is usually negative. But China's system is also the oldest, and therefore can be considered as the most successful—a point to which I will return.

Failure of Existing State Formation Paradigms

The study of states extends back to the ancient philosophers, and thenceforth to Enlightenment *philosophes*: Hobbes, Locke, and Rousseau. Tension between social contract (integration models), and social conflict (coercive models) extends throughout, as argued effectively by Haas (1982). Indeed, the greatest methodological problem that scholars face in interpreting archaeological data for archaic states is in establishing causal links to support or reject conflict or integration positions.

Attempts by evolutionary biologists to explain the state emergence have used the term 'evolution' in a purely reductionist sense of an increase in adaptive fitness to a particular environment. Jack Hill suggests that human beings inevitably seek greater prestige for the reproductive advantage it will provide. States, then, are the culmination of a never-ending quest for greater prestige to obtain more offspring (Hill 1994). Hill's analysis, however, is wholly teleological. Why, for instance, do states not evolve among chimpanzees, since it is also true that the great apes have dominance hierarchies that give them greater reproductive success? Have hunter-gatherers such as the !Kung San somehow missed out on the opportunity to gain reproductive success by not reaching a 'state' level of organization? While Hill is certainly right that a desire for power and prestige is an essential part of any group leader, any increase in reproductive fitness in the leader would necessarily be offset by the loss in reproductive success of the underlings. Hill does not consider that non-prestigious members of a given society do accept laws and ordinances of those who hold prestige. Why would one not simply leave or eliminate one's leaders, or use other means to reduce the resultant inequalities? Another issue with Hill's argument concerns hunter-gatherer bands. Stratified by age and sex, young men know that they have only to wait a few years until their status rises, along with their reproductive success. There is no reason to overthrow leadership in such a stable situation, and there is no evidence that this is how social evolution occurred. While there are certain correlations between the acquisition of power and the continuation of one's line, Hill has reduced a complex situation to such a ridiculous degree that his argument has no merit.

Figure 9.2 Olive tree.

Roger Masters equates political evolution with evolutionary biology game theory. Masters contends that the inevitable result of individual rational choices is some 'social contract' where it is 'natural' that the benefits of law and government outweigh its costs. His sources on state origins are limited to Hobbes, Rousseau, Kant and Hegel. Masters' contention that a state is formed when equals gather to determine codes of proper or 'altruistic' conduct supposes that a 'natural state of equality' once existed (Masters 1982: 442). There is no such evidence. This analysis falls prey to the same sort of fault as Hill's, by failing to consider the non-emergence of states as an equally relevant fact as their actual formation. It is clear that while there may be correlations between state formation and biological adaptive advantages, evolutionary biologists have failed to identify adequate causal agents.

Marxist and neo-Marxist scholars, argue that both material conditions and societal modes of production are essential to transform its political structures and ideological behavior. Another group, called 'vulgar Marxists' by some, are cultural ecologists who argue that a society's environmental conditions are primary determinants of its social structure and changes. While both arguments fail, they fail for different reasons. Marxists have certainly come farther than many in their emphasis on historical processes and structural or ideological change in societies. However, many Marxist scholars still regard state formation according to an orthodox Marxist scheme for which there is little evidence. For instance, Patterson's description of the 'pre-capitalist' Inca state requires that one accept that 'capitalism' is the inevitable successor to whatever sort of 'pre-capitalism' existed among the Inca (Patterson 1991). Furthermore, the direct translation of material conditions into ideology is overly simplified; while certainly one's subsistence method and production influence one's way of thought, the notion that they are thereby determined is far-fetched. Many cultural ecologists have studied state evolution, arguing that the primary mechanisms of cultural evolution and state creation derive from the physical environment. There is no basis for that paradigm either.

Some researchers have even proposed that warfare is the chief causal agent in state formation. In general, advocates for this position combine the two orientations of integration and conflict. Webster notes that warfare facilitated 'the emergence and survival of privileged managerial groups' (Webster 1975) to co-ordinate military efforts and marshal resources. However, this integrative role contrasts with his assertion that 'concentration of power is integrally related to concentration of wealth, and derives from it' (Webster 1975:483). This apparent contradiction suggests that while initially, the need for integration enabled meritorious or cunning individuals to acquire control over resources, coercion and differential access to resources reinforced this position in a resulting power differential.

Warfare is clearly a factor in state formation, but it is insufficient to account for all developments. However, Cohen has advocated this position (1978) as part of complex events that synthesize various factors leading to authority centralization. Equally problematic is the conclusion of Naroll and Divale that since cross-cultural studies fail to show a correlation between warfare and territorial growth 'peaceful diffusion is more likely than warfare to be the primary mechanism of selection in cultural evolution' (Naroll and Divale 1976). Both causes and consequences of warfare are varied and closely intertwined with other societal events, a matter that I will subsequently identify under more broadly defined terms. Warfare is neither indicative of 'coercion' nor 'integration'. It requires that both factors operate simultaneously. Surely war seriously influences political leadership and social structure, but it is overly simplistic to argue that its presence somehow determines the future of any society.

In anthropological literature concerning states, most Marxists and materialists adopt coercive models, while those emphasizing managerial functions propound integrative theories of state formation. However, there is considerable evidence on both sides of the debate, which leads one to suspect that neither theory is wholly satisfactory. Turning to the original authors themselves, it is possible to extract some useful principles. As already noted, Marx envisioned our current *globalization*:

> Modern industry has established the world-market, for which the discovery of America paved the way. This market has given an immense development to commerce, to navigation, to communication by land. This development has, in its time, reacted on the extension of industry; and in proportion as industry, commerce, navigation, railways extended, in the same proportion the bourgeoisie developed, increased its capital, and pushed into the background every class handed down from the Middle Ages. ... The need of a constantly expanding market for its products chases the bourgeoisie over the whole surface of the globe (Marx and Engels 1888).

His view of prior conditions is rather naïve and utopian. By contrast, Charles Darwin's exploration of species diversification, which is less directly associated with human society, is more analogous to the process of *socialization*. We can extract a principle from Darwin, that distinctions between social groups did not occur immediately, but resulted from population pressure and competition for resources. Darwin states:

> It seems clear that organic beings must be exposed during several generations to new conditions to cause any great amount of variation; and that, when the organization has once begun to vary, it generally continues varying for many generations. No case is on record of a variable organism ceasing to vary under cultivation. Our oldest cultivated plants, such as wheat, still yield new varieties: our oldest domesticated animals are still capable of rapid improvement or modification.

Likewise, his observations concerning competition between species for existence parallel the global limitations that social groups face,

> as more individuals are produced than can possibly survive, there must in every case be a struggle for existence, either one individual with another of the same species [= social groups], or with the individuals of distinct species [= social groups], or with the physical conditions of life. It is the doctrine of Malthus applied with manifold force to the whole animal and vegetable kingdoms; for in this case there can be no artificial increase of food, and no prudential restraint from marriage. Although some species [= social groups] may be now increasing, more or less rapidly, in numbers, all cannot do so, for the world would not hold them (Darwin 1860).

My direct association of his point to social groups is not out of line, because the doctrine from which Charles Darwin has drawn this point, that of Thomas R. Malthus, concerns human population, and how it was kept in check. Malthus saw the 'struggle for existence' as the great stimulus for labor and a cause of human improvement. He also wrote, 'It is an obvious truth, which has been taken notice of by many writers, that population must always be kept down to the level of the means of subsistence; but no writer that the Author recollects has inquired particularly into the means by which this level is effected'. Furthermore, Malthus notes, 'the power of population is indefinitely greater than the power in the earth to produce subsistence for man'. Three of his main conclusions are as follows:

> That population cannot increase without the means of subsistence is a proposition so evident that it needs no illustration. That population does invariably increase where there are the means of subsistence, the history of every people that have ever existed will abundantly prove. And that the superior power of population cannot be checked without producing misery or vice, the ample portion of these too bitter ingredients in the cup of human life and the continuance of the physical causes that seem to have produced them bear too convincing a testimony (Malthus 1798).

Accordingly, one of the chief aims of *socialization* is to regulate population. Hence, the breakdown of traditional social structures through rampant *globalization* yields both increased population and wide-scale social unrest. Interestingly, the world currently faces these two major problems.

In general, the study of state formation, and social change in general, has fallen out of fashion in recent years, particularly among ethnologists. Existing models of cultural and technological evolutionism, or various re-visitations of diffusionism are incapable of resolving the problem of how social structures function. The method adopted by Claessen and Skalník in their Early State Project attempted to define the state by a number of structural characteristics (Claessen 1978). While useful for purposes of description, the model had little explanatory value.

Until recently, theorists concerned with state formation have polarized into two schools: conflict theorists, who emphasize the coercive role of the state in increasing and legitimating inequality, and integration theorists, who point to the state's greater redistributive ability as its primary causal feature. Neither extreme position is wholly satisfactory for every state, and neither sufficiently explains the dynamics of any state. Whether a mechanism is coercive or integrative is not a primary determinant of its importance for state formation. The excessive focus on the polar opposition of these two principles may stem from the *philosophes*. Thus, while we may maintain that organizing irrigation systems is 'integrative' and enslaving one's conquered enemies is 'coercive', there are more important guiding principles of state formation, yet to be defined. As Machiavelli astutely noted almost four centuries ago, both laws and arms make a good prince, and it is impossible to have one without the other.(Machiavelli, *The Prince*, ch. 12).

A New Paradigm Based on Globalization and Socialization

Returning to the interaction between *globalization* and *socialization*: is there a way to resolve the old debate in establishing causal links to support or reject either conflict or integration positions? Could an application of *globalization*, in the sense of Manuel Castells' *The Information Age: Economy, Society and Culture* lead to an answer or at least to some new questions? I believe it can. It appears that conflict chiefly arises in response to tensions within the *globalization / socialization* dichotomy, while integration is the positive and balanced result of *globalization* and *socialization* functioning in harmony and in balance. The man with the flying machine represents the technologically driven *globalization* of our current age. The emperor's fear was that he would lose control. The counterbalance of interest between *globalization* and *socialization* is clearly functioning in this example to create a non-emergence of a technological breakthrough that would have hurled the Chinese state further forward than any other state at the time. By extension, we could imagine localized *socialization* conditions that would not allow the creation of any state at all. This model allows for this possibility, as an equally relevant fact of the actual formation of states. While many causal factors lead to state development, trends of increasing political complexity are evident in widely divergent societies, until they collapse.

Our particular current situation involving intense *globalization* is fueled by technology, but technology alone has not always been the main driving force of *globalization*. Karl Marx was no friend to *globalization*. He clearly perceived it as the enemy of the social fabric and traditional systems, leading to a world with little or no diversity.

> The bourgeoisie [*globalization*] has through its exploitation of the world-market given a cosmopolitan character to production and consumption in every country. ...They [old established industries] are dislodged by new industries, whose introduction becomes a life and death question for all civilized nations, by industries that no longer work up indigenous raw material, but raw material drawn from the remotest zones; industries whose products are consumed, not only at home, but in every quarter of the globe. In place of the old wants, satisfied by the productions of the country, we find new wants, requiring for their satisfaction the products of distant lands and climes. In place of the old local and national seclusion and self-sufficiency, we have intercourse in every direction, universal inter-dependence of nations. And as in material, so also in intellectual production. The intellectual creations of individual nations become common property. National one-sidedness and narrow-mindedness become more and more impossible, and from the numerous national and local literatures, there arises a world literature (Marx and Engels 1888).

Largely, Marx points out aspects of *globalization* that are potentially good. We have a modern perception that all societies and the factors that influence them are neither infinitely particular nor widely general. Just as when we eat a potato or piece of corn, we do not ask, 'Where does it come from?' or 'How was it grown?' so too, our pre-conceived paradigms about society are increasingly global. The danger is that we do not even stop to ask what it is about a given society, past or present, that makes it function as it does. Let us then consider several ethnocentric positions concerning technology and information we in the West are prone to accept uncritically:

1. that increased technology is basically good; inventions will ALWAYS make life better and solve problems, including problems created by pre-existing technologies.
2. that increased communication is basically good, the more quickly ideas get transferred and the bigger the web of communication the faster problems will be solved.
3. that increased commerce is basically good, leading to higher living standards for all involved, or what is good for business is good for everyone.
4. that relatively greater technology and faster communication is the hallmark of more developed civilizations and, conversely, less technology and slower communication is the hallmark of backward societies.
5. that wise leaders always embrace technology and communication while foolish ones react like Emperor Yuan and reject innovations.
6. that in some sort of 'survival of the fittest' model those technologically advanced civilizations will always beat out the technologically backwards ones.

To support this paradigm, historians are quick to cite the Spanish with their greater technology easily vanquishing the Incas and Aztecs, of course ignoring factors such as disease, a standing army with nothing to do at the end of the *reconquista*, native American political struggles, coincidence, timing, and blind luck. With closer scrutiny, Alan Kolata (1997) and other researchers have been able to discern how the native American cohesive systems of *noblesse oblige* worked against their ability to defend against the invading snatch and grab empire-building. A millennium before the Incas built their empire, the city of Tiahuanaco sat at the center of a great empire of its own. Located on Lake Titicaca, the world's highest at 13,000 feet, in what is now Bolivia, at the very limits of agriculture, the people of Tiahuanaco developed an ingenious system of cultivation based on raised planting beds alternating with trenches that served as irrigation ditches. From AD 400 to 800, the temples of Tiahuanaco glittered with gold and the empire supported as many as 250,000 people. They were not destroyed by the impact of *globalization*, when the Spanish arrived. Instead the Aymara formed a spiritual bond with nature that industrialized society fails to comprehend. In their culture, which survives to this day, time and space merge to provide with a strong coherent *socialization* that provides them a lasting identity (Kolata 1996). In this instance, *globalization* has fostered *socialization*. This process has sometimes been called 'secondary state formation' (Esse 1989), but the process can even occur without the creation of a secondary state.

The archaeological record is filled with data concerning the processes of *globalization* and *socialization*. 'Data relevant to most, if not all, components of past socio-cultural systems are preserved in the archaeological record', argued Lewis Binford (1968). The problem has been interpretation. One of the problem has been in the focus on stages of social organization, as if there were a series of social revolutions through which societies had to progress. V. Gordon Childe (1956) had identified the Neolithic and Urban Revolutions as an interaction between human cultural evolution and developing social organization. Leslie White and Elman Service developed a simple model of societal evolution through prehistory that still attracts wide attention. In his classic *Profiles in Ethnology*, Elman Service (1971) defined broad levels of socio-cultural evolution from primitive family structures of the earliest hunter-gatherers to highly complex state-organized societies of early civilizations. What is lacking in his model, and others, is any clear engine that fuels the change from one level of social complexity to another. Ultimately, such models are derived from the paradigms of Darwinian evolution or Marxism though the Hegelian dialectic. While the two approaches stand in theoretical opposition to one another, they are both based on observed occurrences of random variations, governed by principals of selection and adaptation, or set patterns and stages of development. Therefore, in both cases, the theoretical problem postulated by such models is one of assessment (extent of presence or operation of an element in question). Thereby, all human behavior is analytically reduced to special cases of more general laws. Darwinian models view these laws as thresholds of change. Marxist models view the laws as stages in standard social progression. Rather than questioning the core concepts of either paradigm, or searching for an engine that would move and govern these 'laws', scholars have focused on developing increasingly elaborate models for stages of social development to explain how and why the 'laws' don't really explain observable conditions. In short, existing archaeological models are inherently flawed because they are unidirectional and progressive in their outlook, assuming that greater complexity equates to improved conditions. They fail to explore the ever-present tension and cooperation between the internally driven force of *socialization* in the local group and the externally driven force of *globalization*.

The concept of secondary state formation comes close to dealing with this issue, but only to the extent that it observes the most transparent factors. In the 'old world' most states, other than Egypt and Mesopotamia, were secondary, and the result of a *globalization* force from the earlier state interacting with developing states. The appearance of a secondary state is by definition the result of regular interaction and/or competition with expanding states, *vis-à-vis* non-state-organized populations (Price 1978). Warfare has long been noted as a factor of cultural interaction (Cohen 1985). Two additional case studies are Habuba Kabira South in northern Syria, and Ebla in Syria (Bucellati 1967).

The forces of increased technology and faster communication, culminating in *globalization*, is neither good nor bad in itself, just as strong forces of socialization are neither good nor bad. The technologically fit society does not always have the survival edge, not does the society with strong traditions. Each case must be considered individually. That survival and development of a given human society is dependent on a far more complex set of influences, stretching back to remote antiquity, into what seems to us a pre-technological dark age of conceptual isolationism. I will later elaborate on the complexity of these factors, but in general, it consists of a balance between a desire for innovative exchange (*globalization*) and conservative values that define the group (*socialization*).

Here is an example to illustrate my point. In numerous instances, state officials have employed imagery and texts to establish their legitimacy of authority. The archaeological record from many regions attests to this fact. Carved stamp or cylinder seals from Greece, Egypt, Mesopotamia, Persia, India and China all attest to this principle. The administrative system in the Third Dynasty of Ur is an excellent example of this particular type of *socialization*. This period witnessed an unprecedented standardization of cylinder seal designs, as pointed out by Irene Winter (1987). This Ur III period also corresponds to an equally unprecedented concentration of and distribution of resources within a highly centralized bureaucracy. Within the administrative system, the seals functioned as both coinage and identity cards, serving as markers of systemic unity and indicating an individual's place within the system. The imagery and text on the seals argued for both the king's and the official's legitimacy. Thus, on several levels, these seals were powerful markers of *socialization*. Interestingly, the standardization of these seals as indicators of rank and status may be unique to the Ur III period, representing in particular the control exerted by king *Šulgi*, and the rulers immediately following him. In later periods of Mesopotamian history, seals were not used in the same way and, of course, they are not used that way in modern-day Iraq.

As a group becomes larger, it gains increased opportunity for exchange. It also requires more complex symbols and systems to exert its own unity, such as King *Šulgi*'s innovative use of cylinder seals to promote and legitimize his power base. However, in Mesopotamia the use of seals in this way ended, as it did in much of the ancient world at various times. The system ended in India after the Harappan period. In Egypt, the administrative cylinder seals gave way to scarab seals, which had less of an administrative purpose than a religious and commemorative purpose. In Persia and Greece the seals became personal signet rings. In China, the People's Republic still uses administrative stamp seals. When I lived in China, my students encouraged me to take a Chinese name and have a stamp seal carved. There are stamp seal carvers in every corner of the public marketplaces. No official document is without at least one official stamp seal, and to get permission for legal events of a social nature, such as a marriage, legal paperwork must have the stamp seal from each tier of authority—from the apartment block leader, to the district official, to the regional office, to the provincial office. At each stage, if a lower ranking stamp seal is missing from a document, approval is denied and the petitioner is sent down the hierarchy rungs to obtain the proper stamp seal. The question that no one has bothered to ask is why did this ancient system of administrative seals never end in China?

Socialization is the implementation of societal codes that provide definition and cohesion, even loyalty to the group. We see evidence of this in the names given to work groups laboring on the great pyramid of Khufu in Giza. They proudly wrote their patriotic slogans on the massive blocks buried over the main burial chamber. One can easily imagine a competition to get them in place. Some *socialization* codes are constructed by an elite, such as their administrative seals, while others are more ancient, predating the elite, but used by them to exert and maintain authority (Kemp 1994).

Sometimes such codes become too specialized, so that when an intrusive system appears, the elite become helpless to call upon the defensive forces of *socialization*. This was one of the major factors in the Spanish conquest of Latin America. The Native American civilizations had systems that were completely undermined by the invading forces. Like *globalization*, this *socialization* is a basic form of human interaction. It preserves society. It makes us feel safe. It is either in anticipation to or response to a threatening force of *globalization*, and as such is perceived by the forces behind that *globalization* movement as terrorism. It is also manifest in laws, cultural habits or even a flag waving on a car driving down the road, in protest against 'terrorism'.

It must be stressed again that *globalization* and *socialization* are neither good nor bad, and the one needs the other, otherwise a given society goes into decline. For example, the political, technological and cultural isolationism of Ching dynasty China and the Roman Empire's intense polymorphic internationalism of 'anything goes' both led to corruption and decline. Constant growth and development of a civilization requires a healthy balance of both forces. What Marxist models view as thresholds of development (clan, tribe, chieftain, state, and empire) are simply manifestations of the *socialization* responses to a given need or localized advantage, which may be fueled internally or externally by forces of *globalization*. Marxism inherently views all change as being socially driven. By contrast, the perspective of evolutionary models is more in tune with forces of innovative *globalization*. In that paradigm, society is basically static, until some external or internal variation pops up. There is nothing in the makeup of any society to suggest that it evolves over time. What is Egyptian was always Egyptian. What is Roman was always Roman. The one cultural paradigm will never become the other one and as long as there are Egyptians and Romans, some aspects of Egyptian and Roman culture will always persist. Probably the greatest effort to exterminate a people and culture was committed by the Nazis, carried out with misplaced goals of evolutionary zeal. It was tragic, but it also failed. Adaptation and selection (or rejection) of the new element is the only driving force in the evolutionary model. As such, it is also incorrect.

In fact, there is a built-in catch-22 situation which prevents *globalization* from completely dominating, even now in our age of instant communication. As any given social group expands its sphere of influence to create a cultural hegemony, it encounters other social groups that confront it, both aggressively and passively. The only way for an invading force to be successfully accepted by other social groups is for that invading force to adopt the socialization markers of the conquered group(s). Such apparently submissive gestures of reconciliation are counterintuitive to any invader. It is little wonder that this tactic has rarely been carried off tactfully. Alexander the Great was perhaps the first leader to pull this maneuver off with any amount of finesse. However, his subordinates were often bewildered by his *esprit de corps* with the natives, as he became Pharaoh in Egypt and

Figure 9.3 Representation of camel caravan at Avdat.

Silkunder in India. The concept did not last beyond his lifetime, as his generals carved up his empire. What Alexander managed to pull off amounts to a parlor trick sleight of hand when compared to the present-day localized social groups acting against *globalization*. We define the most aggressive units as terrorists, and their numbers inevitably will grow in step with growing *globalization*, unless our leaders can achieve an identity makeover similar to that which Alexander accomplished.

Furthermore, I propose that *globalization*, or the intense interconnectedness of idea exchange, is a basic byproduct of all human creativity and interaction. For example, the creator of the flying machine interacting with Emperor Yuan was a microcosm of the *globalization* process that failed. Alexander the Great brought about a *globalization* process that succeeded, for a time. When such a contact is productive, the byproduct serves to fuel increased contact. As a counterbalance, *socialization* is an intense compartmentalization of ideas, exemplified by Emperor Yuan. It is also exemplified by Alexander the Great, but for different reasons.

I am not proposing that societies or even individuals persist unchanged. The key to understanding what fuels change in human society is in part a reconciliation between these two paradigms, Marxism and Darwinism, which separately, by themselves, fail to explain why change occurs. Much ink has been spilled over the question of societal typology. The classic theories of Service (1962) and Fried (1967) are seminal discussions. In general, each is concerned with how egalitarian (or band) societies changed through intermediate stages into modern states. Upham pointed out that Service's 'band-tribe-chiefdom-state' and Fried's 'egalitarian-ranked-stratified-state' models 'do not exist in their entirety in the real world; they are categorical representations of reality that condense meaningful variability' (Upham 1990). That these typologies are constructs does not eliminate their analytical value, as long as we understand their limited explanatory value. They cannot reflect the fullness of social reality.

The paradigm that I am proposing functions in conjunction with and expands the usefulness of one existing theoretical model, which we have not yet discussed, systems theory. Systems theory developed from cultural evolution. In it, 'multivariant causality' allows for various factors to be interrelated in a complex of feedback loops, causal chains and other relationships (Flannery 1972: 399–426). By limiting 'prime movers' such as population pressure or warfare, without denying their importance, multivariant causality allows those factors to operate in different directions. The limitation is that this approach does not lend itself to easy analysis.

Furthermore, systems theory has been used to study instances of state formation among archaic civilizations known archaeologically. Examining evidence in southwest Iran from Mesopotamian sites, Wright and Johnson concluded that 'only multiple variable changes' could produce vast shifts in the political economy and exchange networks present (Wright and Johnson 1975:284). According to them, the shift toward greater political centralization and loss of autonomy among smaller centers may have overloaded an existing system's capability to process information, leading to the creation of hierarchies to govern the new system. While Wright and Johnson admit that their research is unable to answer what specific causal factors led to the creation of centralized redistributive centers, they offer a model that can be tested in order to explain specific instances of state formation. I propose that the factor leading to the creation of these centralized redistributive centers was the interplay between *socialization* and *globalization*.

J. Stephen Athens criticized the systems approach of Flannery, Wright and Johnson. He argued from an ecological perspective: 'an understanding of the evolution of complex social systems can only proceed through an examination of factors relating to the stability of agricultural production and the use of relevant variable dimensions of analysis' (Athens 1977:377). He claims that system theories 'are unsuccessful because they cannot predict state formation' (1977:360). However, if we begin accounting for influences of *socialization* and *globalization*, his argument vanishes. Taking my model a step further as I do in the next section (to propose an organic pattern of societal development, peak, and decay), it becomes possible to even predict when state formation, apex, and decline will occur. Athens assumes that a theory which successfully addresses the question of causation will be fully equipped for prediction. By arguing that any successful theory of state formation should be universally applicable, Athens is calling for exactly the type of model that I am proposing.

Systems theorists have tried to formulate a response to Athens' qualms regarding causation with the concept of equifinality. This is defined by Buckley (1967:60) as a final condition of a system that may be achieved by any number of developmental routes. On the surface, it is true that distinct causes can come together in different ways to yield similar events. One may attempt to emphasize one cause as primary, but any theoretical 'cause' may not turn out to be useful, because the result is unknown until it finally emerges. The 'final' result of the interplay of factors is not merely the collimation of causes to produce an effect, but a process of interaction and amplification. Where I differ from systems theorists is that they claim it is not possible to predict the emergence of the state with any regularity, or to separate causes from their results. They are looking at the problem the wrong way. Particular events or situations do not actually shape a given society. Rather, the way in which a particular social group is patterned to deal with situations truly shapes that society. That is what I will be referring to as 'societal DNA'. Of course, there is no single factor sufficient to shape all societies. What would function as a catalyst for change in one, would destroy another, just as one plant prefers dry acidic soil and another prefers wet base soil. The many factors acting upon each human social group are without a doubt multivarient. What is not multivarient is how a particular group is likely to respond. That is what we need to study in order to begin understanding the processes of human society.

As a model, systems theory is generally headed in the right direction. It creates testable hypotheses, not complete accounts of state formation incidences. These are human creations, subject to the vagaries of human existence and random chance. We must recognize that something as simple as the untimely death of one's leader can have profound consequences on history (as it did on the Mongol hordes), and there is nothing like a hurricane to crush an incipient rebellion and unite individuals in a rebuilding effort. However, the specific response of one social group may be very different from the response of another. It is important to note that these responses are not random. They are encoded in the particular group's *socialization*. Charles Spencer discusses the effect of the eruption of the volcano Xitle as a precipitating event for the conquest of Cuicuilco by the early Mesoamerican state of Teotihuacan (Spencer 1990:22). As noted above, the consequence of this randomizing factor is that we never know exactly what parts of the system have priority in a given society, rendering prediction impossible. In no way do I mean to imply that because a system is stable (has achieved equilibrium or *homeostasis*) that it is 'adaptive', to use a much-misused term. As Rappaport notes, 'Social systems ... can make mistakes of which biological systems may be incapable' (Rappaport 1977:51). Still, recognizing this fact, we should proceed with the knowledge that even an imperfect system is not a random aggregate, but a structured somewhat predictable grouping. Above all, the focus of our investigation needs to be in the realm of monitoring social responses to situations, not the situations themselves.

The Organic Nature of Globalization and Socialization

Now that we have established that a delicate balance between *globalization* and *socialization* fuels all change in society, I will endeavor to illustrate how complex human societies follow an organic process of birth, growth, decay and sometimes renewal through the developments of *socialization*, the catalysis of *globalization*, and continual interplay between the two. This force of connectivity motivates all change, now and throughout antiquity. The proper model for this change is neither evolutionary transformation, nor jumps from one stage of development to another. By 'organic', I mean both a natural process of human interaction with the exchange of ideas and that this human process correlates with adaptations that an organic creature might make to changing environmental conditions.

This perspective introduces a new goal for anthropology—to search for something akin to societal DNA, or put another way, that the semiotics of a culture should be viewed as its genetic code. This societal DNA functions in much the same way as biological DNA. The strength to survive comes from the core elements, that is, societal DNA of a given culture reapplied and reinterpreted simultaneously making use of borrowed and foreign elements when useful. This concept should not be confused with biological determinism. Carneiro made such an egregious conclusion, placing descriptive characteristics of states above factors causing them. He noted that the number of autonomous political entities extant in the world has declined steadily from the human beginnings to the present, and that as the number of states grows smaller, their size grows larger—fair enough, so far. He then asserted that the curve of declining polities leads inevitably to the emergence of a world state (Carneiro 1978). To do so, he invoked a principle of competitive exclusion (an idea borrowed from biological evolution), which states that two species cannot coexist using the same niche indefinitely, and one will eventually prevail, forcing the other to evolve or die out (Carneiro 1978:221). We must also consider whether conditions of harsh competition and warfare required for this model actually existed. Furthermore, it is by no means a foregone conclusion that a world state is inevitable. Carneiro confuses directionality with teleology. It is entirely unknown where the curve of autonomous polities might be leading. We cannot predict where social developments may go, simply because they do not 'go' anywhere at all. Rather, processes of *globalization* and *socialization*, acting at the present, shape a future without any inherent goal or endpoint. Even now, new *socialization* units are emerging though a primary tool of *globalization*—the internet. One of the most popular features of that communication tool is the 'chat room' where people can meet and socialize over a topic of common interest. Who is to say that these social groupings may not someday form into distinct socio-political units, thereby subverting the same integrative system that created those same groups.

Societal DNA is most easily associated in our thinking with *socialization*, but it also determines how a group will interact through *globalization*. Some groups are missionaries by virtue of the cultural template to which they are subscribing. Islam and the Church of Latter Day Saints clearly fall into this category, while Judaism primarily functions in the realm of *socialization*. The key point is that any given societal DNA will concern itself differently with *globalization* and *socialization*. A primary *globalization* function of societal DNA is how it defines and deals with foreigners, either in peace or at war, at home or abroad. Concerns of sexuality and procreation are major ways that societal DNA functions in matters of *socialization*. Jewelry, body ornamentation, rituals, rites of passage and even toys all serve to shape the gender constructs of a groups members (Gosline 1999).

Sometimes, amazing changes in social structures happen through the process of *globalization*. When people in the river valleys of the Fertile Crescent needed more food they borrowed and applied the growing of grains, first developed by people living at a higher elevation, leading to the earliest civilizations. They did not simply grow the grain the same way, but developed new methods to suit their environmental conditions. When Egyptians wanted a governmental system and symbols of authority, they borrowed artistic and architectural elements from Mesopotamia, including administrative seals, but soon after the Egyptians made their own new corpus of semiotic indicators, according to their own *socialization* template. For example, we know that human sacrifices were carried out at Ur in Mesopotamia, at sites such as the grave of King *A-bar-gi* (Woolley 1965). In Egypt, we have no conclusive evidence of human sacrifices, but some Pre-dynastic pallets depict human sacrifice and some hymns in the Pyramid Texts indicate ritual cannibalism of all the Egyptian gods and men to take on their powers (Wilson 1951:52, 85, 146–7, 151). The Egyptian cases are probably borrowed references to Mesopotamian practice.

Linguistically, we also see *globalization* at work. When the Caananites needed a writing system, they borrowed Egyptian hieratic phonetic signs and developed the first alphabet with far reaching influence. Their language did not evolve into Egyptian; they maintained and promoted their own language by adapting a borrowed symbolic structure with phonetic values. Written English came about the same way, which explains why there are so many sounds without proper letters: for example, 'th', 'sh', 'ch', and totally useless letters like 'c'. Despite these shortcomings, we are still writing in English, not Latin. True, the languages of North America were not always English, Spanish and French, but these can easily be identified as invasive foreign societal DNA strains that have nearly wiped out all traces of the native species. Traces mostly remain in place names, such as 'Susquehanna', 'Potomac', or 'Towanda'. Time does not permit the elaboration of this point, but similar trace societies have been identified in Sumerian place names.

The way civilizations both borrow and set up barriers can also be seen in this model. The borrowing process increases flexibility, while the barriers maximize strength. I will elaborate with a technological study of irrigation in the Persian Empire. The Persians are generally credited with inventing the *qanat* system of irrigations (Briant 2001). This was a system of underground canals to trap ground water coming down a slope and directing it to a location where agriculture and/or settlement was desired. By being underground, there was less evaporation, and it also provided a source of water along the way to its destination. What is *not* generally known is that the *qanat* system of irrigation is attested both archaeologically and textually in at least one Egyptian oasis in the Libyan desert, Bahariya, at a much earlier date: the reign of Ramesses II. In Bahariya Oasis, there are extensive tracts of land now covered by desert sands crossed by ancient *qanat* systems. These were abandoned since the late New Kingdom, according to the pottery remains. Textual records from Egypt clearly state that Ramesses II constructed a massive irrigation system in Bahariya to cultivate grapes for royal wine production. Likely, Ramesses II himself only borrowed this technology. Life in the oases of the Libyan desert lends itself to an organic development of the *qanat*. Its invention was most likely local to that region and ancient. Other factors, such as local gods inhabiting underground caverns and waterways, lend further support. Curiously, in his recent book on *qanat* systems, Pierre Briant (2001:109–36) makes *no* mention of these facts. While the authors describe various local variations of the *qanat* system in neighboring Kharga Oasis, they fail to realize that variations are more likely in a region where a technology was begun, in much the same way that greater biodiversity of a crop is found in its native habitat.

The most likely scenario is that the Persians discovered *qanats* being used in these Egyptian oases at the time they took over the country. Then the Persians took that technology, modified it to their own cultural system and needs. They replicated a standardized version of it throughout their vast empire, thus creating a golden age of irrigation and agriculture, which not only fed their own empire, but also sustained Alexander's empire, the Hellenic empires of his generals and finally the Roman empire, after which the systems collapsed from neglect, overuse, salination and other factors. I would like to extract the principle that the source of a particular societal DNA is most likely not an invading culture, but rather the location where there was greatest variation, just as one would find for a plant or animal. The potato was not cultivated by Spain, it was found by them and transplanted through globalization, with the results of increased food worldwide, increased population, increased social pressures, increased famine, increased migration, etc.

The 'rise' and 'fall' of civilizations follows a natural process, triggered by the degree of adaptability to the given situation. The concept of 'other' is taught to socialize individuals into a strong unified group. It is akin to the constructors of identity, according to Castells. The leaders determine symbolic content of societal hallmarks, and what it means to those who embrace or reject them. Again, the American flag is a good example. It is burned in protest and worn in tribute. Barry Kemp (1994) described this a similar way in his book on ancient Egypt. He claimed that late prehistoric Egyptian leaders invented their own high culture. This view could be seen as an extension of Karl Marx's doctrine of class struggle. In Ramesside Egypt there was a religious conservative backlash against the extreme doctrines of the Amarna Period. The artistic code also reflected a return to strict rules and a preservation of Egyptian elements. Ramesses II is famous for looting ancient monuments and reinscribing his own name on them to be set up in new temple cities with giant propagandistic billboards proclaiming the evil influences of foreigners and how he personally controlled them. Meanwhile, there were many foreign queens in this period, and Egyptians enjoyed numerous foreign luxury goods. The two processes, *globalization* and *socialization*, are not only present at the same time, they fuel one another!

The social desire for group identity often intensifies in response to increased *globalization*. Often a less socialized group will be more flexible while a less globalized one will be ideologically stronger. The Babylonian captivity of Israel is commonly acknowledged as the time when Jewish culture and the Bible itself was molded (Isbell 1999:112–26). There are countless other examples to illustrate this dualistic process. In the period when the Persian Empire dominated Egypt, there was a renaissance of traditionally Egyptian culture. In some respects, that period saw many slavish copies of earlier Egyptian masterpieces, but there was also an active interest in *being* Egyptian.

On the whole, the most successful moments throughout history occur when the two forces of *socialization* and *globalization* are most intense and balanced. There also needs to be a certain amount of pressure on the given society to spur on both cohesion and creativity. That pressure often has come from a particularly energetic ruler. Yet when that ruler is no longer in power, the force of *socialization* persists. When we look at the literature of Middle Kingdom Egypt, after the collapse of the Old Kingdom, social upheaval and redefinition of kingship, we see a deep understanding of the human condition. How is it that some societies can pick up the pieces, pull themselves together and even become stronger after the demise of their globalizing power, while other social groups simply vanish like smoke in the wind? The great nation of the Hittites is gone, and completely forgotten, except for a small group of Hittitologists, but Israel survived! Theoretical models of systems collapse do not fully account for some societies' survival of such political events (Renfrew 1979; Tainter 1988).

Consider the golden age of Greece as manifest in the marble of the Parthenon, when Athens was confidently victorious against Persia and open to new ideas. The development of Greek society goes against the model of center-periphery. The Italian Renaissance is yet another era when there was no fear of embracing foreign influences; yet, each city-state was confident in its own identity. Again, the Spanish *reconquista* was a time when a strong religious nationalism was fused with a desire to take risks and explore the unknown with obvious results. This balance between strong self identity and a strong desire to interact with others is the catalyst that makes room for greatness. In all these instances, the great change did not take place in the center, but in what was then considered the periphery of civilization, a fact that goes against what seems logical (Rowlands, Larsen and Kristiansen 1987; Edens 1992).

Thus just as the model of primary and secondary state formation is misleading, so too is the model of core and periphery. Both models place too much emphasis on visible factors of a society's might. They imply an ethnocentric bias that one society was intrinsically superior to another in the *globalization* process. Often the core of any civilization as it matures is too busy maintaining its own identity to be concerned with expanding globally. In fact, this paradigm presents confusion between process (affect) and result (effect). I am not even convinced that the inheritors of democracy hold any patent to success; the jury is still out. We are beginning to witness the same contractions toward ideological demagoguery in United States society as existed in the late Roman Republic. In both cases, the leaders played on the passions and fears of the populace to bolster their own interests. Where are the 'weapons of mass destruction'? What is the financial benefit for defense contracts? We are now living in that world, where the 'emperors' have lost control of the *globalization* process. As in the story of the Chinese emperor, those in power have turned to military might to reassert authority.

You might have noticed that I have not yet addressed the issue of economics to any great extent. My model differs from Castells' in that I view the modern multi-national corporation as a pseudo-society or even pseudo-nation undergoing the same pressures of globalization and socialization. Conversely, all (other) social groups can be seen as corporations, being enterprises organized to regulate production, meet the needs of its members and particularly to benefit the elite of the group (elders, priest-king, pharaoh, or CEO) at the expense of the laboring masses.

The particular issues of a multi-national corporation directly relate to earlier institutions that competed with the nation states for control of resources. Some of the earliest corporations that functioned outside the control of the state, similar to the modern multi-nationals, were the pyramid complexes that provided for the 'needs' of the deceased pharaoh in Old Kingdom Egypt. Over the course of the Old Kingdom, they account for an alarmingly high percentage of the gross national product, which could not be taxed by the given administration in power (Lehner 1997). As a reigning pharoah's control over the country's resources diminished, over time the system eventually came to a standstill. Part of the evidence is the decreased size and quality of pyramids and the land area allowed for later rulers. Eventually, by the New Kingdom, pyramids were no longer a royal prerogative. Private citizens of the Ramesside Period built small pyramids for religious reasons, especially in the Theban necropolis (Seyfried 1987:219–53; Manniche 1987).

Finally, an exciting line of inquiry concerning the question of societal DNA concerns the predictability of societal success given a variety of situations. Historically, the most resilient and long-lived social pattern is that of China. A detailed study of its elements of adaptability to a host of situations would yield profound observations. It would be interesting to see how Chinese societal DNA compares with that of ancient Egypt, which was also long-lived, but not as resilient to change. Do particular circumstances explain the survival of the one and the demise of the other society, or as I propose, is there a combination of factors, functioning as a cultural template, that have come together to make the Chinese social system the most resilient. In the end, we may learn more from

Emperor Yuan than we ever bargained for. In brief conclusion, I view the processes of technology and communication leading to *globalization* as the affect that has always brought about the historical effects of change, as different cultures cope with the pressures of that change over time. Without the constant flux of *globalization*, 'history' could not exist as we perceive it in human society.

References

Athens, J. (1977) Theory building and the study of evolutionary process in complex societies in *For Theory Building in Archaeology*, edited by L. R. Binford. New York: Academic Press.

Binford, L. (1968) Archaeological Perspectives. In *New Perspectives in Archaeology*, edited by L. R. Binford and S. Binford. Chicago: Aldine.

Briant, P. (2001) *Irrigation et Drainage dans l'Antiquité*, Persika 2, Paris: Thotm éditions.

Buccelatti, G. (1967) Cities and nations of Ancient Syria. *Studi Semitici* 26. Rome: Instituto di studi del vicino oriente.

Buckley, W. (1967) *Sociology and Modern Systems Theory*. Englewood Cliffs, NJ: Prentice-Hall.

Carneiro, R. (1972) *Primitive Social Organization*. Random House: New York.

Carneiro, R. (1978) On the relationship between size of population and complexity of social organization. In *Southwestern Journal of Anthropology* 23:222.

Childe, V. G. (1956) *Man Makes Himself*. London, reprinted Bradford-on-Avon: Moonraker Press.

Claessen, J. (1978) The early state: a structural approach. In *The Early State*, edited by Henri J. M. Claessen and Peter Skalník. The Hague: Mouton, pp. 533–96.

Cohen, R. (1978) State origins: a reappraisal. In *The Early State*, edited by H. J. M. Claessen and P. Skalník The Hague: Mouton, p. 46.

Cohen, R. (1985) Warfare and state formation. In *Development and Decline: The Evolution of Sociopolitical Organization*, edited by H. J. M. Claessen, P. V. de Velde and M. E. Smith. South Hadley: Bergin and Garvey.

Darwin, C. (1860) *The Origin of Species by Means of Natural Selection; or, the Preservation of Favored Races in the Struggle for Life*. 6th edn. London: John Murray.

Edens, C. (1992) Synamics of trade in the Ancient Mesopotamian world system. *American Anthropologist*.

Esse, D. (1989) Secondary state formation and collapse in Early Bronze Age Palestine. In *L'urbanisation de la Palestine a l'age du Bronze ancien*, edited by P. de Miroschedji. BAR Int Series 527. Oxford: British Archaeological Reports, pp. 81–96.

Flannery, K. (1972) The cultural evolution of civilizations. *Annual Review of Ecology and Systematics* 3: 399–426.

Fried, M.H. (1967) *The Evolutuion of Political Society*. New York: Random House.

Gosline, S.L.(1999) *Archaeogender: Studies in Gender's Material Culture*. Warren Center, PA: Shangri-La Publications.

Haas, J. (1982) *The Evolution of the Prehistoric State*. New York: Columbia University Press.

Hill, J. (1994) Biology, prestige and the origin of states. In *Journal of Social and Evolutionary Systems* 17(2):224.

Isbell, C. (1999) *God's Scribes: How the Bible Became the Bible*. Warren Center, PA: Shangri-La Publications.

Kemp, B. (1994) *Ancient Egypt: Anatomy of a Civilization*. London: Routledge and Kegan Paul.

Kolata, A. (1996) *Valley of the Spirits*. New York: John Wiley and Sons.

Kolata, A. (1997) Of kings and capitals: principles of authority and the nature of cities in the native Andean state. In *City States*, edited by D. Nicholson and T. Charlton. Washington, D.C.: Smithsonian Institution Press.

Lehner, M. (1997) *The Complete Pyramids*. London: Thames and Hudson.

Malthus, T. (1798) *An Essay on the Principle of Population*. London: printed for J. Johnson, in St. Paul's Church-Yard.

Manniche, L. (1987) *City of the Dead: Thebes in Egypt*. London: British Museum Publications.

Marx, K. and Engels, F. (1888) *Manifesto of the Communist Party*. English edition. London: William Reeves.

Masters, R. (1982) Evolutionary biology, political theory and the state. *Journal of Social and Biological Structures* 5:446–47.
Naroll, R. and Divale, W. (1976) Natural selection in cultural evolution: warfare versus peaceful diffusion. *American Ethnologist* 3:121.
Patterson, T. (1991) *The Inca Empire: The Formation and Disintegration of a Pre-Capitalist State*. New York: Berg.
Price, B. (1978) Secondary state formation: an explanatory model. In *Origins of the State: The Anthropology of Political Evolution*, edited by R. Cohen and E. R. Service. Philadelphia: Institute for the Study of Human Issues, p. 165.
Rappaport, R. (1977) Maladaptation in social systems. In *The Evolution of Social Systems*, edited by J. Friedman and M.J. Rowlands. London: Duckworth.
Renfrew, C. (1979) Systems collapse as social transformation: catastrophe and anastrophe in early state societies. In *Transformations: Mathematical Approaches to Cultural Change*, edited by C. Renfrew and K. L. Cooke. New York: Academic Press, pp. 64–85.
Roth, A. (1987) The organization and functioning of the Royal Mortuary Cults of the Old Kingdom in Egypt. In *The Organization of Power*, edited by M. Gibson and R. D. Biggs. Studies in ancient oriental civilization 46. Chicago: Oriental Institute, pp. 115–22.
Roth, A. (1991) *Egyptian Phyles in the Old Kingdom: The Evolution of a System of Social Organization*, SAOC 48, Chicago: Oriental Institute, pp. 8, 145–95, 208–9.
Rowlands, M., Larsen, J. and Kristiansen, K. (eds) (1987) *Centre and Periphery in the Ancient World.* Cambridge: Cambridge University Press.
Service, E. (1962) *Primitive Social Organization: An Evolutionary Perspective*. New York: Random House.
Service, E. (1971) *Profiles in Ethnology: An Evolutionary Perspective*, rev. edn. Harper and Row: New York.
Seyfried, K. (1987) Entwicklung in der Grabarchitektur des Neuen Reiches als eine Weitere Quelle fur Theologische Konzeptionen der Ramessidenzeit. In *Problems and Priorities in Egyptian Archaeology*, edited by J. Assmann, G. Burkard and V. Davies. London: KPI, pp. 219–53.
Spencer, C. (1990) On the tempo and mode of state formation: neo-evolutionism reconsidered. *Journal of Anthropological Archaeology* 9(1):22.
Tainter, J. (1988) *The Collapse of Complex Societies*. Cambridge: Cambridge University Press.
Turner, V. (1969) *The Ritual Process: Structure and Anti-Structure.* Cornell, NY: Cornell University Press.
Upham, S. (1990) Analog or digital? In *The Evolution of Political Systems*, edited by S. Upham. Cambridge: Cambridge University Press, p. 89.
Webster, D. (1975) Warfare and the evolution of the state: a reconsideration. *American Antiquity* 40(4):469.
Wilson, J. (1951) *The Culture of Ancient Egypt*. Chicago: University of Chicago Press, pp. 52, 85, 146–7, 151.
Winter, I. (1987) Legitimation of authority through image and legend: seals belonging to officials in the administrative bureaucracy of the Ur III State. In *The Organization of Power*, edited by M. Gibson and R. D. Biggs. Studies in ancient oriental civilization 46. Chicago: Oriental Institute, pp. 59–99.
Woolley, L. (1965) *Excavations at Ur*. Thomas Crowell: New York
Wright, H. and Johnson, G. (1975) Population, exchange and early state formation in Southwestern Iran. *American Anthropologist* 77:284.
Yoffee, N. and Cowgill, G. (eds) (1987) *The Collapse of Ancient States and Civilizations*. Tucson: University of Arizona Press.

Section Three: Antiquity and the Power of Identity

Introduction to Section Three: Antiquity and the Power of Identity

In Castells' conception of the network society the primary oppositions and dialectical moving forces in social, economic and political life today are the Net and the Self. The Net represents a pattern of communications between organizations at all levels of society—from corporations to social movements. The Self represents the affirmation of identity and the communities that form around such identities.

For Castells in *The Power of Identity*, identity is not synonymous with culture or nationality. It is rather constructed on the basis of certain cultural attributes, or a related set of cultural attributes that social actors give priority to and internalize. Constructors of identity and their motives for thus constructing them determine the symbolic content of the identity, and 'its meaning for those identifying with it or placing themselves outside of it'. He distinguishes three types of identity. The first of these is legitimizing identity, a product of dominant institutions. The second is project identity, formulated by those who are out to 'change the world' through a specific social, economic or political enterprise. The third is resistance identity—the potent weapon of the disenfranchised.

The three essays in this section represent the authors' explorations into the power of identity as an historical concept. Manger in his discussion of the Hadrami migrations explores the different forms of identity constructed by émigrés and the ways in which those identities interact in their new environments. Manger gives us a new understanding of globalization in the past relating to the Hadrami migrations in contrast to Castells' fairly entrenched view of globalization as a modern phenomenon. Scham brings the discussion into the modern world with an examination of how resistance identities constructed with the use of internet technology make use of the past.

Cashman's examination of identity in New Kingdom and Ramesside Egypt provides a new look at this society which is often seen as unchanging and which she characterizes as dynamic and globalizing. She looks at the shifting concept of 'foreign' in this period of Ancient Egypt in terms of both people and goods and further discusses the consumer and production shifts that embraced new technologies and fostered a demand for mass production of non-consumable goods. With these philosophical and economic changes she also posits a concomitant expansion of literacy, an increase in the range of literary genres, and an individualization of private (non-royal) and royal representation.

In contrast, Manger deals with the more fluid boundaries of the Hadramis from South Yemen. Tracing over one thousand years of Hadrami movements between Arabia and South Asia and Hadrami involvement in the historical events occurring in these regions, he connects the people and places through technological developments that enabled these people to continue and expand upon an already well established pattern of movements. Looking at the bin Laden migration to Saudi Arabia as a Hadrami movement, Manger makes a convincing case that this 'globalizing' long-term historical trend has wrought significant changes in the modern world as well.

Figure 10.1 Bedouin protest in Israel.

Figure 10.2 Bedouin at Petra, Jordan.

Scham explores two unusual situations where resistance identities have been formed via the 'space of flows' that exemplify Castells' main argument that the societies of the 'information age' are being irrevocably changed by the relationships between the self and technology. Antiquity plays a significant part in the formation of these identities that, strangely enough, can be traced to the printed word. Marija Gimbutas' *The Civilization of the Goddess* and Martin Bernal's *Black Athena*, in opposition to the consensus of scholarly opinion, take a decidedly global approach to the advance of civilizations and they have had a clear appeal to disenfranchised groups. The movements that have been formed around these concepts interact with technology in unique ways and are, in themselves, affirmations of the importance of the self.

Connectivity in the *Longue Durée*: Hadrami Muslims in an Indian Ocean World

Leif Manger

Introduction

In his wide-ranging trilogy *The Information Age: Economy, Society and Culture* (1996, 1997, 1998) Manuel Castells tries to make sense of broad global social dynamics that characterize our time. At a general level, Castells is interested in the inter-connections between the new global technologies of information communication, how this level of technology interacts with, and helps shape, the material basis of society, and the various types of collective identities that are emerging as a result of the general developmental processes that he discusses. Castells presents a sophisticated analysis of the various types of changes, developments and transformations that brought about this information-based society, and how it works. All these factors are pulled together in a perspective seeing societies as being organized around 'human processes structured by historically determined relationships of *production*, *experience* and *power*' (1996:14). By this he means that this type of modern technology creates 'space of flows' that replaces the 'space of places', and thus changes the ways people are rooted. It creates a polarization between those within the flow of power and those without: the first characterized by 'spaceless power', the second by 'powerless space'. But such developments are not neutral. People experience the developments in different ways, as winners and losers, and react to them in different ways. Thus one important point that Castells makes is his emphasis on the many ways these developments are being challenged by various *social movements*. The situation brought about by the new information technology leads to processes defining a global order that is being reacted to by members of social movements, and that in the process new types of identities emerge. Contemporary identities are to a large extent influenced by what Castells calls 'the bipolar opposition of the Net and the Self' (1996:3). Drawing on Alain Touraine, he identifies three types of collective identities coming out of all these processes. They are *legitimizing identities*, that play along with dominating trends in society; *resistance identities*, which I think is self-explanatory; and *project identities*, that aim at building new 'projects' that can transform society. In parts of the second volume (1997) of the trilogy Castells offers analyses of such social movements, exemplified by religious fundamentalist movements, environmental movements and feminist movements.

I find Castells' focus on the ways the emergence of a new global order brings about reactions, represented by different types of identities, to be interesting and worthwhile pursuing. In this paper I shall put Castells' perspective to use on historical material, arguing that a more historical perspective, opening comparisons in time as well as in space, open up even more avenues to Castells' interesting project. Although there are many references to historical works and to historical periods in which important changes in communication technologies have changed, indeed indicating that Castells himself is aware of these possibilities, he offers no analysis of specific *historical transformations* that such earlier developments led to. Rather, by focusing on the period since 1920, and most particularly dealing with the last decade, Castells places himself in the camp of scholars arguing that contemporary globalization is a new phenomenon. What is *now* is *new*. By doing that he also limits his ability to exploit the comparative potential embedded in his analysis in which the modern information technologies can be seen in a comparative light of earlier technologies of communication, be they through direct human interaction, letter-writing, telephones or e-mail. The same can be said about travel technologies, for instance the various ways the development of new types of ships and sails have created important effects. And, most importantly, such a perspective could also show how collective identity-making processes in earlier periods evolved in ways similar to what Castells is arguing for with reference to contemporary identities.

In the paper I want to present such an analysis. I shall focus on the region of the Indian Ocean and on the particular history of Muslims in that region. My time dimensions shall be defined by a period stretching from about 1000 AD to about 1900. My focus on the region of the Indian Ocean and its history in the *long dureé* constitutes an attempt to establish relationships between technological and general socioeconomic and political developments, and how the Muslim reactions to those developments, helped shape particular Muslim identities within this region. Although I stop my discussion at the time Castells starts his (about WWI), the story of the Muslims in the Indian Ocean carries several lessons of relevance to a discussion of Castells' perspective. I claim that by historicizing our perspective we can see that claims that our contemporary, globalized world is a new historical construction, radically different from earlier societies, should be modified. Certainly there are new trends. Certainly things are more global. But still there are differences in the distribution of these global forces, and also in the extent to which different groups of people participate in a globalized world. Using the same type of logic, I think that there were sectors of communities and certain groups of people who were more involved in world economies and global economies of the day. I think that a focus on those sectors that also in earlier epochs were based on flows of information that crossed oceans and continents and on groups of people who presented themselves as bearers of a 'global' perspective, we can see many of the same processes going on. We see a 'space of flows' emerging that is defined by a certain technology (for instance the technology of navigation in the Indian Ocean, the change from sail to steam, from land to air etc.), certain places (the trade towns, which represented the 'global cities' of the day) and certain people (like groups of Muslim traders) that operate such spaces. We can say now, of course, that these processes were limited and that it is only today that the system is really global. But I want to argue that seen from the perspective of the participants of the day, what they were doing must have appeared global, and that they believed they knew the world, and that the dynamism of their lives was different from the (primarily) peasant lives of the (traditional) populations with whom they interacted.

We also see that in earlier epochs of global restructuring there were reactions and a restructuring of identities. But reactions among Muslims were not uniform. They were shaped by the various ways the Muslims themselves were placed in the broad processes, in support of the developments of the day, against them, or ignoring them. We also see that identities emerge as a result of specific organizational histories, through which particular individuals played central roles in formulating ideas about what was going on, and mobilizing people in support of such ideas. Castells' work then becomes useful to me in that it prepares the ground for such a comparative effort, by specifying the relationships beween 'the Net and the Self' in a certain historical period, and avoids reducing relationships to a unidirectional process of basis-superstructure dynamics or one in which culture and identity float around, freed from all links to other sectors of society.

Early Muslims in the Indian Ocean

Our story about the Muslim presence in the Indian Ocean region starts not with the coming of Islam, nor with the first Muslim Empires, the Ummayyad and the Abbasid, but rather with the decline of the Abbasid and the rise of the Fatimid dynasty in Cairo. This is because this period from about 1000 AD represents the emergence of several smaller regional centres within the Muslim world, also leading to more regional trade circuits which differed from the state controlled trade of the Abbasid, and to the emergence of the Red Sea and Aden as important points in that trade. Other centers also emerged throughout the Indian Ocean region. They stretched from the Philippines and Southeast Asia to the city states of East Africa to the trading states in West Africa. They were only joined together again under the big 'gunpowder empires' of the 16th and 17th centuries, the Ottomans, the Safavids and the Mughals.

There were trade links between the Arabian peninsula and South India and Southeast Asia. Whereas traffic from South Arabia would cut across straight to the Indian coast, the return journey would go via the Maldives. The reason for this was to exploit the monsoon so that the journey was quicker. And because everyone did the same, the Maldivian town of Male became an important entrepot. S. Bayly (1989) notes the settlement of such traders in India from the 8th and 9th centuries and that their appearance was related to the increase in the international textile trade which linked these South Indian entrepôts of West Asia and the Indonesian archipelago (1989:74). Arabian horses were also an important trade item for the pre-colonial kingdoms, and Muslim traders controlled this trade, as they controlled the region's trade in gemstones, pearls and chanks (which are important in Hindu rituals) and cotton piece goods (1989:78). This means that the Islamization process of the south Indian towns started well before the Muslims invasions from Central Asia which brought Islam to north India. By the 12th and 13th centuries the coastal towns had well-established Muslim communities, and the Islamization of the inland Tamil communities is dated in the 13th and 14th century.

In the 14th century, power was also consolidated in a series of Muslim trading states in Java, and these new states attracted Gujaratis, Chinese and Ryukyu islanders and Southeast Asians like Burmese, Siamese and Javanese. Islam, which had begun to influence northern Sumatra just before 1300, spread under the patronage of Malacca. From there it spread to the north Javanese trading towns, to the spice islands, north Borneo and to Mindanao, only to be stopped by the Spanish seizure of Manila in 1571. Islam then took hold in insular southeast Asia, whereas Theravada Buddhism remained strong on the mainland, with the exception of Vietnam, where Confuscianism spread, in a mixture with Mahayana Buddhism and Taoism.

This period also represents the coming of the European powers into the Indian Ocean. But, as traders and travellers in the Indian Ocean had discovered long ago, the European employees of various East India companies also found the region already to be integrated, by the rhythm of the monsoon as well as by economic interdependencies. Cotton textiles from the coast of Coromondel in India were vital for the purchase of pepper and spices in the Indonesian archipelago. Precious metals imported from the Middle East, East Africa and Japan supplied monetary liquidity without which rich and powerful centralized empires in Asia could not have functioned properly (Chaudhuri 1985:83). This forced the Companies to develop organizations that could meet the needs for participating in the trade. They needed access to the most profitable and regular sources of supply, the long-term capital need necessitated institutional systems, ships had to be bought or hired, and they had to think of the financial capacity of buyers thus also operating as bankers. However, all through the period, Asian traders had also operated providing as much dynamism as the Europeans. The total volume of trade increased tremendously for all carriers and several groups could participate with a profit. *Armenian* merchants were there, as were the *Bugis*, Indian *Banians* and the *Chinese* (Curtin 1984:158–78). This reality makes it necessary to look closer at the development of merchant communities in the Indian Ocean. Abu Loghod (1989) argues that in the 13th century there was a world economy centered around highly commercialized cities linked to each other through systemic exchange networks and economically dominated, or at least 'driven', by private merchants (often in control of production and involved with private finance as well), albeit coexisting with bureaucratic or imperial state structures. But these states were often themselves a direct result of the location and direction of international commerce. From about 1000 AD onwards the most important ones were Aden, Hormuz, Cambay and Calicut in the Western Zone, Kilwa, Mogadishu, Aden and Jedda providing links to Africa and the Red Sea. In the East, Samudra-Pase, later Malacca, Canton and Zaiton were central. If we look at the long-term picture we see that after 1600, Surat took over from Cambay in Gujarat, Bandar Abbas replaced Hormuz and Mocha competes with Jedda in the Red Sea. The city states of East Africa and the towns of Malabar declined. In the East Masulipatam, Hugli, Malacca, Acheh, Bantam, Tongkin and Canton, Oa, Batavia, Madras and Calcutta rose due to imperial presence and power.

The identity games that resulted from this situation are interesting. First of all, it took centuries before the Europeans became dominant in the region, the early Europeans only being able to dominate limited geographical areas and limited parts of the trade systems of the Indian Ocean. As Taylor (1983) showed for the Dutch, rather than dominate the area they were swallowed by it. For centuries it was more an Indian Ocean world than a European one. Given the strength of the Muslim 'gunpowder empires' (Ottoman, Mughal and the Safavids) the Muslim trade system discussed above could operate also in areas with European presence. The early centuries of European capitalism did not change the basic parameters of this world. The Portuguese were the first to appear, but the British and the French were also there, as were the Spaniards and the Danish. A similar story could be told for the various groups of Muslims. They settled in the trade cities which offered a choice of commodities, a variety of currency and banking services, and shipping space. And political stability and peace provided by local leaders was important. But such communities were not only trading communities but also the focal points of a series of developments that were to shape the history of the region for the coming centuries. Processes of creolization and of assimilation were going on, and were counteracted by various forces from within the Muslim community itself. Several processes can be mentioned. The *ulema* developed independence from the political rulers. *Sufism* developed and *tariqas* were to play an important role from the 12th century onwards. All this was reflected in the Muslim communities in the region. *Qadis* arrived to administer justice and adjudicate disputes among Muslims; theologians arrived, serving both as intellectual links to the larger world and as agents promoting a degree of standardization in the transregional culture of Islam; Sufis arrived and sought to penetrate existing cultural boundaries by spreading Islam broadly among native inhabitants. Meanwhile, new converts made pilgrimages to Mecca, where they became acquainted at first hand with Islamic customs and traditions. They became initiated, as it were, into the larger world of Islam. Finally, in many cases, ruling elites recognized political or economic advantages provided within Islam, and as a result they lent official support that enabled the new faith to establish itself securely in their lands (Bentley 1993:125). In spite of all intermingling in such towns, the Muslims remained a distinct group, organized religiously around the mosque. Members of the groups did not intermarry, but kept close trade relations and dealt with members of the other groups. Arabic was important as a language of communication, of religious and literary expression, and of administration, even though Iranian and Turkish were rival languages. Membership in the group of Muslims was through faith. And basic symbols to define group-membership were food habits, articles of clothing and housing, which all signaled social and religious identities, and helped to keep groups apart. Rules about avoidance of pork for Muslims, beef for Brahmanic Indians, milk and dairy products for the Chinese were thus basic markers for members of the various communities. Clothes also helped to differentiate, based on whether people were wearing trousers and robes as dress, whether they were sewn or unsewn. The role of public buildings in Islam expressed the spiritual force of the new religion, but also linked imperial power and architecture.

Figure 11.1 Blue Mosque, Istanbul, Turkey.

The Emergence of a New, Imperial World

The 18th century history in the Indian Ocean is one in which we see a basic change in the macro-situation of the region, related to the change in the involvement of European colonial powers from an earlier interest in controlling trade to a focus on controlling territory, thus initiating the period of Imperialism. Bayly (1989) argues that the rise of British power in the 18th century must be related to the decline of existing political powers in the various regions, of the Ottomans, the Safavids, the Mughals and also of the smaller state of Mataram in Java. The glorious past of the Muslim empires was over, and new realities appeared as a consequence of the emergence of new regional economies and of new classes. The unifying effects of trade had produced processes of local differentiation. But trade was not the only factor. Population growth in the 16th century stagnated in the following centuries and led to uneven developments. Increasing rural differentiation developed. Commercialization led peasants into bondage of larger landowners who held large landed estates. Earlier state lands were also broken up and commercialized, being less dependent on political office and more as 'freehold property'. Revenue farming made it possible for the rulers to shift the burden of expenditures over to regional leaders, who pushed it downwards to the peasants themselves.

Commercialization, urbanization and the growth of landed classes were processes that were to bring changes. Such changes were also affected by external links, for instance trade links with the Europeans. The export of raw materials and the import of precious metals played a significant role, leading to the establishment of a financier class. But the export link also increased vulnerability to price fluctuations elsewhere, thus increasing systemic interdependencies. The new regional power-centers that developed within this context weakened the old imperial centers. Egypt under Muhamed

Ali is a case in point from within the Ottoman areas. Hyderabad under the Asaf Jahs, Bengal and Awadh from within the Mughal area and the Qajars in Iran. At the same time 'military tribes' rebelled. Afghan and Turkik tribes from Central Asia (the Rohillas, 'men of the hills') challenged both the Safavids and the Mughals. The Wahhabis in Arabia also belong to this pattern of 18th century rebellion as did the Maratha Hindu soldiers in India. Tribal societies were also transformed into military dynasties, often creating internal unity by attacking others. But trade links were important also, and many of the areas in which tensions developed were areas in which trade and economic development had led to increased economic tensions. Puritanical movements like the Wahhabis constituted an ideological response to these developments. The leaders of Awadh in India promoted Shi'ism against the Sunni Mughal. One basic consequence of these processes of revolt was the emergence of new political units that were more effectively organized than the loose imperial confederacies they replaced. In fact they might be said to be a first step towards nation-states. The rulers sought to monopolize and protect trade and settle people to tax them (Bayly 1989:47). Professional armies were employed, often recruited from minority groups such as Circassians, Georgians, Afghans and Arabs, including the Hadramis. New areas of land were cultivated, new sources of labour power were sought, and nomads were settled. Thus control of primary producers was important. But so was trade, and wars for the control of trade routes flourished. As export of primary agricultural products flourished the two things were linked. Raw cotton is a case in point; the quest for revenue was on.

It was the period in which we see the processes so common under colonialism and imperialism, when the colonial state began seriously to discipline and control marginal groups, and there is development towards privatization of land and market-oriented economies. Rather than the spread of free trade, it was territorial revenues that the colonialists were after, both the British and the Dutch, and it was in this context that the notion of Britain as a 'Christian Roman Empire' was born (Bayly 1989:11, see also Cooper and Stoller 1997). The new political units could threaten Imperial rule and the new rulers became symbols of tyranny, and, as in the case of Tipu Sultan in Mysore, of *Muslim* tyranny. A clearer racial hierarchy was also appearing, as were other types of British prejudices. Urban elites were despised. Nomads and tribes were to be protected. A number of 'Consuls' appear representing European powers, playing roles similar to the *maigida*, *wakil al-tujjar*, or *shabandar* who were already there, but over time during the 19th century developing into key agents of commercial Westernization. They also represented the new European arrogance, no longer adapting to local Indian Ocean realities but seeking to control and dominate them.

19th-century Globalization

The 19th century represents an intensified development of various globalizing forces. One important field is the continuous maritime technological developments. European industrialization and urbanization were forwarded by the introduction of iron, then steel-hulled sailing ships, and eventually steam ships from the early 1800s, developing through the 19th century (Hugill 1993:30) reducing transportation times as well as costs. The innovations came first in the commercial sphere, but the military sector followed, on which the *Pax Britannica* developed after 1815. Wood and coal were the first major fuel sources, with a number of coaling stations appearing around the major shipping lines. The opening of the Suez canal dramatically affected this by reducing the number of stops required, and hence the number of secure coaling stations. Oil fuel freed ships from many of the problems of coal, the diesel engine further making shipping more efficient into the 20th century.

Thus there were underlying forces of restructuring of the international economy due to the forces of Industrial Revolution. The search for raw materials such as raw cotton or timber was only one element, which foreshadowed the shift in the global division of labor due to industrialization. But tools for Western influence were also the changes in banking, finance, transportation and communication. Ocean shipping developed to steam and steel. Long-distance communication improved. In the 1830s a letter from Europe to India took five to eight months to round the Cape on a sailing ship. To receive an answer might take up to two years. By the 1850s the letter from London to Calcutta could go in 30–40 days. By the 1870s submarine cable had been laid and a message from Britain to India could be answered in the same day. And those who wanted to use them had to follow European rules. The postal service was directed by the Universal Postal Union founded in 1874. In the sectors of new technological developments the 'diasporic' ways of doing things disappeared, and links between various points in the diaspora were replaced by direct links to the center. The British shipping, with coal stations around the world, and telegraphs to increase efficiency both in terms of sailing orders as well as commercial contracts were run from England. Exploitation of rivers made this system also reach far inland towards the major grain-producing areas of the world. These developments were only to be surpassed when oil and petroleum took over as the main energy sources into the 20th century, producing diesel engines for ships, cars and tractors, and later aeroplanes which not only changed trade but also the technological basis for warfare (Hugill 1993). On the social side, an enormous migration out of Europe (O'Rourke and Williamson 1999) also helped change the world order in the 20th century, first towards German, later American power. The production in this system revolved around wheat and cotton: wheat to feed the people, and cotton to provide raw material for the factories. And as populations grew the British import of wheat grew, and America, Argentina, Australia and Russia became important wheat producers, but only after Ireland had failed to provide wheat after the Potato Famine. Cotton could not be grown in Britian and had to be brought from the colonies. Among the colonies India remained the most important one. Railroads, steamships and the Suez Canal transformed India into a major source of cheap food and raw materials for Europe. Tea, wheat, oil seeds, cotton and jute came from there. At the same time India was the market for British products. The large surpluses originating from the India trade were at the base of British capital accumulation and London's central position in world finance (Arrighi 1999:263).

The integration of the world's economy into a single interdependent whole further developed in the period 1870–1914. Three aspects were central. The further improvement of the means of communication, spreading railways outside Europe and North America, the expansion of world shipping in tonnage and the shift from sail to steam which increased speed and regularity. Canal constructions, like the Suez Canal in 1869 and the Panama Canal in 1914, helped save distance and time (41% on a trip from Liverpool to Bombay, 60% from New York to San Francisco). Finally, cables laid beneath the oceans linked the continents, followed by the telephone (international lines from 1887), and wireless stations (from 1897). All this paralleled a boom in commerce, with a tripling of foreign trade volumes between 1870 to 1914. This is the period of 'finance capital' in the imperial age, an expansion that is related to increasing pressure on the profitability of capital within Britain itself, and which led investors and financial houses ('The Age of the Rothschilds') to channel capital through City to distant places, directly linking up with the imperial project (see, e.g., Hobson1938). However, most of this was a development between the major countries. Only 11% of the world's trade took place between the primary producers themselves. Investments from the West into these areas helped colonize them rather than develop them. These investments related to the introduction of the gold standard for European currencies in 1863–74. The flow of capital was paralleled with a flow of labour power leading to the Europization of territories.

But other non-European areas also tried to modernize. Some of the areas were colonies, like the Indian and Indonesian states, others were quasi-independent, like Egypt. As we have seen, the decline of the old urban artisan communities in the Islamic world were replaced by new forms of indigenous capitalism partly, but only partly, linked to the Industrial Revolution in Europe. And in the wake of the French Revolution peasant rebellions flourished. Rural sufi groups also followed suit.

Millennarian movements signaled this breakdown of the old order and the onset of colonialism. People sought new legitimizations. Local issues were replaced by universal issues like Islam versus Christianity. The Sanusiyya in North Africa, the Naqsbandiyya in China, the Salawiyya in the Nile Valley, the Padri in Indonesia (1803–37), all were movements that brought such reformulations. Southwestern India also provides an example of a conflict over the old pepper trade controlled by the Muslim Mappilas, competing with Hindu Nayyar chieftains and also with the Christian Portuguese. Tipu Sultan's success in Mysore helped the Mappilas, but the British defeat of Mysore in 1793 turned the tables and the Nayar retaliated. This case shows the intensification of religious and ethnic identity through actions of the indigeneous state and the violence of popular resistance, the role of indigeneous petty capitalism and, ultimately, intervention by colonial power. The most important movement of popular resistance was the Wahhabiyya in Arabia. Challenged were orthodox Muslim leaderships and also European colonialists.

The printing press helped 'textualize' issues in new ways. People were more in touch with each other than before within the regions, as between the regions and Europe. Indonesian Muslims had been in Mecca during the Wahhabi attacks and brought back the message of purification to the Padri. New groups adopted to the new situations, like the Parsis of Bombay and the Hindu gentry of Calcutta, by founding schools, newspapers and reform societies. In Southeast Asia the Chinese filled these roles as go-betweens for the colonialist and local groups.

Two Muslims attempts of modernization stand out in the 19th century, the most outstanding cases being Muhamed Ali (1805–49) in Egypt and the Ottoman *Tanzimat*, started by Mahmoud II in Istanbul, but there were others. And they all looked to the West to find solutions. This in turn brought Islamic fundamentalist reactions. In Istanbul, the opposition from the Young Ottomans was liberal in nature, whereas the more Islamic reaction took various forms. One was to emphasize the role of the Sultan as a pan-Islamic ruler (Abdel Hamid II from 1876). The other was to debate with the West, developing a Muslim understanding of Modernism. Al Afghani was a key figure here (1839–97). The third theme was a growing absolutism of the Ottoman ruler, as exemplified by Abdel Hamid II who used Muslim clerics to obtain legitimacy. This ended when the Young Turks revolted and took power in 1908. Nationalism, Arab and Turkish, also appeared, thus making the Ottoman empire a case that shows many of the dilemmas and tensions Muslims found themselves in towards the end of the 19th century. In Egypt Muhamed Ali's successors (Abbas 1849–54, Said 1854–63, and Ismail 1863–79) modernized and rebuilt cities and transportation systems. The end result of this policy was that Egypt, rather than developing as a regional Red Sea and Gulf of Aden power, became financially dependent on the West, and, with the revolt of Ahmad Urabi, also lead to the British political take-over in 1882, bringing in Lord Cromer as the key figure. Also here Afghani played an important role formulating critiques, and his follower Muhamed Abduh (1849–1905) even more so. Abduh's aim was to integrate modern Western and Islamic ideas and techniques, and his public positions (mufti of Egypt from 1899) made him able to propagate them. He inspired both fundamentalism and revivalism.

But in other areas the local states were not strong enough to act as reformers, and European colonial powers were the ones spearheading modernization, also leading to Islamic reactions. In India a series of movements appeared as Islamic reactions. Ahmad Brelwi (1786–1831) is a case in point in Northern India, basing himself on links with the Prophet Muhamed. But after the Mutiny in 1857, the British controlled the areas, and a new development started in which Indian Muslims also related to modernism and had to accept the British presence. Sayyid Ahmad Khan (1817–98) was a key figure in this, trying to combine Western learning with Islamic and establishing schools for such integrated learning. And as with Muhamed Abduh, his thoughts were developed in different directions by later people (Chirag Ali's fundamentalism, or the Deoband position linking back to a traditionalist Islamic identity). The Ahmadiyya also appeared, eventually, to engage in missionary activities outside India. In Kerala the famous Hadrami *sayyid*, Sayyid Fadl b. 'Alawi b. Sahl played a central role in a Muslim inspired rebellion (*jihad*) against the British. His family held the title of *tannals* of the Mappilas and in the middle of the 19th century Sayyid Fadl inspired several attacks by Kerala Muslims on Hindu groups. The attacks were more in the tradition of earlier skirmishes with Hindu groups over the spice trade than real resistance against the British. Nevertheless, Sayid Fadl was expelled by the British in 1852 and left for Istanbul, Mecca and Dhofar (see Dale 1997, also Bang 2000). In Southeast Asia the tension between a localized, syncretist faith and a rigorous, cosmopolitan faith existed alongside the conflicts over how to react to Dutch colonialism. Opposition movements were active all through the 19th century. The early one was the Padri movement in Sumatra. The Java War from 1825–30 was a second incident. A third one appeared in Acheh after the Dutch invasion in 1873. All uprisings had the element of holy wars, led by *ulema*. All were affected by Pan-Islamism.

All these movements benefited from the new modern situation in transport. Their leaders could themselves travel to Mecca on pilgrimage, thereby keeping in touch with the centers of the Islamic world. New communicative technologies also helped the organizations keep open their links to the general intellectual currents in the Muslim world. For instance, Shaykh Muhammad Tahir ibn Jalal al-Din (1867–1957) spread the ideas of Muhamed Abduh's Salafiyyah in the region, and he started a newspaper *al-Imam* in Singapore. He accepted the realities of his times, but continued the efforts to place them in a Muslim intellectual context, leading to organizations that were to characterize 20th-century Southeast Asian Islam.

Mecca and Medina were also affected, although their religious leadership was conservative, cooperating with the Egyptian and Ottoman rulers against neo-Sufism. Rather it was the Sharif of Mecca who kept in touch with the world. The Wahhabis continued to struggle for control after their defeat by the Egyptians in 1818, culminating in the 20th-century state of Saudi Arabia. In Oman the maritime empire declined, and Oman became increasingly dependent on British control. The British takeover of Aden in 1839 created a new situation in southern Arabia which hindered the development of any particular reactions.

Towards a Globalized Muslim Religious Identity

Conventional Western historiography on Muslims in the 18th century has portrayed the period as a 'dark age', with a focus on the disintegration of the gunpowder empires and a general defeat to Western powers. The Western views of Islam came to dominate, portraying Muslim societies as stagnating, as barbaric and so on. Not surprisingly the situation is more complex (see, e.g., Watson 1983; Al Hassan and Hill 1986 and Tibbetts 1981 for counterexamples in the fields of agricultural innovations, scientific knowledge and technology, and seafaring and navigation). John Voll points at four styles of Islamic reactions to the developments in the 18th century, styles that are similar to Castells' and Touraine's types of identities. One *pragmatic, adaptionist* style through which Muslims were able to settle in strange territories; a *conservative* style, trying to perserve earlier gains; a *fundamentalist* style, not looking at society but at the Quran for guidance, unwilling to accept compromises, being politically activist and upsetting social stability; the fourth style is the *personal acceptance of the religion*, focused on local holy men, on the Mahdi or the Shi'a Imam as political representations. We see all these streams represented in the hostorical overview presented above. Muslim success in building alliances with power-holders illustrates the line of accommodation. The early resurgence as represented by the Mappilas may tell a story of resistance, perhaps related as much to issues about trade as religious issues. Other reactions were motivated by religious developments, particularly *sufism*. New theological interpretations that signaled a new fundamentalism was known, for example through the work of Ibn Taymiyyah. Such ideas were also transformed into political action, as represented by al-Wahhabiyya in Arabia. Shah Wali Allah al-Dihlawi (1702–62) and his establishment of schools rather than a social movement is a local Indian example of a reaction to the disunity of Muslim society. He reformulated Islam on a broader basis than any one tradition, thus making Indian Islam more receptive to outside influences than, for instance, the Arabian version of Wahhabism. Also Southeast Asian Islam was affected by these trends. The many trading states in the region had introduced Islam, but the religion was by no means dominating. Also, Muslims had adapted to local traditions of Hinduism and Buddhism, making the pantheistic elements of Islam come to the fore. The Dutch presence in Indonesia gradually made the Muslim leaders depend on them for support, thus accepting many Western ways, which again is one backdrop against which to see the growth of fundamentalism. And we see a development of the social organization of the basic unit in sufism, the *tariqah*. Better organized and more activist *tariqahs* appeared, and became vehicles of revival rather than adaptation. The general economic and political situation developed in ways that made these groups able to mobilize also outside the religious platform. Increased travelling brought these groups into contact with each other. Indonesian Muslims traveled regularly to Mecca, and it is an interesting fact that some of the leaders behind the Padri movements in Sumatra had been in Mecca during the time of the Wahhabi revolts. It is likely that there was crossfertilizations between the different Muslim resistances to developments that made them feel marginalized. Scholars traveled widely, being part of transnational networks (Eickelman and Piscatori 1990), often centered on Mecca and Medina, because of the *hajj*, but other centers like Cairo and Damascus were also important. Religion also became a basis for the emergence of new local identities and we find the new types of religious scholars in alliance with new political leaders.

Muslim Identities in the Making

The presentation above certainly shows that there are 'world system' dynamics at play, that the Indian Ocean region is a meeting place of 'civilizations' and that, indeed, from a very early time there have been elements we now think of as typical of 'globalization', both through significant population movement across the ocean and the early formation of diasporic communities, primarily in trading towns perhaps better described as 'world cities'. Several general conclusions of relevance to Castells' analysis appear. First, the presentation shows that we can indeed point to a systematic pattern of interrelationships going back to the very early historical period. Rulers in political centers played a role, as did traders and their trading activities, to promote both political integration and economic commercialization. Technological developments affected traveling, but also provided dynamics into other fields of communication. Second, the overview also shows that the European presence in the history of the Indian Ocean is rather late. The story is not organized around a Wallersteinean pre-1500 and post-1500 period. The early European involvement in the region is shown not to radically change the basic pattern of the Indian Ocean region. Rather than dominating the Indian Ocean the early Europeans who came in the 16th century were swallowed by it. Only much later, towards the end of the 18th century do we see that European Colonialism, Imperialism and Capitalism produce structural changes. Rather than depicting the early historical periods as examples of periods in which there is general social and cultural homogeneity, and then show how the contemporary world is characterized by flexibility and movement, the paper provides evidence of processes that indicate flux in all periods. But how the flux is organized and how continuity is organized is a matter of empirical research, not pre-existing notions. And, significantly, the understanding of all these factors can not be reduced to one type of dynamics alone. Rather, it requires a presentation ranging from economic factors, such as long-distance trade, to local economic factors that allow for local variation; from political factors, such as the rise and fall of political centres to the coming and going of powerful groups at more local levels; from the settlement of traders and missionaries in distant lands to the interaction of these diasporic groups with other people from other cultural backgrounds. By looking for alternative social and cultural ways of organizing our being in the world, both in space (i.e. in the contemporary world), but also in time (i.e. historical examples of such interaction), we might actually enrich our perspectives and thus also improve our chances to find more promising avenues by which to deal with our current cultural differences.

My discussion is clearly inspired by the type of discussion we know as 'Globalization Studies'. With this we are also back to Manuel Castells' work. Along with many others, Castells takes the concept of globalization to mean the rapidly developing and ever-denser network of interconnections and interdependencies that characterizes modern social life. Castells (1996, 1997) calls this '*connectivity*', and he joins a host of other contributions that address the issue of interconnections. The interconnections we are talking about come in different modalities, such as social institutions, relationships between individuals and groups, the increases in the flow of goods, people, information etc., across borders, and the more concrete travel technologies. Words such as 'interconnections', 'networks' and 'flows' are typical. David Harvey (1989) talks about this as 'time-space compression', meaning that due to the radical change in time taken to cross distances, both physically and representationally, new situations arise in which social relationships get stretched across distance. Hence, although 'locality' still exists, a number of things happening in far away places will affect us, and people are increasingly becoming aware that it is happening. Thus the worlds *appear* to us in new ways, with distant places being routinely within reach. And the journey between such places is becoming standardized. But again, the focus of these authors is on the contemporary world.

This leads to a problem of 'beginnings'. Castells and many others (see, e.g., Ong 1999) seek to limit the concept of globalization only to describe the new corporate strategies evident in the new globalized economy. Which is fair enough, but does not leave us much room to discuss the term's usefulness for understanding historical developments. But there are other points-of-view as well. Just like Wallerstein limited his world system to a period characterized by Western capitalism, Giddens (e.g. 1990) and Tomlinson (1999) seem to limit the notion of globalization to the period of Modernity. But when did Modernity arise? All institutions have their different times. Should our focus be on Wallerstein's 'long 16th century' with the economic responses to the crises of feudalism, that is, capitalist modernity? But what about political democracy (17th century—the English civil war, or 18th century—French and American revolutions), industrialization in the 18th and 19th centuries (the Industrial Revolution)? The problem is that there is no agreement about what should be dated. And as Zygmunt Bauman (1995:140–54) says, as we try to date, the object disappears, because modernity is ambigous. Like Giddens, Bauman dates it to 17th-century Europe. It is easy to understand why this is so if the starting point is to understand contemporary globalization. But if we want to make use of this general perspective also to understand earlier moments of reconfiguration, then we should focus on historical 'epochs' in general, that is, eras or ages that denote major shifts in social organization or cultural imagination, expressed in distinctive formative events. We can focus on the Axial Age in which universal religions appeared. Another relevant focus would be on private property and the individual. And we have already mentioned the time-space compression represented by various technological changes implied in terms such as 'Steam Age', 'Atomic Era', 'Computer Age', 'Digital Age' to mention some recent shifts (e.g. Eickelman and Anderson 1999). But technological developments such as the domestication of the camel which revolutionized the crossing of deserts, or the importance of the lanteen sail for crossing the Indian Ocean would be a comparable shifts to those mentioned. What is common to all our examples is that they represent developments that provide people with new futures, characterized by new ways of thinking (reflexivity), but also developments that bring new forms of inequality and collective identities. Such trends become evident if we expand focus outwards from a single historical epoch to look at several epochs and the transformations between them. What I am after here is not the epoch of a specific historical classification, but epoch as heuristic device, that is, not to get lost in 'the banality of dating' (Tomlinson 1999:39) and be terrorized by detail, but to focus on what the ideas are that inform the different epochs. Through such a procedure we can carry out comparisons not only in space, but also in time. By this I believe we can counter one important criticism of globalization theory—that it has a Western bias. My argument is that globalization is not Westernization, a West against the rest type of thing, or Oriental vs. Occidental to speak with Edward Said. It can be that too, but is not necesarily so. It is an empirical question, and we can allow for Featherstone's 'Global Modernities', in plural (Featherstone *et al.* 1995:1–21). And it does not by necessity undermine plurality in the world. The world does not develop by necessity towards a certain goal, as defined by the West. Nor is culture revolving only around notions of 'difference'. Culture is about establishing all kinds of meaning, through collective symbolization woven into a set of material practices that sustain a viable form of life, not only meaning about difference. The focus on difference is a result of specific types of cultural activity, not its essential function.

Obviously, the above shows the process of globalization to be multidimensional, characterized by all sorts of dynamics and resistances be they local or global, particular or universal (Castells 1996, 1997, 1998; Featherstone *et al.* 1995; Giddens 1990; Lash and Urry 1994; Robertson 1995). Such multi-dimensionalism should not keep us from empirically based analysis, but we have to be careful how we do those studies. Hence, there is a need to discuss how we can pull together this complexity, for example, studying human praxis as well as the discourses relating to globality. The problem is not new and consists of how to combine meaning production as well as other more instrumental acts.

I have tried to do this by focusing on Muslim communities in the Indian Ocean world and how their identity as Muslims placed them in different types of relationships, both to other Muslims and to people of other groups living in the various areas of the Indian Ocean. The paper describes the Indian Ocean world as part of a wider *dar al-islam*, a dynamic world in which the Muslims were active players, as missionaries, as traders, as sailors or whatever occupations they represented. The analysis thus develops the argument I have put forward earlier (Manger 1999) about building our understanding of Muslim communities less on ideas about a static Islam and more on notions of dynamic communities engaging in 'world systems inter-relationships'. Certainly, Islam is a religion made up of specific *texts*, the Quran, the *Sunna*, the *Shari'a* and so forth. But the Muslim religion is also one with a particular history of *events*, starting with the Prophet Mohammad, followed by four *khalifs*. They are part of an imperial history of political expansion, of waves of political rise and decline, but also processes of intellectual development and tides of reformism and of accommodation, not reflecting the sequences of political and economic developments. To capture the dynamism in this type of situation a static, Orientalist image of Islam and Muslims will not do. We need perspectives that allow for specific histories to come more clearly to the surface and the lives of Muslims to be portrayed against that history, lives not only affected by integrated localities organized according to Islamic principles alone, but as lives lived in arenas in which complex historical processes have taken place and indeed do take place. The trade relationships in the Indian Ocean activated not only capital, but organizational patterns handling credit, legal patterns creating security around contracts and so on. In such situations Islam was not only a religion, but the *Shari'a* provided a legal code for handling business and for dealing with conflicts. People well versed in the *Shari'a* therefore also acted as judges, arbitrators and so on, drawing on knowledge about earlier cases from elsewhere as well as their interpretation of the text itself. But the same processes also provided arenas in which Muslims met, and in which Muslims met with non-Muslims thereby experiencing themselves as Muslims in their particular world.

References

Abu Lughod, J. (1989) *Before European Hegemony: The World System AD 1250–1350*. New York: Oxford University Press.

Alatas, F. S. (1997) Hadhramaut and the Hadhramaut Diaspora: problems in theoretical history. In *Hadhrami Traders, Scholars and Statesmen in the Indian Ocean, 1750s–1960s*, edited by U. Freitag and W. G. Clarence-Smith. Leiden: E.J. Brill, pp. .

Al Hassan, A. Y., and Hill D. R. (1986) *Islamic Technology: An Illustrated History*. Cambridge: Cambridge University Press.

Anderson, B. (1991) *Imagined Communities: Reflections on the Origin and Spread of Nationalism*. London: Verso.

Anderson, B. (1998) *The Spectre of Comparison: Nationalism, Southeast Asia and the World*. New York: Verso.

Appadurai, A. (1990) Disjuncture and difference in the global cultural economy. In *Global Culture: Nationalism, Globalisation and Modernity*, edited by M. Featherstone. London: Sage, pp. 295–310.

Appadurai, A. (ed.) (2001) *Globalization*. Durham, NC: Duke University Press.

Arrighi, G. (1999) *The Long Twentieth Century: Money, Power, and the Origin of Our Times*. London: Verso.

Asad, T. (1986) *The Idea of an Anthropology of Islam*. Center for Contemporary Arab Studies Occasional papers series. Washington: Georgetown University.

Bang, A. K. (2000) Sufis and Scholars of the Sea: The Sufi and Family Networks of Ahmad ibn Symayt and the Tariqa Alawiyya in East Africa c. 1860–1925. Dr. Art Thesis, University of Bergen.

Barendse, R. J. (2000) Trade and state in the Arabian seas: a survey from the fifteenth to the eighteenth century. *Journal of World History* 11 (2):173–225.

Barth, F. (1989) The analysis of culture in complex societies. *Ethnos* 54 (I-II).

Bauman, Z. (1995) Seeking for a center that holds. In *Global Modernities*, edited by M. Featherstone, S. Lash and R. Robertson. London: Sage, pp. 140–54.

Bayly, C. A. (1983) *Townsmen and Bazaars: North Indian Society in the Age of British Expansion, 1770–1870*. Cambridge: Cambridge University Press.

Bayly, C. A. (1989) *Imperial Meridian: The British Empire and the world, 1780–1830*. London: Longman.

Bayly, S. (1989) *Saints, Goddesses and Kings: Muslims and Christian in South Indian Society, 1700–1900*. Cambridge: Cambridge University Press

Bentley, J. H. (1993) *Old World Encounters: Cross-Cultural Contacts and Exchanges in Pre-Modern Times*. New York: Oxford University Press.

Bluhm, J. E. (1983) A preliminary statement on the dialogue established between the reform magazine *al-Manar* and the Malayo-Indonesian world. *Indonesian Circle* 32 (35.42).

Burawoy, M., *et al.* (2000) *Global Ethnography: Forces, Connections and Imaginations of a Post-Modern World*. Berkeley: University of California Press.

Castells, M. (1996) *The Rise of the Network Society: The Information Age: Economy, Society and Culture* 1. 3 vols. Oxford: Blackwell.

Castells, M. (1997) *The Power of Identity: The Information Age: Economy, Society and Culture* 2. 3 vols. Oxford: Blackwell.

Castells, M. (1998) *The End of the Millennium: The Information Age: Economy, Society and Culture* 3. 3 vols. Oxford: Blackwell.

Chaudhuri, K. N. (1985) *Trade and Civilization in the Indian Ocean: An Economic History from the Rise of Islam to 1750*. Cambridge: Cambridge University Press.

Chaudhuri, K. N. (1991) *Asia before Europe: Economy and Civilization of the Indian Ocean from the Rise of Islam to 1750*. Cambridge: Cambridge University Press.

Collins, R. (1999) *Macrohistory: Essays in the Sociology on the Long Run*. Stanford: Stanford University Press.

Cooper, F. and Stoller, A. L. (eds) (1997) *Tensions of Empire: Colonial Cultures in a Bourgeois World*. Berkeley: University of California Press.

Curtin, P. (1984) *Cross-Cultural Trade in World History*. Cambridge: Cambridge University Press.

Curtin, P. D. (2000) *The World and the West: The European Challenge and the Overseas Response in the Age of Empire*. Cambridge: Cambridge University Press.

Dale, S. F. (1980) *Islamic Society on the South Asian Frontier: The Mappilas of Malabar 1498–1922*. Oxford: Clarendon Press.

Dale, S. F. (1997) The Hadrami Diaspora in South-Western India: the role of the sayyids of the Malabar coast. In *Hadrami Traders, Scholars and Statesmen in the Indian Ocean, 1750s–1960s*, edited by U. Freitag and W.G. Clarence-Smith. Leiden: Brill, pp. .

de Jonge, H. (1997) Dutch colonial policy pertaining to Hadhrami immigrants. In *Hadhrami Traders, Scholars and Statesmen in the Indian Ocean, 1750s–1960s*, edited by U. Freitag and W.G. Clarence-Smith. Leiden: E.J. Brill, pp. 94–111.

de Jonge, H., and Kaptein, N. (eds) (2002) *Transcending Borders: Arabs, Politics, Trade and Islam in Southeast Asia*. Leiden: KITLV Press.

Deliar, N. (1973) *The Modernist Muslim Movement in Indonesia 1900–1942*. Singapore: Oxford University Press.

Eaton, R. M. (1978) *Sufis of Bijapur, 1300–1700*. Princeton: Princeton University Press.

Eaton, R. M. (1990) *Islamic History as Global History: Essays on Global and Comparative History*. Washington DC: American Historical Association.

Eickelman, D., and Piscatori, J. (1990) *Muslim Travellers: Pilgrimage, Migration and the Religious Imagination*. London: Routledge.

Eickelman, D., and Anderson, J. W. (eds) (1999) *New Media in the Muslim World: The Emerging Public Sphere*. Bloomington: Indiana University Press.

Featherstone, M., Lash, S., and Robertson, R. (eds) (1995) *Global Modernities*. London: Sage.

Freitag, U. and Clarence-Smith, W.G. (eds) (1997) *Hadrami Traders, Scholars, and Statesmen in the Indian Ocian, 1750s-1960s*) Leiden: E.J.Brill.

Friedman, J. (1994) *Cultural Identity and Global Process*. London: Sage.

Gallagher, J., and Robinson, R. (1953) The Imperialism of Free Trade. In *The Economic History Review*, second series, vol. VI, no. 1:1–15.

Giddens, A. (1981) A contemporary critique of historical materialism. In *Power, Property and the State*. Berkeley: University of California Press.

Giddens, A. (1982) *Profiles and Critiques in Social Theory*. Berkeley: University of California Press.

Giddens, A. (1984) *The Constitution of Society: Outline of the Theory of Structuration*. Cambridge: Polity Press.

Giddens, A. (1990) *The Consequences of Modernity*. Cambridge: Polity Press.

Goody, J. (1996) *The East in the West*. Cambridge: Cambridge University Press.

Hardt, M. and Negri, A. (2000) *Empire*. Cambridge, MA: Harvard University Press.

Harn, L. C. (1963) The Arab Population of Singapore 1819–1959. Unpublished BA thesis, Dept. of Geography, National University of Singapore.

Harvey, D. (1989) *The Conditions of Postmodernity: An Inquiry into the Origin of Cultural Change*. Oxford: Blackwell.

Hobsbawm, E. (1979) *The Age of Capital 1848–75*. New York: New American Library.

Hobson, J. (1938) *Imperialism: A Study*. London: George Allen and Unwin.

Hugill, P. J. (1993) *World Trade since 1431: Geography, Technology and Capitalism*. Baltimore: John Hopkins University Press.

Huntington, S. (1996) *The Clash of Civilzations and the Remaking of the World Order*. New York: Simon and Schuster.

Issawi, C. (1998) *Cross–Cultural Encounters and Conflicts*. Oxford: Oxford University Press.

Jenkins, R. (1996) *Social Identity*. London: Routledge.

Lash, S. (1999) *Another Modernity: A Different Rationality*. Oxford: Blackwell.

Lash, S. and Urry, J. (1987) *The End of Organized Capitalism*. Madison: University of Wisconsin Press.

Lash, S. and Urry, J. (1994) *Economics of Signs and Space*. London: Sage.

Mandal, S. K. (1997) Natural leaders of native Muslims: Arab ethnicity and politics in Java under Dutch rule. In *Hadhrami Traders, Scholars and Statesmen in the Indian Ocean, 1750s–1960s*, edited by U. Freitag and W. G. Clarence-Smith. Leiden: E.J. Brill, pp. 1–36.

Mandaville, P. (2001) Reimagining Islam in diaspora: the politics of mediated community. *Gazette* 63 (2-3):169–86.

Manger, L., (1992) On the study of Islam in local contexts. *Norwegian Journal of Development Studies*, no. 1.

Manger, L. (1999) Introduction. In *Muslim Diversity: Local Islam in a Global Context*, edited by L. Manger. London: Curzon Press.

Mann, M. (1993) *The Sources of Social Power 2: The Rise of Classes and Nation States, 1760–1914.* Cambridge: Cambridge University Press.
Metcalf, B. D. (1999) Nationalism, modernity, and Muslim identity in India before 1947. In *Nation and Religion: Perspectives on Europe and Asia*, edited by P. van der Veer and H. Lehmann. Princeton: Princeton University Press, pp. 129–43.
Meyer, B. and Gesciere, P. (eds) (1999) *Globalization and Identity: Dialectics of Flow and Closure.* Oxford: Blackwell.
Miller, R.E. (1976) *Mappilla Muslims of Kerala.* Madras: Orient Longman.
Nash, J. (1991) Ethnographic aspects of the world capitalist system. *Annual Review of Anthropology*, 10:393–423.
Ong, A. (1999) *Flexible Citizenship: The Cultural Logic of Transnationality.* Durham: Duke University Press.
O'Rourke, K.H. and Williamson, J.G. (1999) *Globalization and History: The Evolution of a Nineteenth-Century Atlantic Economy.* Cambridge, MA: MIT Press.
Othman, M.R. (1997) Hadhramis in the politics and administration of the Malay states in the late eighteenth and nineteenth centuries. In *Hadhrami Traders, Scholars and Statesmen in the Indian Ocean, 1750s–1960s*, edited by U. Freitag and W. G. Clarence-Smith. Leiden: E.J. Brill, pp. 82–93.
Pan, L. (ed) (1991) *The Encyclopedia of the Chinese Overseas.* Singapore: Archipelago Press and Landmark Books.
Reid, A. (1967) Nineteenth century pan-Islam in Indonesia and Malaysia. *Journal of Asian Studies* 26 (2):267–83.
Reese, S. S. (1996) Patricians of the Benadir: Islamic Learning, Commerce and Somali Urban Identity in the Nineteenth Century. Unpublished PhD thesis, University of Pennsylvania.
Robertson, R. (1995) Glocalization: time-space and homogeneity-hetereogeneity. In *Global Modernities*, edited by M. Featherstone, S. Lash and R. Robertson. London: Sage, pp. 24–44.
Roff, W. (1964) The Malayo-Muslim world of Singapore at the close of the nineteenth century. *Journal of Asian Studies* XXIV no. 1:75–90).
Scott, A. (ed.) (1997) *The Limits of Globalization. Cases and Arguments.* London: Routledge.
Shannon, T. R. (1996) *An Introduction to the World-System Perspective.* Boulder: Westview.
Stagl, J. (1995) *A History of Curiosity: The Theory of Travel 1550–1800.* Chur, Switzerland: Harwood.
Taylor, J. G. (1983) *The Social World of Batavia: European and Eurasian in Dutch Asia.* Madison: University of Wisconsin Press.
Tibbetts, G. R. (1956) Early Traders in South-East Asia. *Journal of the Malaysian Branch of the Royal Asiatic Society* 30/1/177:1–45
Tibbetts, G. R. 1981) *Arab Navigation in the Indian Ocean before the Coming of the Portuguese.* London: Royal Asiatic Society.
Tomlinson, J. (1999) *Globalization and Culture.* Chicago: University of Chicago Press.
Udovitch, A. (1970) *Partnership and Profit in Medieval Islam.* Princeton: Princeton University Press.
van der Veer, P. (1994) *Religious Nationalism: Hindus and Muslims in India.* Berkeley: University of California Press.
Voll, J. (1994) *Islam: Continuity and Change in the Modern World.* Syracuse: Syracuse University Press.
Wallerstein, I. (1974) *Modern World System*, vol. 1. *Capitalist Agriculture and the Origin of the European World Economy in the 16th century.* San Diego: Academic Press.
Watson, A. (1983) *Agricultural Innovation in the Easrly Islamic World: The Diffusion of Crops and Farming Techniques, 700–1100.* Cambridge: Cambridge University Press.
Wolf, E. (1982) *Europe and the People without History.* Berkeley: University of California Press.

Perceptions of Antiquity and the Formation of Modern Resistance Identities

Sandra Arnold Scham

The opposing dialectical moving forces of the Net and the Self in Castells' formulation creates an almost infinite series of interactions impacting on both micro and macro levels of society. Castells is certainly not the first to posit this relationship between social relations and technology but he is the first to introduce the idea that global information and communication technology, combined with individual user control, has effected such far-reaching changes in modern society. For Castells, however, the definer of the Self, identity, is not culturally prearranged. Rather, as the introduction to this section made clear, it is constructed on the basis of attributes selected by social actors and the motives for constructing identities determine their content. Constructions of Castells' three types of identity, *legitimizing identity*, that of powerful institutions, *project identity*, that of social reformers, and *resistance identity*, that of subjugated people, are all dependent to some extent on the past, and social explanations of the past (Castells 1997; Scham 2001).

Marija Gimbutas (1982, 1989, 1991) and Martin Bernal (1987) inspire such antipathy among archaeologists that most would refer to their views as 'misperceptions' of antiquity. I would venture to suggest, however, that a more appropriate reaction on the part of other professionals might be admiration—not for their scholarship which is, I would hasten to agree, flawed, nor for their popularity. Rather, because the notions espoused by these two scholars have so perfectly, and in some ways paradoxically, made antiquity a prominent part of the network society, we should feel impelled at least to scrutinize them with more interest than we may have, heretofore, displayed. Indeed, it might be said that any exploration of the association between connectivity and antiquity would be incomplete without referencing the Goddess and the Egypt in Africa movements.

The Civilization of the Goddess and *Black Athena* have become cultural icons because of the resistance identities that have been formed around them and the Net has been highly instrumental in that formation. Insofar as the sheer number of internet sites referencing these works is concerned, they even outdistance the Bible—a book that has been around for considerably longer. No other scholar, regardless of renown in the profession, is mentioned in websites relating to archaeology and antiquity as many times as Gimbutas and Bernal. The only rival for their preeminence on the web is von Däniken (of *Chariots of the Gods* fame, 1974)—a writer with whom Gimbutas and Bernal are sometimes compared though, as may be already apparent, I do not believe this association is a just or valid one.

Unlike von Däniken's rather eccentric allure (primarily, it seems, to UFO-sighters) eco-feminism, neo-paganism and Afrocentrism have a powerful appeal as categories of identity. In order to fully appreciate the degree to which *The Goddess* and *Black Athena* have engrossed women and people of African descent in Europe and North America, we need only examine the veritable cottage industries in Bernal and Gimbutas criticism that have been inspired by their ideas (Conkey and Tringham 1995; Davis 1998; Goode 1994; Lefkowitz 1995; Lefkowitz and Rogers 1996; Meskell 1995 and 1998). It is safe to say that any theory that scholars devote entire volumes to refuting must be taken seriously. How seriously depends upon the orientation of the observer.

Postprocessualist archaeologists like Shanks (2001), Gosden (2001) and Hodder (1999) have more soberly addressed these ideas in their written and fieldwork. Hodder's excavations at Çatal Höyük have attracted numerous 'goddess tours' and his website, in part, caters to the interests of eco-feminists. In his recent book on *The Archaeological Process*, Hodder challenges both traditional and political archaeologists who suggest that encouraging 'goddess groups' to engage with the past at Çatal Höyük promotes an idea of the past as a 'theme park'. He asks his critics rather vehemently, 'who are you to judge the role of archaeology for individuals who believe in the goddess? ... Who are you to say that discovering the goddess does not help them to gain a stronger sense of what it means to be a woman after centuries of subjugation?' (Hodder 1999:83).

Meskell, however, has suggested that goddess worship presents a vision of the past that employs premises that are in themselves patriarchal and anti-feminist. Labeling eco-feminism as the 'archaeology of desire' she proposes that goddess worshippers, in arguing for the innate superiority of women today as evidenced by their supreme status in the remote past, construct *woman* as a category that is natural, biologically bound and emotional. As she so articulately expresses it, 'This concept of an abstract masculinity against which we women must struggle is perhaps just as offensive as blatant androcentrism has been for women and suggests, ironically, that things have failed to move on.' She believes that the goals of goddess worship, supporting a modern feminist identity rooted in the past, are better served 'not by artificially interpolating [gender difference] for its own sake but simply in recognizing the horizon of possibilities in the past' (Meskell 1997:63–4).

Bernal, as was mentioned above, has no shortage of detractors and some of the arguments that have been made against his ideas have approached the hysteria level. How else is one to account for Mary Lefkowitz's dire warnings that Afrocentrism 'has a destructive side, which *cannot and should not* [italics mine] be overlooked. First of all, it offers them a "story" instead of history. It also suggests that African-Americans need to learn only what they choose to believe about the past' (1995:101). Roth, while acknowledging that Bernal is a 'scholar and presumably adopts a scholarly critical attitude', believes that the main problem with his work is that, by viewing ancient Egyptian culture through an 'Afrocentric' lens, it fails to examine the real nature of the society (1998:123). North similarly suggests that Bernal's work is 'deeply problematic' because of 'the crucial links that Bernal makes (or allows to be inferred) to contemporary concerns...first that the Egyptians were black; secondly that their blackness was connected with their being denied "credit" in the evolution of culture; thirdly, that the restoration of their "credit" has relevance to relations between contemporary groups'. He maintains, however, that 'the problem for ancient historians is not just to say that this whole agenda is misconceived, but to define what would be a better one. Attributing colour to Egypt may be conceptually anachronistic; that does not destroy the power of the idea' (North 2000:2).

The consensus of these scholars' opinions are that goddess worship and Afrocentrist Egyptology have messages to communicate to archaeologists—however deficient we may view the media through which those messages are expressed. The messages may not occur in the form of questions, but questions are precisely what they convey to us. First of all, we need to discuss the charges that have been implicitly laid at the door of 'traditional' archaeology by Gimbutas and Bernal. Does archaeology, in fact, fail to address the roles played by women in the creation of western civilization? Has it neglected to credit African civilizations properly for their part in the creation of Western culture? Were there, in fact, great feminine and African-controlled cultures of the past that we have ignored because they do not reflect the current masculine and European-controlled present?

Figure 11.1 Early Bronze Age fertility idol (Louvre).

As many feminist archaeologists are now pointing out, in a less grandiose manner than Gimbutas, western civilization is a product of the labors of both men and women—as well as commoners and elites. There has been a recognition in more theoretical circles for some time that the traditional emphases for archaeology and history have been both sexist and elitist (Conkey and Gero 1991 and 1997; Gero 1995; Spector 1991; Wylie 1992). Perhaps Classical scholars have failed to acknowledge that predecessor ancient Egyptian and Semitic cultures, as alleged by Bernal, created 'the grandeur that was Greece'. Perhaps Egyptologists have attempted to divorce Egypt from its African context. Certainly, women's roles in Classical and Near Eastern antiquity are still uncharted in the standard archaeological literature, despite the proliferation of newer works on these subjects.

These realizations do not inevitably lead, however, to the certainty that the ancient 'old world' was a multi-cultural mosaic led by a class of strong but benevolent African women. The Queen of Sheba may provide an intriguing role model for generations of girls of African descent but it is unlikely that she ruled an empire equal to Alexander's and it is equally unlikely that Alexander must attribute all of his success to his mother.

The Net and Resistance Identities

Having examined, however briefly, the resistance identities supported by the work of Gimbutas and Bernal and their probable basis in the reality of the past, I would like to discuss the impact of the internet with respect to the construction of these identities by highlighting two prominent narratives that have had wide circulation in cyberspace.

The first narrative is an old one about the damage to the nose of the Sphinx. It is unclear when and where this story originated but for some time now many have believed that Napoleon's soldiers were responsible for this damage. The Afrocentric twist to the story is that the reason behind the French soldiers' destruction is their alarm at the supposed African features of the Sphinx—in effect, that it was a monumental depiction of Black Africa that was offensive to European eyes. Many African-Americans repeat the story of Napoleon's soldiers because it symbolizes for them the great European 'cover-up' of the true nature of Egyptian civilization (Crawford 1994; James 1992).

The second story is the popular myth concerning a divine woman, the goddess Sophia. In very early Christian days, so this narrative goes, before the male-centered church supplanted and suppressed them, the Gnostic Christians believed in a Trinity that included both male and female aspects. They also supported the equal treatment of women in the Church, allowing both men and women into the priesthood. Sophia at this time had the place later accorded to the 'Holy Spirit'. She was worshipped by Jews as well as Christians and celebrated in such biblical books as 'The Song of Songs'. Sophia in this popular literature is often allied to Adam's first wife Lilith who, according to Medieval legend, was banished from Eden for disobeying her husband (Stone 1976; Goode 1994).

Both of these narratives underscore the three enterprises at which the Net excels and which are so conducive to promoting resistance perceptions of the past. I characterize these enterprises as *the unmasking of conspiracy, the construction of collective memory* and *the sharing of power*.

I am not the first to observe that the Net is the quintessential means for exposing conspiracies—or would-be conspiracies. The Net, as yet, is unregulated by government, is global in scope and can absorb and distribute a broad range of information. It is also a 'closeted' activity. When we are using the Net, we are alone with it. Thus, in the privacy of your own home you can discover via this medium how European white males have gotten together over the centuries to destroy the great and glorious histories of women and Africans. No matter that the Sphinx destruction, most probably, was caused in 1378 AD when a religious zealot found it offensive to Muslim eyes and that there is no evidence for an early 'Wisdom goddess' figure in the Christian Church—if there are enough people in the world who think it to be so, it can become true.

The Net also offers a means of calling up and collectivizing the past. Certainly, we can see archaeological and historical programming on television but we cannot do this in our time, in our space and for our purposes—and we cannot share our insights about it with strangers. We can read about the past in books but we have to purchase or borrow them and they lack the wonderful ability of Google to self-direct us to the information we want. The Net offers us a way of treating our imaginations as memory and our experiences as history. We don't speculate that women were once powerful in the church and that the Ancient Egyptians were like African-Americans—we remember it.

Finally, the Net enables us to share power—our own power and that of other users. We can create gods, change the past, uncover the present and know the future. We are all empowered together within this great framework of modern communication technology.

Power Vacuums, the Past and the Space of Flows

Foucault has been primarily responsible for informing the postprocessual position that knowledge in the West is constituted by 'regimes of truth' that serve to reinforce society's powerful institutions (Foucault 1979). Culture and its products—books, magazines, entertainment media, academia, the arts, literature—are all subject to the overbearing effects of this authority. Foucault saw resistance as a hopeless but nonetheless necessary reaction to the imposition of power through the production of knowledge. He saw 'knowledge', always it seems, as the exclusive property of the powerful (Foucault 1993). Castells' work has exposed the basic flaw in Foucault's thinking—or rather has demonstrated his lack of prescience in imagining the advent of global internet communication before his death in 1984.

The Net has already altered our system of cultural production as well as our concepts of space—sacred space, social space, cultural space. When Foucault dealt with 'space', he envisioned it as a dynamic force constituted by both knowledge and action and he discusses the uses of space for imprinting regimens on the mind (1979 and 1993). Cyberspace, the 'space of flows', is constituted by neither knowledge nor action but by information once the exclusive province of governments and other institutions of control. The Net can effectively imprint new 'regimens of information' on the susceptible minds of millions. It fills the power vacuums created by traditional knowledge production mechanisms. Thus, the disenfranchised have a voice that can be heard across a broad spectrum of geographical, social, educational and political statuses. In her recent book, whimsically entitled Give Me That Online Religion, Brasher states that, because of internet technology, 'We are more aware of others than ever before—not in a modernistic sense, where we see people from other cultures as exotica that spice up our own life ... but in a postmodern sense whereby people live according to divergent moral, ethical and aesthetic perspectives' (Brasher 2001:21).

The Internet has become the source of 'alternative' data *par excellence*. This was recently brought home to me when a student of mine, a Pakistani whose family was originally Persian, questioned the traditional characterization of Alexander the Great as a conqueror who practiced religious and cultural tolerance. In his tradition, he told me, Alexander was an unrepentent villain—a barbarian who burned libraries and massacred innocent people. I consulted any number of texts for information about this and found basically the same Western historical clichés about Alexander incessantly repeated. In desperation to find information on the view of Alexander from the East I turned to the internet. By net standards the sites were few on this, only about 400, but I found what I was looking for.

Increasingly, unless we are willing to critically examine our assumptions, we will find that our evidence will become less persuasive to a generation of Net-educated young people. In fact, the boundaries between specialist and non-specialist websites are already blurred. Part of the education that we should be offering to our students is the ability to distinguish erudition from rhetoric and propaganda. Thereafter, they may still reject the former in favor of the latter but at least they will know the differences between them. This is part of what Ian Hodder has called 'the overall process of a shift from a hierarchical to a networked structure of archaeological knowledge'. As he further states, 'The archaeologist has to argue for an authority, not assume it' (Hodder 2001:14).

Conclusions

In an essay called 'The Pact', Emmanuel Levinas characterized the ills of a society on the eve of the internet and communications revolution:

> [B]oundaries have become, in a sense, planetary: a society, in which, due to the ease of modern communications and transport, and the worldwide scale of its industrial economy, each person feels simultaneously that he is related to humanity as a whole, and equally that he is alone and lost. ... [O]ne understands that one's personal destiny, freedom or happiness is subject to causes which operate with inhumane force. One understands that the very progress of technology ... which relates everyone in the world to everyone else, is inseparable from a necessity which leaves all men anonymous. It is a world in which men find themselves side by side rather than face to face (Levinas 1989:212).

The loneliness that Levinas postulated as a consequence of communications technology has been abated somewhat by the Net but his last cogent comment is still evocative of today's world. Our ability to exchange the details of our lives with strangers has masked the essential truth that we are just as hidden from each other as individuals as we were before. The Net, however, offers us the illusion of relatedness and of group solidarity. It is this illusion that has always sustained disenfranchised people throughout history but today the illusion has more power to effect change than ever before.

References

Bernal, M. (1987) *Black Athena: The Afroasiatic Roots of Classical Civilization*, vol. 1: *The Fabrication of Ancient Greece 1785–1985*. New Brunswick, NJ: Rutgers University.

Brasher, B. (2001) *Give Me That Online Religion*. San Francisco: Jossey-Bass.

Castells, M. (1997) *The Power of Identity: The Information Age: Economy, Society and Culture* 2. 3 vols. Cambridge, MA and Oxford, UK: Blackwell.

Conkey, M. and Gero, J. (1991) Tensions, pluralities and engendering archaeology: an introduction to women and prehistory. In *Engendering Archaeology: Women and Prehistory*, edited by J. Gero and M. Conkey. Oxford: Blackwell, pp. 3–30.

Conkey, M. and Gero, J. (1997) Programme to practice: gender and feminism in archaeology. *Annual Review of Anthropology* 26:411–37.

Conkey, M. and Tringham, R. (1995) Archaeology and the Goddess: exploring the contours of feminist archaeology. In *Feminisms in the Academy*, edited by D. Stanton and A. Stewart. Ann Arbor: The University of Michigan Press.

Crawford, C. (1994) *Recasting Ancient Egypt in the African Context: Toward a Model Curriculum Using Art and Language*. Trenton, NJ: African World Press.

Davis, R. (1998) *The Goddess Unmasked*. Oxford: Blackwell.

Foucault, M. (1979) *Discipline and Punish: The Birth of Prison*. New York, Vintage.

Foucault, M. (1993) Space, power and knowledge. In *The Foucault Reader*, edited by P. Rabinow. New York: Pantheon Books, pp. 239–56.

Gero, J. (1995) Railroading epistemology: paleoindians and women. In *Interpreting Archaeology: Finding Meaning in the Past*, edited by I. Hodder, M. Shanks, A. Alexandri, V. Buchli, J. Carman, J. Lastand and G. Lucas. London and New York: Routledge, pp. 175–80.

Gimbutas, M. (1982) *The Goddesses and Gods of Old Europe*. Los Angeles, CA: University of California Press.

Gimbutas, M. (1989) *The Language of the Goddess*. San Francisco, CA: Harper.

Gimbutas, M. (1991) *The Civilization of the Goddess: The World of Old Europe*. San Francisco, CA: Harper.

Goode, S. (1994) Sophia and feminist theology. *Insight Magazine*:1–16.

Gosden, C. (2001) Postcolonial archaeology: issues of culture, identity and knowledge. In *Archaeological Theory Today*, edited by I. Hodder. Malden, MA: Blackwell, pp. 284–305.

Hodder, I. (1999) *The Archaeological Process: An Introduction*. Oxford and Malden, MA: Blackwell Publishers.

James, G. (1992) *Stolen Legacy: Greek Philosophy is Stolen Egyptian Philosophy*. Lawrenceville, NJ: Africa World Press.

Lefkowitz, M. (1995) *Not Out of Africa: How Afrocentrism Became an Excuse to Teach Myth as History*. New York: Basic Books.

Lefkowitz, M. and Rogers, G. (1996) *Black Athena Revisited*. Chapel Hill: University of North Carolina Press.

Levinas, E. (1989) The Pact. In *The Levinas Reader*, edited by S. Hand. Cambridge, MA: Basil Blackwell, pp. 211–26.

Meskell, L. (1997) *Archaeologies of Social Life: Age, Sex, Class Et Cetera in Ancient Egypt (Social Archaeology)*. Oxford and Malden, MA: Blackwell Publishers.

Meskell, L. (1995) Goddesses, Gimbutas and 'New Age' archaeology. *Antiquity* 69:74–86.

Meskell, L. (1998) Oh My Goddess! *Archaeological Dialogues* 5(2):126–42.

North, J. (2000) Attributing Colour to the Ancient Egyptians. Paper presented at the conference on Encounters with Ancient Egypt, University College London, London.

Roth, A.M. (1998) Ancient Egypt in America: claiming the riches. In *Archaeology Under Fire: Nationalism, Politics and Heritage in the Eastern Mediterranean and Middle East*, edited by L. Meskell. London and New York: Routledge, pp. 217–29.

Scham, S. (2001) The archaeology of the disenfranchised. *Journal of Archaeological Method and Theory* 8(2):183–209.

Shanks, M. (2001) Culture/Archaeology: the dispersion of a discipline and its objects. In *Archaeological Theory Today*, edited by I. Hodder. Malden, MA: Blackwell, pp. 241–61.

Spector, J. (1991) What this awl means: toward a feminist archaeology. In *Engendering Archaeology: Women and Prehistory*, edited by J. Gero and M. Conkey. Blackwell: Oxford, pp. 388–406.

Stone, M. (1976) *When God Was a Woman*. San Diego: Harvest/HBJ.

Wylie, A. (1992) The interplay of evidential constraints and political interests: recent archaeological research on gender. *American Antiquity* 57:15–35.

von Däniken, E. (1974) *Chariots of the Gods?* New York: Bantam Books.

Foreign Self and Familiar 'Other': The Impact of 'Global' Connectivity on New Kingdom Egypt

Jenny Cashman

The New Kingdom (1550–1070 BC) in ancient Egypt was a time of expansion and social change. Its sphere of influence extended beyond earlier limits and its rulers formed new political alliances with old neighbors. Egypt played a major role in the ancient Near East's evolution from an international system to an 'international society in the making' (Ragionieri 2000:42–6).

But was it a 'new' society in a 'global' world? The purpose of this paper is to explore in what ways the conceptual framework that Manuel Castells applies to globalization in the 20th century can be used to better understand ancient Egypt during this phase of its history. Castells proposes that a 'new' society is one in which there are changes in relationships of production, relationships of power and relationships of experience (Castells 1998:340). I will address all three aspects of this conceptual frame, but with an emphasis on the latter two components. For the first one—relationships of production—I provide a brief discussion of certain aspects of modes of production and technological innovations in the New Kingdom. The focus of this paper is on changes in relationships of power and experience, especially in relation to the foreign 'other' in the world outside Egypt—and their visible and preserved expression in ancient material.

In this investigation, the evidence is inherently fragmentary, distanced from modern society by almost 3,000 years and experienced within a very different economic and cultural frame. The reaction of ancient peoples to 'global' networks therefore cannot be evaluated in the same ways that modern society in an 'information age' can be assessed.

When attempting to understand societal mechanisms through the use of written sources, one of the crucial issues is the interpretation of ancient language. In considering Egypt's relationships with other cultures, it is particularly important to recognize that the modern translation of terms lacks the cultural texture of their original usage. When inscriptions use the term *inw*, for example, it means something very different to 21st-century readers if it is translated as 'tribute'—a traditional translation that suggests an unequal, even dominant-subservient relationship of power—rather than 'gift' or 'supply' or 'product'. It is also important to consider the context of the text in which it appears: an administrative document recording incoming goods, a diplomatic letter between sovereigns, or a caption in a tomb scene depicting foreigners carrying splendid and exotic luxury goods.[1]

In the interpretation of visual material other issues arise, especially in terms of royal power and responsibility regarding the world outside Egypt. It is an integral part of the social contract for the king to control the forces of chaos and subdue enemies. The standard iconography of kingship includes the 'smiting' scene, in which the king stands poised to strike, holding a mace in one hand and in the other, the hair of the enemy. The enemy, or group of enemies, is distinguished as representatives of various foreign peoples by dress and hair (Hornung 1995:1727–8).

Traditional representation of an Egypt against and in control of foreign lands and peoples does not disappear in the New Kingdom, and in certain ways gains greater emphasis in royal identity, as seen in the explicit representation on numerous temple walls of battle scenes, capture of foreign cities and subjugation of foreign populations. Royal action and success are vital to the king's legitimation, an important component of Egyptian society (Baines 1995:6–8). This prominent display, however, coexists with new forms of depiction and expression of the foreign, suggesting a changing and more complex relationship. There are striking differences in the roles and identities selected and emphasized by the various rulers.[2] By looking at the unique instances that emerge across time rather than the patterns seen in multiple or widespread use of standard representations used by a particular ruler, it may be possible to see the development of a 'global' community, transcending national boundaries and going beyond royal alliances.

This paper proposes that the analysis of the representation of the foreign 'other' in the construction of identity, focusing on monumental display and changes in expressed relationships, provide an avenue for exploring the 'global' nature of New Kingdom Egypt.

For this purpose, a few examples from each of eight rulers are considered in terms of their innovative representation of the foreigner or incorporation of foreign elements. These rulers—Hatshepsut, Thutmose III, Amenhotep II, Thutmose IV, Amenhotep III, Akhenaten, Ramesses II and Ramesses III—have been extensively studied, and this paper does not attempt to comprehensively review the building programs, policies or literary achievements during their reigns.[3] Rather, the intention is to examine the utilization of the 'foreign' in the construction of *legitimizing identity*, and perhaps alternative forms of *resistance identity*, as Castells defines these (Castells 1997:6–12), during a time in which Egypt was developing new relationships of power with foreign rulers. Parallel but different changes in the representation of foreigners and foreign lands among non-royal elite during this period are also discussed.

Before this consideration of construction of identity, however, I will briefly discuss changes in the relationships of production in New Kingdom Egypt. The New Kingdom economy is far different from the capitalist mode of production that is the focus of Castells' study, but the changes in the nature of Egypt's economic structure during this time period may have had significant impact on social change. Egypt had certain key features of a redistribution economy in which the institutions of government played a central role. The transactional mode was the barter of goods. Although there was no coinage, equivalence values expressed in weights of copper and bronze were used (Janssen 1975:127–85).[4] Components of a market economy existed, and may have had more influence than is yet completely understood. The most significant change in the New Kingdom was the rise in the power of the temple, and its interdependence with the king:

> By virtue of its dominance, the Egyptian state was able to direct employment and to transfer the title of land ownership to the temples, and the Pharaohs of the New Kingdom increasingly sought their legitimacy through the gods, which increased the power of the temples...which guaranteed a continuous reciprocal relationship (Warburton 1997:318).

Also during the New Kingdom there was a shift to mass production of goods in several industries. Archaeological evidence suggests that the manufacture of certain types of pottery points to specialist craft organization, producing vast quantities of vessels showing standardized features and uniform fabrics (Bourriau, Nicholson and Rose 2000:139–42). In the production of faience objects, a new, open-faced mold was developed, making it possible to produce large quantities of small items such as amulets and jewelry (Nicholson and Peltenburg 2000:182). New techniques in stone bead manufacture also indicate mass production (Stocks 1989:526–31).

In agriculture, the introduction of the shaduf marked an important technological innovation in irrigation practices. The shaduf was a simple device for transporting water from a river or canal up to a higher level of ground. At one end of a pole was an open vessel which could be lowered into the water, and at the other end, a weight that served as a counterbalance to lift up the water-filled vessel. It is first attested in 18th-Dynasty tomb scenes.[5] Its major use was in the irrigation of vineyards and gardens rather than fields of grain (Eyre 1994:63–4 and 1995:182–3; Butzer 1976:44–7). It allowed for the cultivation of land not suitable for farming and resulted in the expansion of the Egyptian wine industry, not only for local use but for export and trade (Murray 2000a:512, 2000b:595). Increased wine production, in turn, called for specialized pottery production, especially in the use of marl fabrics that were particularly suited for the transport and storage of wine (McGovern 1997: 69–108; Bourriau and Nicholson 1992:29–91).

One of the results of international trade alliances was the importation of glass, usually dated to the reign of Thutmose III and attributed to his political relationship with the Mittani kingdom. Glass used in the jewelry and grave goods in the Egyptian tomb of three Mittani princesses, who may have been sent for the purpose of diplomatic marriage, suggests both the date and source of this material's substantial entry into Egypt, although there may be some earlier examples (Lilyquist and Brill 1993:5–12). Glass vessels appear both in the archeological record and in depictions in Theban tombs in the 18th Dynasty (Shortland 2000:159–61). Glass working reached new heights in the production of decorative arts in the reigns of Amenhotep III, which continued under Akhenaton (Kozloff and Bryan 1992).

Another import in New Kingdom Egypt was the chariot, which came into use in Egypt just prior to the 18th Dynasty during the Hyksos wars (Schulman 1979:105–13). While not a technological advance in the traditional sense, it is a foreign technology with enormous impact on Egyptian elite identity. It becomes an integral component of royal iconography during the New Kingdom, and enters many spheres of expression in depiction and literature. The significance of this, and the ways in which the chariot illustrates how the foreign 'other' becomes part of the 'self' in Egypt, will be considered further in the discussions that follow.

Egyptian Identity and 'Global Connectivity'

Castells' investigation into processes of identity construction and social change recognizes the necessity of grounding the analysis in a specific social context. His study focuses on societies at the end of the 20th century, using data from numerous sources to examine global economic dynamics, the use of information technology, and selected social movements. His analysis of the rise of the network society concludes that new forms of social change result from the 'systemic disjunction between the local and the global for most individuals and social groups'. (Castells 1997:10–11)

In any attempt to analyze the processes in ancient Egypt with respect to local and 'global' interaction, a distinct constraint is that the majority of evidence available was generated by the literate and privileged elite, much of it designed for mortuary and religious contexts. This body of evidence is further distorted by the selective character of what there is left to study, due to ancient alterations and reuse, and the accident of preservation. These contextual considerations are integral to interpretive approaches to the material. That said, this elite material provides important access to a stratum of society that was both involved and invested in the power structure and policies of the Egyptian state. This is useful for studying social processes using Castells' framework, since, as he observes:

> who constructs collective identity, and for what, largely determines the symbolic content of this identity, and its meaning for those identifying with it or placing themselves outside of it...the social construction of identity always takes place in a context marked by power relationships... (Castells 1997:7).

Tombs provide one such context, and are a primary source of data, especially for personal self-presentation. The presence of the foreigner in non-royal constructions will be discussed after consideration of royal representation. Royal individuals, as legitimized rulers with control of key resources, had access to another important canvas for identity construction on a monumental scale: the temple. In ancient Egyptian society, temples played a crucial role in social structure and societal identity. As 'guarantors and participants' of the civilization, temples provided venues for ritual devotion and social memory, they 'enhance reality, enacting, celebrating and enriching an ideal order' (Baines 1997:217–18).

The monuments of Thebes played an important role in the construction of legitimizing identity and manifest power in the New Kingdom. Thebes was a political and religious center, and the temple complexes at Karnak and Luxor were major sites for royal dedication and monumental building. Military victories were attributed to the support of Amun, and vast quantities of goods from the spoils of war were donated to the cult. The royal mortuary temples on the other side of the Nile in Western Thebes were another forum for display. Public festivals and processionals linked these sites and provided a forum for Egyptian society's involvement.

As Baines says, 'a distinctive development of the New Kingdom was the integration of temples into cosmically elaborated cities, inscribing a meaning that their structure and decoration had always had into the environment on a much grander and more socially inclusive scale' (1997:226).

Two rulers of the mid-18th Dynasty were crucial to the transformation of the sacred landscape of Thebes, and each of them incorporated their activities in foreign lands into royal display as an important element in legitimizing their position. The death of Thutmose II (c. 1480 BC) left these two individuals in positions of potential power. One was Thutmose III, the king's son—though by a minor wife—but still a logical heir to the throne. The other was the widowed queen and principal wife Hatshepsut, who as half-sister to Thutmose II was also the royal daughter of the previous king, Thutmose I.

It was not unusual in Egyptian history for a regent to serve as ruler while a royal heir reached an appropriate age, and there is ample evidence to suggest that co-regencies had existed at numerous times in Egypt's past, providing a transition period for the transfer of power. What evolved instead was a power dynamic that is still not fully understood, and unparalleled in recorded Egyptian history. Thutmose III became king, but by Year 7 of his reign, Hatshepsut proclaimed herself 'king', as well, and remained as such until at least Year 22.[6]

There had been relatively few women who had ruled as kings in Egypt's past, but she would not have been the first,[7] and royal women in the 17th and early 18th Dynasties had wielded considerable power. Her approach to legitimization, however, took her into unprecedented territory. In monumental statues and building projects, Hatshepsut chose to be depicted as a male king, complete with ceremonial beard and the king's crowns or *nemes* headcloth. In a series of scenes narrating her birth, in her temple at Deir el Bahari in Western Thebes, she is shown as a young male child—the offspring of her royal mother and the god Amun (Naville 1894, vol. II: Pls. xlvii–lv). The claim to power through divine birth was reinforced by other narrations to show that she was the chosen heir of her father, Thutmose I. In contrast to her royal male image, parts of her royal titulary utilized feminine endings and emphasized alignment with female deities (Robins 1999:103–12).Thus she utilized male and female representations of power in her construction of identity.

She also used the foreign world in a new way. In one section of the temple at Deir el Barahi she represented her divine origins, and in another she shows her devotion to the god through an expedition to Punt, the 'God's Land'. Representations of foreign lands in temple reliefs were generally confined to showing foreign fortresses under seige. The reliefs showing the expedition to Punt are replete with details: huts built on stilts, foreign types of trees, the distinctly foreign king and queen of Punt. The sequence clearly represents a trade expedition. The ships are shown departing Egypt and arriving in Punt. Gifts are presented to the rulers of Punt, and they offer goods in return. When the ships return, live incense trees are unloaded to be planted in the temple garden, to delight the god.

> he put before me to establish Punt in his house, digging up fruit (?) trees in the divine land for the two sides of his dwelling in his garden...the place of his heart. What he loves, he takes hold of it. I brought to him Punt, in his garden, as he put it before me (Naville III: pl. LXXXVI).

Significantly, after a scene in which Hatshepsut presents the gifts to Amun there is another in which the success of the expedition is related to the god *and* the court of officials who form the Egyptian elite. In her legitimizing identity she gains approval of the god, and thus her right to rule, which is then confirmed by those who hold political power.

The 'peaceful' expedition for purposes of trade contrasts the military exploits and battle scenes that are associated with other New Kingdom rulers. Early interpretations speculated that Hatshepsut was not involved in military activity, with some suggesting such action would have been precluded by her gender, but current evidence seems to point the other way, that the foreign policies reinforced by military action were part of her rule (Redford 1967:57–64). The apparent absence of traditional battle scenes at Deir el Bahari might be an accident of preservation rather than their actual absence, since portions of the temple are quite damaged.[8]

Many years later, when it appears that Thutmose III came into sole power, he undertook major projects in the temple complex at Karnak, not only through initiating new buildings but reorganizing and expanding existing temple structures, changing the face of the temple complex. (Björkman 1971:73–93). His military campaigns reinforced his role as a mighty king subduing foreign forces, royal service on behalf of the god. His building in Karnak includes two constructions that present his interaction with the foreign in new ways.

The first is a lengthy inscription on several walls which describes his battles, beginning in Year 22, and details the spoils of war that he has brought back for Amun. The king is prominently figured with obelisks and numerous cult objects and precious gifts, including foreign items of prestige, which he is offering to a seated image of the god Amun. Beneath this depiction begins a lengthy inscription whose purpose is explicit:

> His majesty commanded to record [the victories his father Amun had given him] by an inscription in the temple which his majesty had made for [his father Amun so as to record] each campaign, together with the booty which [his majesty] has brought [from it, and the tribute of every foreign land] that his father Re had given him (Lichtheim 1976:30).

The tradition of royal annals is an ancient one in Egypt, but both the location and the extensive use of descriptive narrative mark this as an unusual innovation. There is no other instance of texts of this genre being monumentally displayed in such sacred space, which is normally devoted to religious themes. By placing these texts near the sacred bark shrine of the god, Thutmose III may be evoking a direct connection between royal and cult action. It is from this shrine that the image of the god is carried forth for processional display, and it is implicitly through the king's devotion and donations that this ritual act can be performed (Baines 2003).

Another construction at Karnak relating to the king's foreign campaigns is a 'botanical garden' dedicated to Amun. This 'garden' is a small room within the sanctuary of Thutmose III's newly erected Festival Hall, which is itself a structure that departs from traditional forms (Golvin and Goyon 1987:44–7). Its placement within an inner sanctuary, separate from the rest of the temple and thus with highly restricted access, makes it quite different from the king's annals.

The inscriptions by the entrance of the room are dated to Year 25 and announce the king's return from Retenu (the lands to the north) on behalf of Amun, who has ordained it. Inside the room there are no inscriptions, only the representation of hundreds of plants and dozens of birds and animals. Some can be identified as originating in other countries, some are indigenous to Egypt, and many are 'extraordinary' in nature, animals with multiple tails or horns or from the realm of imagination rather than the earthly world. An interpretation of its significance that incorporates the Egyptian attraction to the exotic and the 'monstrous' suggests that this room represents Thutmose

III's expansion of the boundaries of Egypt beyond the lands themselves, an integration of the Egyptian world with the foreign and cosmic unknown (Beaux 1990:315–17).

The Great Sphinx on the Giza plateau is the site of relevant monuments of the next two kings following Thutmose III. The stelae placed here—one by Amenhotep II and the other by his successor, Thutmose IV—incorporate aspects of foreign influence in juxtaposition to their own ancient national past. At the time these kings ruled, the pyramids rising from the Giza plateau were almost 1000 years old, and the Great Sphinx was considered a deity in its own right. The legitimizing character of these stelae drew from conventional Egyptian kingly values: fitness for rule and connection with the ancient past (Baines 1995:24–5). The manner in which they do so, however, are innovations in royal display.

The text of the Amenhotep II stela features the traditional motif of Egyptian dominion over foreigners at the bequest of the god Amun. Both the ancient aspect of the god's power and the legitimizing special relationship between king and god are first emphasized:

> ...Gathered are the crowns of Atum,
> Handed over to his image,
> As ordained by the maker of gods,
> [Amun], the most ancient, who crowned him.
> He commanded him to conquer all lands without fail,
> The Son of Re, Amenhotep, Divine Ruler of On,
> Re's heir, [Amun's son], shining seed...

Resulting in the king's ultimate victory:

> ...He has gathered them all into his fist,
> His mace has crashed upon their heads,
> As [Amen]-Re-Atum, Lord of Gods, has decreed,
> He seized the lands in triumph once and for all.
>
> (Lichtheim 1976:40–1)

The narrative that follows relates a story from the king's youth, presenting him as a son worthy of becoming king, with strength and skill in the soldierly sports of chariotry and archery, and a special affinity with horses (Der Manuelian 1987:181–213). It is through the horse motif that a different relationship to the foreign is introduced:

> Then the king's son was told to look after some horses of the king's stable. He did what he was told, and Reshef and Astarte rejoiced over him as he did all that his heart desired.
>
> (Lichtheim 1976:42)

What is significant here is that royal action results in divine favor from two foreign gods, Reshef and Astarte, both of whom were divinities imported from Syria-Palestine. This stela may be the earliest mention of them in Egyptian monuments, and there is much other evidence that cults to these gods, in addition to the foreign deities Anat and Qadeshet, were active in New Kingdom Egypt. Of these, only the goddess Anat seems to have been incorporated into Egyptian religious belief before the New Kingdom.

A monumental stela erected at the same site by Amenhotep II's successor, Thutmose IV, was prominently placed between the paws of the Great Sphinx. There are thematic similarities with the stela of his father, Amenhotep, especially with regard to the location and the king's sporting activity. This stela, however, narrates a tale showing a relationship between king and god that is a mutual exchange of action and legitimation. As Thutmose IV rested in the shadow of the Sphinx, he had a dream in which the Sphinx spoke to him, promising future greatness and requesting help to clear away the sands that buried the monument:

> ...I shall give to you the kingship...good provisions will be for you from within the Two Lands, and the great produce of every foreign country, and a lifetime of time great in years. My face belongs to you, my heart belongs to you, and you belong to me. [Behold, my condition is like one in illness], all [my limbs being ruined].The sand of the desert, upon which I used to be, faces me (aggressively); and it is in order to cause that you do what is in my heart that I have waited.
>
> (Bryan 1991: 144–6)

The text of the stela uses traditional themes of divine favor in return for royal action, but it presents them within the context of a dream, something new in Egyptian literary expression. The royal message dream is a literary device known earlier in Mesopotamian literature, but its appearance in Egyptian inscription dates to the New Kingdom. The earliest such dream noted in Egyptian sources is found on a slightly earlier stela of Amenhotep II, and there it is a brief mention of the god Amun's appearance in the night between two days of battle, its purpose perhaps to emphasize the god's protection and the king's special relationship with the deity. The dream related on the Thutmose IV stela is unparalleled in known Egyptian sources, and it may have served several purposes, depending upon the intended focus: legitimation of the king's rule, or the deed of the king itself, which would place it within the *königsnovelle* genre of Egyptian literature (Szpakowska 2000:77–93; Loprieno 1996:286–8). On another level, the stela's use of the dream motif may point to deliberate intellectual adaptation of foreign elite culture. Was this another impact of extended and increased social contact in the international sphere?

The reign of the next king, Amenhotep III, is the one most commonly associated with foreign diplomacy because of information from the 'Amarna letters', a partial archive of correspondence in the form of cuneiform tablets recovered from his son's royal city of Amarna.

The aspect of Amenhotep III that I consider here is literally a very small component of the identity construction of a ruler with extensive building projects throughout Egypt and Nubia. In Thebes he initiated numerous building works, rebuilding the Luxor temple on a larger scale, expanding the Karnak complex, and building a massive mortuary temple with a pylon gateway flanked by the two statues now known as the Colossi of Memnon (Johnson 1998:64–80).

On a much smaller scale than his building works, he initiated a new form of historical record, issuing five series of 'commemorative' scarabs, much larger than scarabs that were common in the New Kingdom. These new scarabs recorded specific events or matters of importance in his reign; a number of them have been found in Syria-Palestine and one in Nubia, in addition to those that probably come from Egyptian sites. The events may have been associated with celebrations, and both the form and content of the scarabs suggest that they may have been produced as royal gifts (Baines 2003).

The so-called 'marriage' scarab is the only undated series, and it does not record an event, but instead lists the king's names and titles along with the queen's name and primary title of 'Great Royal Consort' along with her parentage. Its purpose is unclear, but if it was intended to mark the union of Amenhotep III and Tiye it would not necessarily have had any other information provided, since royal marriages were not recorded and dated events in Egyptian inscriptions. The four dated scarab series record various different types of events: a lion hunt, which has the most numerous examples known (123), a wild-boar hunt, the construction of a lake, and, of most interest for the current discussion, the arrival of a foreign princess into Egypt.

There are six scarabs that record Amenhotep III's reception, in Year 10 of his reign, of the Mittanian Princess Gilukhepa, daughter of the 'Prince of Naharina, Shutarna'. It is assumed that these scarabs recognize a diplomatic alliance forged between Mittani and Egypt, an arrangement usually referred to as a 'diplomatic marriage', even though the scarabs do not give Gilukhepa the title of a queen. That status is reserved for Amenhotep III's Egyptian wife, the 'Great Royal Consort Tiyi', whose name and title are written on the scarab directly after the king's. Gilukhepa is referred to as a 'marvel'[9] and the only other information beyond that, and her name, is that her entourage totaled 317 women (Blankenberg-Van Delden 1969:3–18, 128–33, pl. XXIX; and Baines 2003).

The absence of an Egyptian royal title for Gilukhepa may confirm Egypt's approach to diplomatic marriages, an aspect of foreign policy in which Egyptian kings participated, but not in the form of equal exchange. The Amarna letters record both the complaints of foreign allies and Egypt's reply that it did not send its daughters to other countries (Liverani 2001:189–95).

However, the recording of Gilukhepa's arrival on these commemorative scarabs indicates that this was an event of importance to the king, and, if these were indeed royal gifts, also of importance to the intended recipient. The shape and format of the scarabs may have been inspired by a combination of Egyptian tradition and foreign influence. The textual form of the inscription resembles that of Egyptian annals, and their physical design might also be based on bone and wooden tags in royal contexts from a much earlier time in Egypt's history (Baines 2003). An alternative explanation of their physical form, I propose, is that they may have been meant to evoke the cuneiform tablets that were used for foreign correspondence. They are of a similar size, and though oval instead of rectangular, their shapes are roughly the same. The modeling of the scarab body on one side, with text inscribed on the other, gives a uniquely Egyptian flavor to the objects, emphasizing their Egyptian origin.

Before considering the foreign 'other' in the reign of Amenhotep III's son and successor, whose religious 'revolution' altered Egypt's expressions of self and the world, I will now consider the representation of foreigners in elite private tombs of the 18th Dynasty.

Foreigners in Non-royal Tombs

Representations of foreigners in Egyptian tombs are seen occasionally in tombs from earlier time periods, most notably the 12th Dynasty Middle Kingdom tomb of Khnumhotep II at Beni Hasan,[10] but they do not become a common feature until the mid-18th Dynasty.

Depictions of foreigners in the New Kingdom occur in many tombs of the elite from various segments of Egyptian society, particularly during the reigns of Hatshepsut, Thutmose III and Amenhotep II. Some tomb owners are government administrators who had direct responsibilities in relation to receiving the products (*inw*) of foreigners, such as Rekhmire, a vizier under the reign of Thutmose III. Others held positions in the administration of the cult of Amun or were members of the military, and there was a considerable range in the placement and content of the depictions.[11]

The most commonly used depiction showed a procession of foreigners—some identified by name as individuals and known from other contexts—carrying distinctly foreign objects or goods and dressed in recognizably foreign fashion. The level of detail suggests accuracy in depiction, but many of the representations were actually hybridized portraits, combining elements of different foreign peoples, and sometimes even Egyptian components, into a single figure or object, or showing objects from one culture carried by another for the sake of the artistic composition (Wachsman 1987:4–25).

These scenes of foreigners are generally considered to represent the tomb owner as an agent of the king, a logical interpretation since the tomb owner's self-presentation in 18th-Dynasty tombs often emphasized his place in society and relationship with the king. I would suggest, though, that the range of content and frequency of appearance in such depictions may also signify a greater awareness of foreign existence, and, in some cases, reflect the personal experience of individuals with foreign peoples and lands.

Some of the earliest scenes of foreigners in Theban tombs, which date to the reigns of Hatshepsut and Thutmose III, do not include the king sitting in a kiosk, an element that becomes standard in later examples. The dating of such tombs is not precise enough to be able to determine whether the king's presence was consistently depicted once this element was introduced, or whether there were other factors influencing the presence of the king.

The tomb of Puyemre (TT 39) raises some interesting questions in this regard. The scenes of foreigners include Syrians, Aegeans and Nubians bringing goods, and piles of products from Punt.[12] There are also Egyptians bringing goods from the Oases, and it is the Egyptian men who are shown prostrate and crawling on their bellies, while the Syrians are depicted walking upright, with only one bending slightly forward in a deferential pose. Does this indicate a differential treatment in the depiction of foreign elite vis-à-vis the oasis men? Could it suggest that from the perspective of an Egyptian who was a member of an elite priesthood, elite foreigners had more status than Egyptians of a lower administrative level?

Puyemre was a Second Priest of Amun, and it is in this capacity that he is shown receiving and registering foreign goods for the temple of Amun (Davies 1922:79–87, Pl. xxxi and xxxii). Is Puyemre's official function as a representative of the temple the reason that the king's figure is not represented? In Warburton's study (1997) of economic relationships, he concludes that the temple of Amun received foreign *inw* (gifts or products) directly and separately from the *inw* delivered to the king. Do the scenes in Puyemre's tomb represent direct contact between this representative of the temple and foreigners? What was the distribution process for the receipt of materials from foreign lands, and what part did Egyptian officials play in it? An accompanying text indicates that the goods were designated for the temple by the king, but royal action is not emphasized, nor is the king specifically named. It is therefore notable that in these scenes with foreigners, the figure of Puyemre in each row has been erased and in its place is a standard bearing the cartouche of Thutmose III. While Davies suggests that this was done to assert Thutmose III's power over Hatshepsut's (who may be the unnamed king cited in the text; Davies 1922:20–3), another explanation is that the king's role in providing for the temple of Amun is to be explicitly understood, even if the king himself is not present.

Trade missions and military campaigns took many Egyptians into foreign lands, and these experiences are related in numerous inscriptions. The depiction of foreign landscapes is much more rare, especially in private tombs. In the tomb of Amenmose (TT 42), a procession of foreigners bearing tribute or products is set against the backdrop of a forest of tall trees, with a Syrian fortress at one end of the scene (Davies 1933a: Pl. 36). On the adjoining wall, another line of foreigners is depicted before the king. Amenmose, as a captain of troops under Thutmose III, may well have seen such forests during a foreign campaign.

In the tomb of Senneferi (TT 99), the only other known tomb in which a Syrian structure is similarly depicted, the tomb owner's travels are explicitly narrated. Senneferi journeys to Lebannon to obtain wood at the request of the king. Before cutting the wood, he visits the shrine of the local deity and makes an offering to her, and she grants her permission (Strudwick 1999: walls 4 and 5; Sethe 1906:356–63). This relationship with a foreign goddess in foreign territory suggests that the worship of foreign deities in Egypt may have been influenced by similar acts of devotion on foreign soil, and may even have originated there.

A direct and personal relationship between an Egyptian and a Syrian is suggested by the tomb of Nebamun (TT17). In an offering scene, a well-dressed Syrian man is seated in front of an offering table opposite the tomb owner with a row of other Syrians behind him, some bringing offerings (Säve-Söderberg 1957: Pl. XXII). This space is normally where relatives of the tomb owner would appear and the fact that it is instead occupied by foreigners is quite unusual.

The presence of Syrians in Egypt as merchants is suggested by another Theban tomb, that of Kenamun (TT 162). One scene shows vessels coming to port and Syrians engaging in trade for various products in a port town (Davies and Faulkner 1947:40-6).

The chariot's significance as a prestige item is suggested by many scenes as well as inscriptions that list chariots and horses among items of tribute and spoils of war. Another feature of non-royal tombs in the mid-18th Dynasty is scenes of workshops for chariot manufacture. These scenes show various components of chariot-making, suggesting that Egyptian workshops took on the task of making what was originally a foreign import. But an underlying relationship of dependence on foreign trade is implicit in these scenes. The types of wood needed for chariot manufacture—especially birch and willow—were not indigenous to Egypt, and had to be brought in via trade with several different foreign regions (Hoffmeier 1999:193–5).

The chariot was thus both an item of prestige in Egypt, which would become a symbol of royal power, and an object that could not be produced without foreign trade. Egyptian construction of elite identity could not be created without interaction with the foreign.

Two tombs later in the 18th Dynasty that date to the short reign of Tutankhamun illustrate how the construction of identity varies depending upon context, and suggests an interconnection between elite foreigners and Egyptians. In the Theban tomb of Huy, viceroy of Nubia, there is a scene of foreigners bearing gifts that resembles earlier 18th Dynasty tribute scenes. The scene includes a representation of Hekanefer, the Chief of Miam, depicted with the characteristics and dress of a Nubian, followed by a Nubian princess in a wagon-chariot. The only other scenes in Egyptian tombs showing a woman in a chariot are those of Queen Nefertiti in Amarna, so both the presence of the princess and her depiction in a chariot indicate the prestige of these foreigners in the tomb of Huy. A close relationship between Huy, a high-ranking Egyptian, and Hekanefer, a member of the Nubian elite, is seen by the design and decoration of Hekanefer's tomb at the Nubian site of Toshka. His tomb is modeled after Huy's, but in contrast to his depiction in the Theban tomb, Hekanefer is shown as an Egyptian in his tomb in Toshka (Davies 1926; Simpson 1963).

The 'Revolution' of Akhenaten

The processes of identity construction for the five rulers considered above are within the frame of legitimizing identity in a civil society. New Kingdom Egypt certainly experienced internal struggles for power, but that in itself does not mandate social change. The question was *who* would be king, not whether there should be a king. The longevity of ancient Egyptian civilization may well be largely due to the enduring character of its kingship, which was maintained by a social structure with enough flexibility to resolve power conflicts within existing power relationships.[13]

The one major departure from the succession of New Kingdom kings rising to power with legitimization by the divine—represented powerfully during this time period as the god Amun—is the king who came to be known as Akhenaten. His religious 'revolution' was brief, violent in its rise and eradicated with equal violence after its fall, but it had a lasting effect on Egyptian society in numerous ways. His religious 'revolution' has core elements that are strikingly similar to Castell's understanding of *resistance identities*, and it is from this perspective that I will consider the 'foreign' presence in Akhenaten's construction of identity.

Whether the origins and intentions of his religious movement were in reaction to global expansion is difficult to assess, but he does articulate a new concept of world order that is distinctly different from kings before and after his rule.[14] There were, of course, many forces at work in the development of the solar religion of Atenism and Akhenaten's use of power, and it is not my intention to oversimplify a dynamic that has been the source of extensive scholarship and diverse opinion.[15] My focus here is to consider whether Akhenaten's religion and his new royal city of Amarna represent the social construction of a 'community of believers' (Castells 1997:65) that parallels how social movements of resistance create identity through religious fundamentalism in today's global society. This type of identity-building, Castells suggests, is an expression of '*the exclusion of the excluders by the excluded*', a defensive identity that 'leads to the formation of *communes*, or *communities*' (Castells 1997:9).

To begin with, I will consider the emergence of Akhenaten's exclusionist policies within Egyptian society, which are in glaring contrast to his religious conceptualization of a world order that embraces all peoples in all lands.

Akhenaten was initially known as Amenhotep, like his father before him, Amenhotep III. The name Amenhotep, which translates as 'Amun is pleased', affirms the connection and alignment with the god Amun, so it signals a significant shift when the ruler whom we would consider Amenhotep IV changed his name to 'Akhenaten', which means 'one who is effective for Aten'. The rejection of the god Amun was demonstrated in very visible changes of increasing proportion.

In his early years of power, his monumental building in the temple of Karnak included constructions both to the god Amun and to the Aten, a solar concept of god that already existed in Egyptian religious thought and which was represented as a sundisk instead of a human figure. At some point, though, comfortable co-existence ceased, and monuments using traditional motifs—such as the king smiting a group of foreigners—were left unfinished (Murnane 1999:303–16). Did the king abandon dedications to Amun in favor of the Aten, who he was beginning to envision as *the* one and only god, above Amun? Could the priesthood have forbidden further building to the Aten within the temple of Amun, or did the king simply decide to devote all resources to the new god, whose worship required an entirely new type of temple structure?

On open land to the east of the Karnak complex he built a temple in a new form: a large open court, 600 m by 210 m, surrounded by a wall that may have been as high as 9 m, decorated with scenes that differed in content and style from any previous temple. This was probably the largest of at least four structures dedicated to the Aten, and the new construction techniques used suggest that it was built rapidly and involved a vastly different use of resources and labor. The perimeter wall was built of *talat* blocks, sandstone quarried in block sizes of a royal cubit (52 × 26 × 24 cm), a standardization of stone components of small scale, easy to carry, which facilitated rapid construction (Redford 1999:50–9). The form of the temple was dramatically different and incorporated new approaches to ritual action, but the purpose of this temple was fundamentally traditional: the sed-festival, a ritual re-enactment of the coronation of the king. The radicalization of religious expression was still contained within the physical and cultural frame of the Theban power structures.

In the steps that came next, these relationships of power were completely disrupted. The king forbid the worship of Amun, closed temples and seized temple resources. The name and image of Amun were systematically eradicated from public structures, and tombs were opened and similarly defaced, including whenever the name appeared on small objects and burial goods.[16] The king left Thebes to build a new royal city at Amarna, dedicated to the Aten, and thousands followed him.[17] All of these actions represent the substantive break that typifies social movements of resistance: 'cultural communes organizing new resistance emerge as sources of identity by breaking away from civil societies and state institutions from which they originate' (Castells 1997: 66).

Akhenaten did not renounce his rule of Egypt in this process, so Amarna became the new seat of government. His attention seems to have centered on internal matters rather than foreign issues. The ideal world was reconfigured to one in which Egypt and foreign powers are all underneath a single cosmic force, as expressed in the Great Hymn to the Aten:

> You fill every land with your beauty.
> You are beauteous, great, radiant,
> High over every land;
> Your rays embrace the lands,
> To the limit of all that you made.
> You made the earth as you wished, you alone,
> All peoples, herds and flocks;
> All upon earth that walk on legs,
> All on high that fly on wings
> The lands of Khor and Kush,

The land of Egypt.
You set every man in his place,
You supply their needs;
Everyone has his food.
His lifetime is counted.
Their tongues differ in speech,
Their characters likewise;
Their skins are distinct,
For you distinguished the peoples.

(Lichtheim 1976:98)

The Aten is all-embracing and all-powerful, and Akhenaten's role within the religion places him in a privileged position. His special access and knowledge affirmed an unprecedented relationship, and his power-through-association as 'The Unique one of Re' supported his selective exclusivism in religious and political arenas (Baines 1990:30). This uniqueness is another aspect in which Akenaten's 'revolution' mirrors the religious fundamentalism movements that are a major expression of resistance identity in the modern world, which can be defined as 'the construction of collective identity under the identification of individual behavior and society's institutions to the norms derived from God's law, interpreted by a definite authority that intermediates between God and humanity' (Castells 1997:13).

Ancient Egyptian society prior to and after the Amarna period held beliefs that position the king as an intermediary and representative of divine order, but he was not the only access to the divine, nor the sole 'definite authority'. The individual could interact with the deities and directly receive their favor, and priests were of great importance in maintaining good relations with the divine. Under Akhenaten, those relationships were restricted primarily to himself, though the queen and royal daughters could also be active participants in ritual action.

The depiction of the king in elite tombs graphically illustrates how the identity construction of the king shaped non-royal self-presentation. The king is the overwhelmingly dominant figure, occupying the space of the whole wall, while rows of small figures look on. The tomb owner is only centrally situated in the scene when the king is bestowing rewards upon him, and the figure of the tomb owner is shown at a very reduced scale in relation to the royal presence (Meyers 1985:35–51). A frequently represented scene shows Akhenaten in his chariot, sometimes along with Queen Nefertiti in her own chariot, riding along the processional route as the crowds of devoted followers bow. The chariot here is stripped of its military context. The image of the victorious king in battle, riding in his chariot and trampling foreigners underneath, has been replaced by a king whose power is rooted in devoted service to the Aten through ritual action but not conquest. The rows of people lining the sides of the street often include foreigners, and there is a certain visual equality in depiction: foreigners from different countries and Egyptians from various segments of society are represented on the same scale and in the same poses of deference to the king.

What is difficult to determine from present evidence is whether this inclusive world view of the foreigner that appears in an idealized form in both text and image resulted in a truly different attitude towards 'global' connection. Did the residents of Amarna embrace the idea of a worldwide order under the Aten? And if they did, was it acceptance of a 'global' reality or a reaction against foreign influence and an attempt to reassert Egyptian identity as central and dominant?

There is evidence of military activity early in Akhenaten's rule, including battle scenes of the 'First Hittite War' in the talat at Karnak (Schulman 1988), and soldiers are an important element in the scenes of public processionals. Battle scenes were also represented in illustrated papyri, a theme unknown from earlier papyri, although this may be a result of preservation of material rather than an innovation. An unusual feature of these scenes is that Egyptian troops are wearing foreign helmets (Parkinson and Schofield 1995:125–6; Kendall 1999:160). Scenes of tribute in Year 12 were also elaborately depicted in some non-royal tombs, with the king rather than the tomb owner as the central figure (as in the tomb of Meryra II; see Reeves 1999: Fig. 60), suggesting that goods continued to arrive from certain foreign lands, at least on that occasion. The Amarna letters indicate that Akhenaten did not pay as much attention to maintaining foreign alliances as his predecessors, however, and the Hittites' increased power either went unnoticed or unchecked.

In any case, Akhenaten does not seem to have utilized the image of a military conqueror in his public identity in Amarna. The community as a whole was focused on the adoration of the Aten, its identity defined by religious commitment and geographically centered at this one site. The boundary stelae in the desert around Amarna mark the territory of the new city, emphasizing its locational identity:

> ...I shall make Akhet-Aten[18] for the Aten, my father, in this place. I shall not make Akhet-Aten for him south of it, north of it, west of (it) or east of it. I shall not go past the southern stela of Akhet-Aten toward the south, nor shall I go past the northern stela of Akhet-Aten downstream, in order to make Akhet-Aten for him there... (Lacovara 1999:62).

In modern scholarship, the reign of Akhenaten is seen as a demarcation of profound social change, its impact lingering and incorporated into numerous aspects of the society even though the city of Amarna was abandoned, Atenist influence systematically destroyed, and the cult, image and name of Amun restored.

In the succession of rulers after Akhenaten, the military elite proved to have increasing influence, the young and short-lived king Tutankhamun being followed by the Commander of the Chariotry, Ay, and then the Great General of the Army, Horemheb. The 'global' sphere was changing with new powers rising and new threats abroad, and victory was not a guaranteed outcome of any military campaign. Nevertheless, the image of the king as a mighty warrior in his chariot, trampling his foes underfoot in elaborate battle scenes became a standard element in the iconography of power during the reign of the Ramessid rulers who followed. The traditional iconography of the Egyptian king defeating enemies was portrayed against foreign landscapes, showing besieged cities and narrating events in specific battles.

The Battle of Kadesh of Ramesses II would seem, at first glance, to be one such standard depiction. The visual display of the king's dominance is powerfully presented, and the story of this battle is told not only on temple walls of Luxor, Karnak, and the Ramesseum in Thebes, but also in Abydos and Abu Simbel. The king's exploits are narrated in two different versions, one poetic and one in the style of a bulletin. The 'poem' of the Battle of Kadesh also survives on papyri, and this earliest example of a narrative battle poem (Lichtheim 1976:59) is another literary innovation of the New Kingdom.

What is remarkable, however, is that this battle was not a straightforward victory and did not pretend to be—in its *written* form. The pictorial representation looks like a victory, but the accompanying narrative told a different story. Ramesses was tricked by Hittite forces, surrounded by the enemy, and the Egyptian army abandoned him. It was only through the divine intervention of Amun that he succeeded:

> Behold, Amun gave me his strength
> When I had no soldiers, no chariotry;
> He caused every distant land to see
> My victory through my strong arm,
> I being alone, no captain behind me,
> No charioteer, no soldier, officer.
> The lands that beheld me will tell my name,
> As far as distant lands unknown.
> Whoever among them escaped from my hand,
> they turned back to see my deeds...
>
> (Lichtheim 1976:68)

A comparison of Hittite sources with Egyptian ones confirm that Kadesh was far from being an Egyptian triumph, but in this masterful interpretation, the foreigners who survived served a distinct purpose: to witness and communicate Ramesses' victory in the 'global' world.

The chariot and its horses also were emphasized in the poem of Kadesh as a symbol of power, a physical manifestation of divine support: 'I crushed a million countries by myself when I was on Victory-in-Thebes, Mut-is-Content, my great horses. It was they whom I found supporting me when I alone fought many lands' (Lichtheim 1976:70).

In Ramessid literature, the chariot was associated with royal and divine power. Two ostraca survive with poems (possibly two versions of the same poem) in which the parts of the chariot are enumerated and described as embodied with powers in battle over foreign troops. It is unclear from the fragments of the texts whether the chariot referred to is that of the king or of the god Amun. This is a new form of poem in Egyptian literature, and may be the result of foreign influence, since it resembles the tigi of Mesopotamian literature (Dawson and Peet 1933:167–74; Schulmann 1986:19–35, 39–49).

In Ramesses III's temple of Medinet Habu in Thebes, another foreign motif is utilized in an unusual manner. The temple complex, which includes an earlier and smaller 18th-Dynasty temple of Hatshepsut and Thutmose III, is surrounded by a fortified mudbrick enclosure wall that is estimated to have been 18 m high and 11–12 m thick at its base. The entrance gate on its eastern side rose another 2 m higher than the wall, an imposing structure through which processionals would have entered; the canal led to quay right in front of it. The gate is modeled after a Syrian *migdol*, the same type of fortress depicted in battle scenes of Seti I and Ramesses II (Hölscher 1951:4–11; Pl. 1–24). The use of a foreign style of architecture as the primary entrance into sacred space is unprecedented in other Egyptian temples, with the possible exception of another building project of Ramesses III at Tell el-Yahudiya in the Delta (Baines and Malek 1980:174). Remains of a fortified wall and a gateway of similar size and dimensions have been found there, though they are not as well preserved as the structures at Medinet Habu.

This appropriation of foreign architecture for use in Egyptian royal identity construction is another indication that the concepts of 'Egyptian' and 'foreign' were changing, or at least that the foreign 'other' was becoming increasingly familiar.

The value of knowing about foreign lands is explored in a Ramessid 'satirical' papyrus (Papyrus Anastasi I; Wente 1990:98–110), a story written as though it were letters between two scribes. One of its topics is a journey up the coast of Palestine, naming towns and describing the geography of the land in great detail. The superior scribe is the one who knows all of these things, the one who has experienced the outside world and knows how to navigate within it:

> 'See, I have described to you the way of a Maher-warrior and traveled through Retenu for you. I have introduced to you foreign countries at a single time with cities in their proper sequence. O that you might look them over at leisure so that you might be found able to describe them and become with us a well-traveled guide' (Wente 1990:109–10.).

This literary composition may have been a teaching text, with a straightforward message that in order to succeed in the world it was necessary to learn about foreign lands and foreign ways. An alternate interpretation suggests it was actually a criticism of elitist officers, couched in the form of imaginary correspondence (Fischer-Elfert 1986:279–90). What it reveals in either case is an intimate knowledge of the world beyond Egypt's borders.

Another new genre of literature that emerges in the Ramessid period glorifies individual cities (Lichtheim 1980:15–23). This literature relates to Castells' concept of *territorial identity*, a reaction 'on the basis of the most immediate sources of self-recognition and autonomous organization: their locality'. He suggests this focus on familiar territory is the paradox of 'increasingly local politics in a world structured by global processes… the production of meaning and identity: my neighborhood, my community, my city' (Castells 1997:60–4).

In ancient Egypt, poems were written about the delights of the home city and also of the longing for them, a direct contrast to the tales of travel and wonders of foreign journeys:

Behold, I do not want to depart from Thebes
save me from what I abhor!
...Bring me to your city, Amen
Because I love it
I love your city, Amen
more than bread and beer, Amen,
more than clothes and oil.
I love the soil of your town
more than the ointment of another land.

(McDowell 1999:157)

In New Kingdom Egypt, the development of 'global connectivity' impacted social experience and sense of identity in numerous ways. The changes in relationships of power and experience fundamentally challenged Egyptian society. Castells' framework for understanding social processes offered new ways of approaching the past and seeing the mechanisms and interactions at work. From this perspective, I have attempted to illustrate the wide range of expressions and variability of reactions as the foreign 'other' became incorporated into Egyptian representation and construction of identity.

Notes

1. For discussion of *inw* in various economic contexts, see Warburton 1997 and Bleiberg 1996; for discussion of it in diplomatic correspondence in the ancient Near East, including other cultures in addition to Egypt, see Liverani 2001:167–88. Galán's 1995 examination of two other Egyptian terms that are relevant to understanding 'international' relations—'victory' and 'border'—suggests similar difficulties due to modern connotations; expanding the 'border' of Egypt may have had much more to do with extension of power and influence than territorial occupation.

2. See Bryan 1998:27–32 for discussion of different emphases of rulers in the 18th Dynasty

3. While the references for this paper are limited due to the highly selective nature of the material under consideration, many of the works cited contain extensive bibliographies providing access to broader issues and larger contexts than those I consider. For text translations cited, I have chosen works most likely to be accessible for the non-Egyptologist; these also provide bibliographic references to original text sources.

4. Bogoslovsky (1987:227–36) suggests that increasing abstraction towards universal equivalents and labor as a commodity may be linked to administrative destabilization in the Ramessid period.

5. Examples showing its use throughout this time period include the tomb of Neferhotep in the 18th Dynasty (TT49, Davies 1933b:70–3) and TT217 in the 19th Dynasty, see Manniche 1989:12).

6. See Dorman 1988:1–45 for discussion of her accession date; 46–65 regarding her proscription date, which he concludes was not earlier than Year 42. Eaton-Krauss 1998:209 favors an earlier proscription date based on a reassessment of a Karnak renewal text.

7. In our current knowledge, the last woman before Hatshepsut to do so was Queen Sobekneferu who had held the throne some 300 years prior to Hatshepsut. Although little is known about her, she did have the five-name titulary of Egyptian kings. Queen Nitocris from the 6th Dynasty may also have held sole rule, but without the royal titles reserved for kings.

8. New evidence on royal monuments in the New Kingdom is continually emerging. Recent excavations at the Abydos monuments of the early 18th-Dynasty ruler Ahmose have uncovered fragments of battle scenes including horses and chariots, providing the earliest attested evidence of this motif in royal context (see Harvey 1988, esp. pp. 314–43 and 362–72).

9. This same term 'marvel' is used to describe exotic goods from Punt.

10. The row of 'Asiatic' foreigners (Newberry 1893: Pl. XXXVIII, 2); Franke (1991:56–8) has suggested that this representation is related to the prestige associated with Khnumhotep's official role in relation to foreign lands.

11. A comprehensive list of Theban tombs with depictions of foreigners can be found in the index of Porter-Moss; Wachsman's study (1987) focuses on 'Aegeans' in these tomb scenes but also pulls together material from numerous sources and provides a useful overall analysis of the depiction of foreigners.

12. These scenes of Punt produce are markedly similar to those in the Punt expedition reliefs at Hatshepsut's temple at Deir el Bahari.

13. Castells' definition of a civil society includes these features.

14. Assmann summarizes the major features of Akhenaten's 'counterreligion' and the theoretical approaches to its origins, including that which suggests it was in response to Egypt's imperialist policies (Assmann 2002:214–28).

15. The origins of the 'new' religion of the Aten, socio-political dynamics and personal motivations of Akhenaten have been discussed by numerous scholars. Recent studies that synthesize important new material on his reign are found in two major publications: *Pharaohs of the Sun* (Freed *et al.* 1999) which accompanied a major museum exhibition, and *Perspectives on the Reign of Amenhotep III* (Akhenaten's father and predecessor), especially Baines'chapter (see Baines 1998); along with extensive work by Assmann, especially *Egyptian Solar Religion* (1995).

16. The erasures were systematic but the evidence of many mistakes suggests that many agents of the king in this effort were not literate (Der Manuelian 1999:285–98).

17. It is unclear from the evidence available what percentage of the population of Thebes moved to Amarna with Akhenaten, or whether Egyptians living in other parts of the country joined the new community.

18. Akhet-Aten, meaning 'Horizon of Aten' was the ancient Egyptian name for Amarna.

References

Assmann, J. (1983) Krieg und Frieden im alten Ägypten: Ramses II und die Schlacht bei Kadesch. *Mannheimer Forum* 1983–84:175–231.

Assmann, J. (1995) *Egyptian Solar Religion in the New Kingdom: Re, Amun and the Crisis of Polytheism*. Trans. Anthony Alcock. London and New York: Kegan Paul International.

Assmann, J. (2002) *The Mind of Egypt: History and Meaning in the Time of the Pharaohs*. New York: Metropolitan Books.

Baines, J. (1990) Restricted knowledge, hierarchy, and decorum: modern perceptions and ancient institutions. *Journal of the American Research Center in Egypt* 27:1–23.

Baines, J. (1995) Kingship, definition of culture, and legitimation. In *Ancient Egyptian Kingship*, edited by D. O'Connor and D. Silverman. Probleme der Ägyptologie, 9. Leiden: E.J. Brill, pp. 3–47.

Baines, J. (1996a) Contextualizing Egyptian representations of society and ethnicity. In *The Study of the Ancient Near East in the Twenty-First Century: The William Foxwell Albright Centennial Conference*, edited by J. Cooper and G. Schwartz. Winona Lake: Eisenbrauns, pp. 339–84.

Baines, J. (1996b) Classicism and modernism in the literature of the New Kingdom. In *Ancient Egyptian literature: History and Forms*, edited by A. Loprieno. Probleme der Ägyptologie, 10. Leiden: E.J. Brill, pp. 157–74.

Baines, J. (1997) Temples as symbols, guarantors, and participants in Egyptian civilization. In *The Temple in Ancient Egypt: New Discoveries and Recent Research*, edited by S. Quirke. London: Published for the Trustees of the British Museum by British Museum, pp. 216–41.

Baines, J. (1998) Dawn of the Armarna Age. In *Amenhotep III: Perspectives on his Reign*, edited by D. O'Connor and E. Cline. Ann Arbor: University of Michigan Press, pp. 271–312.

Baines, J. (2003) On the genre and purpose of the 'large commemorative scarabs' of Amenhotep III. In *Hommages à Fayza Haikal*, edited by N. Grimal, A. Kamel and C. M. Sheikholeslami. Bibliothèque d'Etude 138. Cairo: Institut Français d'Archéologie Orientale, pp. 29–43.

Baines, J. and Malek, J. (1980) *Atlas of Ancient Egypt*. Oxford: Phaidon.

Beaux, N. (1990) *Le Cabinet de Curiosités de Thoutmosis III. Plantes et animaux du 'Jardin botanique' de Karnak*. Orientalia Lovaniensia Analecta 36. Leuven: Departement Oriëntalistiek / Uitgeverij Peeters.

Björkman, G. (1971) *Kings at Karnak: A Study of the Treatment of the Monuments of Royal Predecessors in the Early New Kingdom*. Uppsala Studies in Ancient Mediterranean and Near Eastern Civilizations, 2. Uppsala: Acta Universitatis Upsaliensis Boreas.

Blankenberg-Van Delden, C. (1969) *The Large Commemorative Scarabs of Amenhotep III*. Leiden: E.J. Brill.

Bleiberg, E. (1996) *The Official Gift in Ancient Egypt*. Norman and London: University of Oklahoma Press.

Bogoslovsky, E. (1987) On the process of appearance of money in ancient Egypt. *Altorientalische Forschungen* 14:227–36.

Bourriau, J. D. and Nicholson, P. (1992) Marl clay pottery fabrics of the New Kingdom from Memphis, Saqqara and Amarna. *Journal of Egyptian Archaeology* 78:29–91.

Bourriau, J., Nicholson, P. and Rose, P. (2000) Pottery. In *Ancient Egyptian Materials and Technology*, edited by P. Nicholson and I. Shaw. Cambridge and New York: Cambridge University Press, pp. 177–94.

Bryan, B. (1991) *The Reign of Thutmose IV*. Baltimore: The Johns Hopkins University Press.

Bryan, B. (1998) Antecedents to Amenhotep III. In *Amenhotep III: Perspectives on his Reign*, edited by D. O'Connor and E. Cline. Ann Arbor: University of Michigan Press, pp. 27–62.

Bulter, S. (1998) *Mesopotamian Conceptions of Dreams and Dream Ritual* (15-19). Alter Orient und Altes Testament, Bd 258. Munich: Ugarit-Verlag.

Butzer, K. (1976) *Early Hydraulic Civilization in Egypt: A Study in Cultural Ecology*. Chicago: The University of Chicago Press.

Castells, M. (1996) *The Rise of the Network Society: The Information Age: Economy, Society and Culture* 1. 3 vols. Oxford: Blackwell Publishers.

Castells, M. (1997) *The Power of Identity: The Information Age: Economy, Society and Culture* 2. 3 vols. Oxford: Blackwell.

Castells, M. (1998) *The End of the Millennium: The Information Age: Economy, Society and Culture* 3. 3 vols. Oxford: Blackwell.

Davies, N. (1922–23) The Tomb of Puyemrê at Thebes, v. 1-2. New York: Metropolitan Museum of Art.

Davies, N. (1933a) *The Tombs of Menkheperrasonb, Amenmose, and Another (nos. 86, 112, 42, 226)*, explanatory text by Norman de Garis Davies. Theban Tomb Series, 5. London: Egypt Exploration Society.

Davies, N. (1933b) *The Tomb of Nefer-hotep at Thebes*. Publications of the Metropolitan Museum of Art Expedition; v. 9. New York: Metropolitan Museum.

Davies, N. (1963) *Scenes from Some Theban Tombs (nos. 38, 66, 162, with excerpts from 81)*. Private tombs at Thebes, 4. Oxford: Griffith Institute.

Davies, N. and Faulkner, R. (1947) A Syrian trading venture to Egypt. *Journal of Egyptian Archaeology* 33:40–6.

Davies, N. and Gardiner, A. (1926) *The Tomb of Huy*. Theban Tomb Series, 4. London: Egypt Exploration Society.

Dawson, W. and Peet, T. (1933) The so-called poem on the king's chariot. *Journal of Egyptian Archaeology* 19:167–74.

Der Manuelian, P. (1987) *Studies in the Reign of Amenophis II*. Hildesheimer Ägyptologische Beiträge, 26. Hildesheim: Gerstenberg Verlag.

Der Manuelian, P. (1999) Semi-literacy in Egypt: some erasures from the Amarna Period. In *Gold of Praise: Studies on Ancient Egypt in Honour of Edward F. Wente*, edited by E. Teeter and J. A. Larson. Studies in ancient oriental civilisations, 58. Chicago: Oriental Institute, University of Chicago, pp. 285–98.

Dorman, P. (1988) *The Monuments of Senenmut: Problems in Historical Methodology*. New York: Kegan Paul International.

Eaton-Krauss, T. (1998) Four notes on the early Eighteenth Dynasty. *Journal of Egyptian Archaeology* 84: 205–10.

Eyre, C. J. (1984) The water regime for orchards and plantations in Pharaonic Egypt, *Journal of Egyptian Archaeology* 80:57–80.

Eyre, C. (1995) The agricultural cycle, farming, and water management in the ancient Near East. In *Civilizations of the Ancient Near East* I, edited by J. Sasson. New York: Charles Scribner's Sons, pp. 175–89.

Fischer-Elfert, H. (1986) *Die satirische Streitschrift des Papyrus Anastasi I. Übersetzung und Kommentar*. Ägyptologische Abhandlungen, 44. Wiesbaden: Verlag Otto Harrassowitz.

Franke, D. (1991) The career of Khnumhotep III of Beni Hasan and the so-called 'Decline of the Nomarchs'. In *Middle Kingdom Studies*, edited by S. Quirke. New Malden: SIA Publishing, pp. 51–67.

Freed, R. E., Markowitz, Y. J. and D'Auria, S. H. (eds) (1999) *Pharaohs of the Sun: Akhnaten, Nefertiti, Tutankhamen*. Boston: Museum of Fine Arts, Boston in association with Bullfinch Press/Little Brown.

Galán, J. (1995) *Victory and Border: Terminology Related to Egyptian Imperialism in the XVIIIth Dynasty*. Hildesheimer Ägyptologische Beiträge, 40. Hildesheim: Gerstenberg Verlag.

Golvin, J. and Goyon, J. (1987) *Les bâtisseurs de Karnak*. Paris: Presses du CNRS.

Harvey, S. P. (1998) The Cults of King Ahmose at Abydos. Unpublished PhD dissertation, University of Pennsylvania.

Hoffmeier, J. (1999) Chariots. In *Encyclopedia of the archaeology of ancient Egypt*, edited by K. Bard. London; New York: Routledge.

Hölscher, U. (1934–54) *The Mortuary Temple of Ramses III: Part II. The Excavation of Medinet Habu, v. IV.* Chicago: University of Chicago Press.
Hornung, E. (1995) Ancient Egyptian religious iconography. In *Civilizations of the Ancient Near East* III, edited by J. Sasson. New York: Charles Scribner's Sons, pp. 1711–30.
Janssen, J. (1975) Prolegomena to the study of Egypt's economic history during the New Kingdom. *Studien zur altägyptischen Kultur* 3:127–85.
Johnson, R. (1998) Monuments and monumental art under Amenhotep III: evolution and meaning. In *Amenhotep III: Perspectives on his Reign*, edited by D. O'Connor and E. Cline. Ann Arbor: University of Michigan Press, pp. 63–94.
Kemp, B. (1989) *Ancient Egypt: Anatomy of a Civilization.* London and New York: Routledge.
Kendall, T. (1999) Foreign relations. In *Pharaohs of the Sun: Akhenaten, Nefertiti, Tutankhamen*, edited by R. Freed, Y. Markowitz and S. D'Auria. Boston: Bulfinch Press/Museum of Fine Arts, Boston, pp. 157–61.
Kozloff, A. and Bryan, B. (1992) *Egypt's Dazzling Sun: Amenhotep III and His World.* Cleveland: The Cleveland Museum of Art in cooperation with Indiana University Press.
Lacovara, P. (1999) The city of Amarna. In *Pharaohs of the Sun: Akhenaten, Nefertiti, Tutankhamen*, edited by R. Freed, Y. Markowitz and S. D'Auria. Boston: Bulfinch Press/Museum of Fine Arts, Boston, pp. 61–71.
Lichtheim, M. (1976) *Ancient Egyptian Literature*, vol. 2: *The New Kingdom.* Berkeley: University of California Press.
Lichtheim, M. (1980) The praise of cities in the literature of the Egyptian New Kingdom. In *Panhellenica: Essays in Ancient History and Historiography in Honor of Truesdell S. Brown*, edited by S. Burstein and L. Okin. Lawrence, KS: Coronado Press, pp. 15–23.
Lilyquist, C. and Brill, R. (1993) *Studies in Early Egyptian Glass.* New York: The Metropolitan Museum of Art.
Liverani, M. (1990) *Prestige and Interest: International Relations in the Near East ca. 1600–1100 B.C.* History of the Ancient Near East/Studies I. Padova: Sargon.
Liverani, M. (2001) *International Relations in the Ancient Near East, 1600–1100 B.C.* Basingstoke; New York: Palgrave.
Loprieno, A. (1996) The 'King's Novel'. In *Ancient Egyptian Literature: History and Forms*, edited by M. Liverani. Probleme der Ägyptologie, 10. Leiden: E.J. Brill, pp. 277–95.
Manniche, L. (1988) *Lost Tombs: A Study of Certain Eighteenth Dynasty Monuments in the Theban Necropolis.* London and New York: Kegan Paul International.
McDowell, A. G. (1999) *Village Life in Ancient Egypt: Laundry Lists and Love Songs.* Oxford: Oxford University Press.
McGovern P. (1997) Wine of Egypt's Golden Age: an archaeochemical perspective. *Journal of Egyptian Archaeology* 83:69–108.
Meyers, E. (1985) Component design as a narrative device in Amarna tomb art. In *Pictorial Narrative in Antiquity and the Middle Ages*, edited by H. L. Kesslaer and M. Shreve Simpson. Washington: National Gallery of Art, University Press of New England, pp. 35–51.
Murnane, W. (1999) Observations on pre-Amarna theology during the earliest reign of Amenhotep IV. In *Gold of Praise: Studies on Ancient Egypt in Honor of Edward F. Wente*, edited by E. Teeter and J. Larson. Studies in Ancient Oriental Civilization, 58. Chicago: Oriental Institute of the University of Chicago, pp. 303–16.
Murray, M. (2000a) Cereal production and processing. In *Ancient Egyptian Materials and Technology*, edited by P. Nicholson and I. Shaw. Cambridge; New York: Cambridge University Press, pp. 505–36.
Murray, M. (2000b) Viticulture and wine production. In *Ancient Egyptian Materials and Technology*, edited by P. Nicholson and I. Shaw. Cambridge; New York: Cambridge University Press, pp. 577–608.
Naville, E. (1894) *The Temple of Deir el Bahari*, vol. 2. London: Egypt Exploration Fund.
Newberry, P. (1893) *Beni Hasan, Pt. 2.* London: Egypt Exploration Fund.
Nicholson, P. and Peltenburg, E. (2000) Egyptian faience. In *Ancient Egyptian Materials and Technology*, edited by P. Nicholson and I. Shaw. Cambridge; New York : Cambridge University Press, pp. 177–94.
Nicholson, P. and Henderson, J. (2000) Glass. In *Ancient Egyptian Materials and Technology*, edited by P. Nicholson and I. Shaw. Cambridge; New York: Cambridge University Press, pp. 195–224.
O'Connor, D. (1998) The city and the world: worldview and built forms in the reign of Amenhotep III. In *Amenhotep III: Perspectives on his Reign*, edited by D. O'Connor and E. Cline. Ann Arbor: University of Michigan Press, pp. 125–72.

Parkinson, R. and Schofield, L. (1995) Images of Mycenaeans: a recently acquired painted papyrus from El-Amarna. In *Egypt, the Aegean and the Levant: Interconnections in the Second Millennium BC*, edited by W. Davies and L. Schofield. London: Trustees of the British Museum by British Museum Press, pp. 125–6.

Porter, B. and Moss, R. (1960) *Topographical Bibliography of Ancient Egyptian Hieroglyphic Texts, Reliefs, and Paintings. I. The Theban Necropolis. Part 1. Private Tombs.* 2nd edn. Oxford: Clarendon Press (Oxford University Press).

Ragionieri, R. (2000) The Amarna Age: an international society in the making. In *Amarna Diplomacy: the Beginnings of International Relations*, edited by R. Cohen and R. Westbrook. Baltimore: Johns Hopkins University Press, pp. 42–53.

Redford, D. B. (1967) *History and Chronology of the Eighteenth Dynasty of Egypt: Seven Studies.* Near and Middle East series, 3. Toronto: University of Toronto.

Redford, D. (1999) The beginning of the heresy. In *Pharaohs of the Sun: Akhenaten, Nefertiti, Tutankhamen*, edited by R. Cohen and R. Westbrook. Boston: Bulfinch Press/Museum of Fine Arts, Boston, pp. 50–9.

Reeves, N. 1999. The royal family. In *Pharaohs of the Sun: Akhenaten, Nefertiti, Tutankhamen*, edited by R. Freed, Y. Markowitz and S. D'Auria. Boston: Bulfinch Press/Museum of Fine Arts, Boston, pp. 81–95.

Robins, G. (1999) The names of Hatshepsut as king. *Journal of Egyptian Archaeology* 85:103–12.

Säve-Söderbergh, T. (1957) *Four Eighteenth Dynasty Tombs.* Private tombs at Thebes, v. 1. Oxford: Griffith Institute.

Schulman, A. (1979) Chariots, Chariotry, and Hyksos. *The Journal of the Society of the Study of Egyptian Antiquities* 10:105–53.

Schulman, A. (1986) The so-called poem on the King's Chariot revisited. Part I. *The Journal of the Society of the Study of Egyptian Antiquities* 16: Part I, 19–35; Part II, 39–49.

Schulman, A. (1988) Hittites, helmets and the First Hittite War. In *The Akhenaten Temple Project*, vol. 2: *Rwd-mnw, Foreigners and Inscriptions*, edited by D. Redford. Aegypti texta propositaque, 1. Toronto: The Akhenaten Temple Project, pp. 53–79.

Sethe, K. (1906) Eine ägyptische Expedition nach dem Libanon im 15. Jahrhundert vor Chr. *Sitzungsberichte der Preußischen Akademie der Wissenschaften zu Berlin*:356–63.

Shortland, A. (2000) Depictions of glass vessels in two Theban tombs and their role in the dating of early glass. *Journal of Egyptian Archaeology* 86:159–61.

Simpson, W. (1963) *Heka-Nefer and the Dynastic material from Toshka and Arminna.* Publications of the Pennsylvania-Yale Expedition to Egypt, 1. New Haven and Philadelphia: The Peabody Museum of Natural History of Yale University/The University Museum of the University of Pennsylvania.

Simpson, W. (1982) Egyptian sculpture and two-dimensional representation as propaganda. *Journal of Egyptian Archaeology* 68:266–71.

Stocks, D. (1989) Ancient factory mass-production techniques: indications of large-scale stone bead manufacture during the Egyptian New Kingdom Period. *Antiquity* 63:526–31.

Strudwick, N. (1999) Website for the tomb of Senneferi (TT 99): http: //www.newton.cam.ac.uk/egypt/tt99/ index.html

Szpakowska, K. (2000) The Perception of Dreams and Nightmares in Ancient Egypt: Old Kingdom to Third Intermediate Period. Unpublished PhD Dissertation, University of California, Los Angeles.

Wachsmann, S. (1987) *Aegeans in the Theban Tombs.* Orientalia Lovaniensia Analecta, 20. Leuven: Uitgeverij Peeters.

Warburton, D. (1997) *State and Economy in Ancient Egypt: Fiscal Vocabulary of the New Kingdom.* Fribourg (Switzerland): University Press / Göttingen: Vandenhoeck and Ruprecht.

Wente, E. (1990) *Letters from Ancient Egypt*, edited by E. S. Meltzer. Society of Biblical Literature Writings from the Ancient World, 1. Atlanta, GA: Scholars Press.

Nothing New Under the Sun?

Manuel Castells

The argument put forward by the essays included in this book is a compelling one, and bears considerable theoretical significance: networks are fundamental forms of social organization throughout human history. Therefore, a network theory of society is a critical component of social theory, and it is relevant to all societies. A corollary to this statement: when, in my own research, I limited the validity of my analysis of the social structure that I theorized as network society to our contemporary society, tentatively identified as the Information Age, I was wrong both empirically and theoretically. Empirically: networks seem to have always been at the heart of social structure and social change, as the impressive body of archeological and historical evidence gathered by the scholars in this volume seems to indicate. Networks did not have to wait for microelectronics to be a decisive tool in organizing production, trade, power and communication. Theoretically: a network theory of society is relevant, and indeed fundamental, for general social theory, without being dependent from a given technological paradigm. So, what this volume suggests is the need to decouple network theory and the empirical analysis of social structure and social processes in the Information Age. 'Our' network society would be a specific form of the network society, as a trans-historical form. Thus, globalization is not new: under different forms, it appears to have happened not only in the 19th century of the common era, but thousands of years ago. Furthermore, my insistence in pointing at collective identity as a primary source of meaning to inform social action hardly qualifies as a historical novelty. Therefore, the conflictive interaction between global networks and communal identities is not a specific feature of the Information Age but a critical social dynamic in all forms of human organization throughout history. In the last analysis, *there is nothing new under the sun*. There are only variations on the theme of the human experience. While identifying the modalities and outcomes of this variation is still a worthy intellectual endeavor, the historical commonality of various social forms of existence of humankind provides the material support for a unifying social theory. A theory in which networks, identities, and their relationships would be key elements to anchor our understanding.

I hope I am not oversimplifying the subtle and well documented analyses that, in a diversity of approaches, are collected in this volume under the general editorship of Professor LaBianca. But what I summarized above seems to be the unifying theme of their contributions, and the one that calls for my engagement in the debate. I must say that I do not feel competent to evaluate the data and interpretations they provide. However, the logic, the theory, and the references follow the rules of scholarship, and therefore I will take them at face value. My discussion refers only to the theoretical and epistemological implications of their general argument, and not to the actual analyses of specific societies and historical processes, that I cannot really challenge or endorse. I would just like to say that I learned a great deal from reading this volume, and that my thinking and theory are likely to be influenced and modified by this reading and by the reflections that the reading has induced.

In principle, I could say I have no real disagreement with the argument, because it does not refer to my explicit research project. I did not set out to elaborate a general theory of society. My aim was, and is, to understand the dynamic nucleus of our evolving, contemporary social structure, and the processes of social change related to it. The frame of reference is the historical period that is popularly known as 'the Information Age' (not a theoretical characterization). The Information Age label is linked to the transformation of the dominant technological paradigm, the one based on microelectronics-based information and communication technologies (including computer networks), as well as on genetic engineering and the technologies that are springing from the interaction between the twin scientific/technological revolutions in electronics and biology. The designation of our period as the Information Age is similar to the notion of Industrial Age/Industrial Society that characterized the preceding form of social organization that was based on the industrial technologies related to the energy revolution. In my case, I went beyond the description of a 'postindustrial society' to formulate a grounded theory of an emerging social structure that I theorized as the network society. I built this theory inductively, from my observation of processes of transformation in various areas of the world, taking place in a wide diversity of cultures, institutions, and levels of development. I tried to document the fact that the strategically dominant segments of all societies are built around a globally interdependent set of networks that, together, constitute the network society. I also tried to study the processes of resistance to the domination embedded in the worldwide expansion of these networks. I observed the importance of collective identity, and particularly of resistance identity in these processes of social change. I also noticed the networking form of organization that many of these processes of resistance were adopting, as well as the crisis of the modern nation-state, and of vertical forms of organization, such as large corporations, both private and public, that did not engage into transforming themselves into other organizational forms, theorized as the network enterprise. Thus, the dialectical opposition between the Net and the Self, and the crisis of institutional control and political legitimacy that ensued in the context of globalization, were some of the central ideas that tried to make sense of our world and our lives in this particular historical and technological context. I explicitly said that the question of newness was not relevant to my inquiry. What I was proposing was a synthetic interpretation of our social dynamics, worldwide, on the basis of my observation, and with the help of a conceptual construction that for me, as all theory, was and is strictly instrumental. Theory helps research and understanding or does not, and if so, it is discarded. It is never a goal in itself. Thus, since I could not pretend to even approach the notion of a mega-historical analysis of the evolution of societies in their multiple dimensions, I remained cautiously silent about the potential usefulness of my conceptual toolbox for other historical periods or social/technological contexts. Now, I am told it could also be used for the understanding of other societies and historical trajectories. Maybe. And if it is so, this is good news—we are finding pieces of theoretical frameworks that can be used generally, albeit with the necessary specifications. I would not hesitate in sacrificing the claim to historical originality of this Information Age social structure or of this process of globalization to the far more noble enterprise of contributing to a general social theory based on observation. I am not a cheerleader of the new age, or a futurologist proclaiming the triumph of the human spirit because our toaster can interact with our refrigerator. If in antiquity networks were essential building blocks of human societies, and if connectivity and globalization were some of the key foundations of power and wealth, using sailing technology and animal transportation power, so be it. My archeology and historian colleagues will do their work at their end, other social scientists will unveil the complex networks that characterize our societies, and we'll meet at the construction site of general social theory. This would be an open-minded, easy answer. Too easy in fact, to the point of not being honest. Because I do not believe it. As much as I am profoundly interested in the networking logic that my colleagues have found present in antiquity, I continue to be convinced of the specificity of the networks, and of identity building in the Information Age. Thus, I do think that we can learn from each other and, together, enhance the chances of cumulative, theoretical understanding of all societies and historical periods. But only on the condition of specifying the conditions under which similar forms operate differently in different social and technological contexts. Therefore, to correspond to their effort, I will try to summarize what I consider specific to networks and identity building in our historical context, and why. Only then could the debate be engaged about the relationship between commonality and singularity in the very *longue durée* perspective of studying the human experience.

The Context of the Information Age: The New Technological Paradigm

Networks, as this volume demonstrates, are as old as humankind's history. There were always prevalent forms of solidarity and personal support. But they also seem to have played a critical role as instruments of power and wealth. So, there is nothing new about networks as social forms of human activity. Yet, the key theoretical question is that any form or element of the social structure cannot be understood in itself, but in its relationships to its environment, and to other elements of the structure, in a web of relationships. Very much like in biology, genes can only be understood in relationship to other genes and by knowing the ways and means of these relationships. So, what is fundamentally new about the Information Age is the kind of information and communication technologies that sprung up from the microelectronics revolution that developed from 1947 onwards, to constitute a new technological paradigm in the 1970s.

These technologies enabled networks to deal with size, complexity, and speed in a way that was qualitatively superior to anything experienced in earlier times. For instance, in the 17th century there was already a world economy of sorts, and the Vicerrcinato of Peru, to take one case, was dependent from its connection to the Spanish colonizing metropolis. But the main material expression of this connection was one convoy between Seville and Lima/Callao once a year. Not exactly the same thing as mega financial transactions realized in a matter of seconds in a relentless global flow of interactions that takes place everyday.

But let me organize the argument in a more systematic way by reminding ourselves of the meaning of technological paradigm and by specifying the features of microelectronics-based information and communication technologies. Then I will try to relate these features to the operation of networks in this new technological context (the empirical question of newness of these technologies is beyond challenge, as transistors, integrated circuits microprocessors, electronic computers, digital telecommunications, computer networks, the Internet, and derived technologies are clearly new technological developments, ushering in the digitalization of communication and information processing in a process that seems to be only in its early stages).

As I have argued in my published work, the Information Age is not characterized by the importance of knowledge and information, since this was true as well in any known society. It is characterized by the constitution of informationalism as a dominant technological paradigm. I take the concept of technological paradigm from Kuhn's concept of scientific paradigm as a sign of scientific revolutions. A paradigm is a conceptual pattern that sets the standards for performance. It integrates knowledge into a coherent system of relationships characterized by its synergy, that is by the added value of the system *vis-à-vis* its individual components. A technological paradigm organizes the available range of technologies around a nucleus that enhances the performance of each one of them. Technology is usually understood as the use of scientific knowledge to set procedures for performance in a reproducible form.

Human history is characterized (but not determined) by the succession of major technological paradigms, each one of them subsuming the preceding ones, and enhancing their performance under the parameters of the newer, dominant paradigm, as is the case for industrialism subsumed under informationalism. We know that there is a new, dominant paradigm because of the systemic relationship of a set of discoveries that, together, ensure a superior performance in the generation and accumulation of wealth and power. We know a paradigm is dominant because, when implemented, it erases competing paradigms by elimination, replacing and subsuming them. This does not mean that human history is marked by progress, because superior technologies may be used for destructive purposes. And it does not mean that technology, and technological paradigms, are the driving force of history. Technological determinism has been abandoned by social science some time ago, and there is no need to reopen the debate. Yet, to say that technology does not determine social action and social structure does not mean that it is irrelevant for society. Technology as material culture provides the ways and means through which people live, love, fight, and die.

My proposition is that there is an Information Age because there is a new, dominant paradigm: informationalism. As all technological paradigm, informationalism refers to social organization, and not to institutions. Informationalism provides the basis for the network society, as I conceptualized the social structure of the Information Age. Without informationalism, the network society could not exist. But this social structure is not produced by informationalism but by a broader process of social evolution, and it takes a variety of forms depending on the historical and cultural specificity of each time and space where the network society emerges. What is common to all of them is their rooting in the material culture of informationalism. By informationalism I understand the technological paradigm based on the augmentation of human capacity in information processing and knowledge generation allowed by the twin revolutions in microelectronics and genetic engineering. The information and communication technologies of our time have ushered a new technological paradigm based on three distinctive features of new information and communication technologies:

a. Their self-expanding processing capacity in terms of volume, complexity, and speed,
b. Their recombining ability,
c. Their distributing flexibility.

Let me briefly elaborate on this. First, self-expanding processing capacity. The issue is how much is much more, compared with previous information processing technologies, such as writing, printing or the telegraph? A first answer to this question is empirical: there has been an exponential growth in processing power and communication transmission, coupled with decreasing cost per unit of operation in the last three decades (Mitchell 2003; Mansell 2001). But, in my view, there is something else: the capacity of these microelectronics-based information technologies to self-expand their processing and transmission power because of their ability to immediately insert feedback loops between technological development and the knowledge generated on the basis of the technology. Nanotechnology, bionic materials, wireless digital networks, and self-generated programming capacity through open source software are relentlessly expanding the boundaries of information and communication power. I would also risk the hypothesis that if and when the physical limits of processing and transmission power on the basis of these technologies will be reached, the ways of dealing with these limits will usher in a new technological paradigm, under forms that we cannot imagine today, except in the science fiction scenarios of futurologists.

Secondly, microelectronics-based technologies are characterized by their ability to recombine information in any possible way, as is the case in the hypertext imagined by Nelson and operationalized by Berners-Lee as the World Wide Web. Recombination is a critical source of innovation, particularly if the products of this recombination become themselves supports for further interaction, in a growing spiral of increasingly meaningful information. While the generation of new knowledge requires the application of theory to recombined information, the ability to experiment by recombining information from multiple sources extends the realm of knowledge, as well as the connections that can be made between different scientific fields and domains of application—the source of knowledge innovation in Kuhn's theory of scientific revolutions.

Thirdly, information and communication technologies of our time are characterized by their flexibility in the distribution of processing and transmission power in various contexts and applications. The explosion of networking technologies and their associated software (Internet, TCP/IP, Java, Jini, Wireless Internet and their corresponding protocols, WiFi, and a plethora of new, alternative communication technologies based on decentralized communication networks) are key developments that point to the growing capacity to have processing and communication power anywhere where there is the appropriate technological and human infrastructure (Mitchell 2003).

The characteristics of informationalism as a new technological paradigm shape and affect the conditions under which networks operate, thus specifying networks of the Information Age in reference to their predecessors in history.

Networks Under Informationalism

Under the new technological paradigm networks take on greatly extended capacities. I will not repeat the three technological features presented above that, together, enable networks to increase their operational power. Using this new source of power, networks enhance their capacity in three main ways, each one of which combines the benefits provided by the three technological features.

First of all, networks become able to handle incomparably greater volume of connections, at much greater speed, and manage much greater complexity. Throughout history networks were clearly flexible and adaptive structures. But they had serious difficulties to marshall resources and keep focus on the unity of purpose beyond a certain level of size and complexity. This is why, in spite of the important role that connectivity played in war and trade, ultimately, vertical bureaucracies, armies, states, religious apparatuses, were able to prevail by the accumulation of resources under a central command. Thus, I have the impression (although I may be factually wrong in a number of instances) that while networks of power and wealth were useful devices, they were dependent for their performance on their insertion within large scale, command and control organizations. Current information and communication technologies allow networks to keep their flexibility and their adaptability while still enabling them to perform coordination functions, and control of the execution of the program of the network. Decentralization of execution and centralization of strategic decision-making: this is the winning formula of networks in our world.

Secondly, as the genial geographer Harold Innis proposed many years ago, new communication technologies create new regimes of time and space, increasingly shrinking the planet and minimizing time per unit of operation. An analysis that David Harvey popularized under the notion of time/space compression, although he attributed it to capitalism, thus confusing property social relationships and technical social relationships. The critical matter here is the capacity of new communication technologies to organize processes at a distance in real or chosen time. Thus, physical proximity is no longer the material support for synchrony. Real time interaction frees itself from the constraints of space. And time itself can be programmed to specific purposes inscripted in the network instructions. This new regimes of space and time, based on ubiquity and chosen time for the processes which embody these regimes is what we call globalization. A global economy is not the same as a world economy. A world economy, or a highly internationalized economy, is simply an economy in which some of its processes take place in different areas of the world in an interconnected manner. This is an old phenomenon, as this volume documents. If this is all it is, there is no reason to invent or use a new term, such as globalization. If there is a global system is because, with the material support of microelectronics-based technologies, there is a system (e.g. a global economy) whose strategically dominant, core components (e.g. financial markets or transnational production of goods and services) have the capacity to work as a unit on a planetary scale in real time or chosen time. This capacity is, at the same time, technological, organizational, and institutional (e.g. international deregulation and liberalization of trade). Global networks, under these conditions, become the backbone of the space/time regimes under which the whole society operates, even if most people in most countries are not included in these global networks. Indeed, this enhanced capacity makes networks able to generalize to society at large their binary logic: on/off, in/out, creating a new, polarizing dynamics of social cleavage, social differentiation, social exclusion, and, ultimately, social domination by exclusion rather than by direct exploitation.

Thirdly, the interactive capacity of communication technologies in real time or chosen time, based on the three technological features presented above, has two fundamental consequences for the global networks that constitute the architecture of our world. Paradoxically, they are contradictory between themselves, but both derive from the same socio-technical matrix. The first one is the capacity of networks to constantly reconfigurate themselves by adding or deleting nodes without losing their effectiveness, as soon as changes in the environment, or in the network's program advise a more effective configuration. The speed and efficiency of this reconfiguration would be simply impossible without high speed telecommunicated computer networks, and particularly the Internet. The second major consequence is that in the case a global network does not change the overarching goal that has been programmed for its performance, the reconfiguration takes place automatically within the network. Furthermore, if changes in the network's environment are out of control, or come from unknown sources, the network itself keeps changing and reconfigurating itself to fulfill its programmed goal under new circumstances, beyond the control of the original programmers. Until the network is modified in its program or in its goals by an external source, the network keeps evolving autonomously: it becomes an automaton. Since these two consequences of the new interaction between networks and technology are fundamental to understand our world, I will try to elaborate on them in a less abstract form, by giving two examples of such reconfiguration processes, on the basis of my documents and observation: global financial markets and the so-called 'antiglobalization movement'. Both are global networks, albeit programmed and constituted around sharply divergent goals, and enacted by opposing social actors.

Networks in Action: the Financial Automaton and the Global Social Movement of the Information Age

There are two strategically crucial networks in conflict in our world. On the one hand, the key institutional arrangement of capitalism and global financial markets. On the other hand, the social movements proposing a more humane form of globalization or fighting against market-driven globalization, trying to organize societies around different values. In both cases, information technology-driven networks (not just networks *per se*) are of essence in the structure and practice of these two essential features of our society.

Global financial markets are made of nodes of stock exchange markets connected by computer networks. Some are physical places (e.g. NYSE, London, etc.) wired and interconnected among themselves and with other stock exchanges. Other financial places are purely electronic networks, such as Nasdaq or Eurex. So, there is a global network of stock exchange trading networks. Through this network circulate flows of a different kind: flows of money, flows of information, flows of instructions about what to do with the money on the markets. This network is programmed to ensure the goals of financial markets. These goals are complicated, but for the sake of illustration, let us say that they are geared to: a) mobilize as much money as possible to invest in the financial market; b) ensure stable, reliable investment conditions so to create trust in the market, since trust is the condition for investment; c) to maximize the rate of return, thus fostering expectations, the driver of investment; d) to absorb erratic variations in market valuation as part of the system, hoping that the market logic will correct excessive deviations from standard criteria over the long term. From these general goals a number of regulations and rules derive. Rules are specific to each market, so there are interruptors, connectors, and switchers in the network. Interruptors: each market has its own regulation, so the flows will stop there, and they will have to be communicated to each different market through a number of procedures. The network may find its own connectors—for instance, investing in hedge funds offshore, from where the funds may come back into the main markets under new regulation. Or a protocol of communication will be found between two markets by transforming investment into derivatives that combine different values belonging to different markets. Or a switcher will be activated by modifying market regulations to make it compatible to other markets—through government action, through advice from the International Monetary Fund, or through changes in the rules of the overseeing bodies. In fact, much of the deregulation process that took place in the planet in the 1990s consisted of an effort to homogenize the conditions of circulation of capital in different financial markets. While the global financial market is still made of connections between nationally based markets, the overall trend is towards the homogenization of codes and procedures for valuation and transaction. Without computer networking this system would not be able to operate.

Now, valuation of stocks and securities are not the result of strict economic calculation. They are influenced by what I call information turbulences (Castells 2000; Volcker 2000). Global financial markets are connected to information flows of all kinds, not generated in the financial network, but affecting the functioning of the financial network (Zaloom 2003). The media, for instance. The connections between media networks and financial networks are uncontrolled and uncontrollable. What is reported in the media, goes into investors' minds, and what investors do with this information ultimately shapes the financial markets. So, the openness of the financial network, the ability of investors to enter it electronically worldwide, increases the size and complexity of the financial network and makes it uncontrollable in its totality—even if government regulation may influence some flows for a short while in some instances.

The global financial market is connected, of course, to networks of production and consumption in every country, and ultimately to the livelihood of everybody in terms of the value of money and assets that people have. Some connections are protected by interruptors institutionally decided: for instance, government-guaranteed bank deposits. Most are not: the ups and downs of financial markets affect the overall economy and, through it, the society at large.

The flexibility, scalability and survivability of the global financial market, as expression of information technology-powered networks, has made it into the heart of the global capitalism. The networked global financial market survives crises by disconnecting markets in crisis instantly, and reconfiguring itself around those markets that are still valuable. Its networking capacity *vis-à-vis* the rest of the economy ensures its expansion and its domination. On the other hand, its openness to information turbulences emerging from other networks blurs its information codes concerning valuation, thus inducing systemic volatility beyond institutional control.

Let us see now the other side of globalization: the movement for global justice, or so-called anti-globalization movement (Juris 2004). It is a network of movements and individual and collective actors connected by the Internet and the media (two specific communication networks). It connects various nodes, from various origins, that become meaningful as anti-capitalist globalization forces only by linking up with other nodes to form a network. The network has spatio-temporal discontinuity: it forms *vis-à-vis* specific events where there is maximum connection to the media network—creation of a media event as a protocol of communication with society at large. Its focus of action depends on the time/space of the global network of power and wealth. Indeed, it is an anti-network network. Each one of this network's nodes has its own logic and specific existence. But they only become activated as a network by focusing on the convergence of some symbolic action, by connecting the minds through the media, forcing a debate on the goals of globalization, and affecting the codes of the network of capital and production. In other words, capitalist globalization was predicated on the disconnection between economic globalization and societies at large: societies were assumed to be the passive consumers of the goods provided by globalization. The alternative globalization movement reconnects societies to the global market, introducing new codes in the logic of the economic system. But it is only able to do it because of the global networking capability (including technological capability) between different groups, from different cultures, and because of its switching capacity to communicate both by the Internet and with the media network.

Thus, the networking logic of our world can be to some extent epitomized by two opposing networks. One, the network of global financial market, is in fact an automaton, since it is beyond control of any single human institution or action. It is not the invisible hand of the market either, since information turbulences create random movements of valuation beyond economic criteria. It is a human creation, but also a source of alienation, as a dominant structure that has escaped the institutional control of societies.

This alienation is fought against by another powerful network, the so-called anti-globalization movement that tries to restore social control over capitalist markets. This is in fact a will-powered network, made of projects, of consciousness, of values, of social action. In this sense, the new historical struggle is not class against class, but the consciousness of humankind against the domination of the automaton it has created.

In both instances, however, information-technology powered networks are both the medium and the organizational form of structure and struggle. This is **our** network society.

Identity in the Global Information Age

Of course identity is the oldest expression of human meaning. How can anyone or any society be without identity? And when the time comes to resist oppression, identities of different kinds, inherited, constructed, and reconstructed, are essential trenches from where emerge first the negation of the negation of self, and then, in a later stage, the affirmation of new values and interest that are acknowledged by the powers that are.

Thus, the scholars contributing to this volume show how global networks of domination in antiquity had to reckon with resistance and identity from societies they were trying to subdue. This is a great service to research. Because while it should be obvious, it is not. We have been preached to by liberal and Marxist rationalism about the false consciousness of identity politics when confronted with the 'true' contradictions of class and power. It seems that class is only one of the many sources of autonomous construction of meaning throughout history, and that, overall, identity rather than consciousness seems to have been and to be nowadays a preeminent form of asserting human experience.

However, while identity (religious, national, territorial, ethnic, gender, age etc.) has always been essential as a source of meaning, we still have to apply here our methodological principle: the same cultural form changes its significance in a different historical context. What is the specificity in the Information Age?

What I have observed is that resistance identity is the fundamental form of organizing collective action and individual meaning in our world. Legitimizing identity works only in some defensive, powerful nation-states in the Western world. Project identity is the main one behind the proactive social movements of our time: anti-globalization, environmentalism, feminism. But in most of the world, including in the dominant West, people who feel threatened build their trenches around resistance identity. This is because domination in our world takes the form of an uncontrollable non-human net such as a global financial automaton that is being enforced militarily when necessary, or the global mass media that capture mental representation everywhere within the hypertext of words, sounds and images they construct. So, against an anonymous master that has no values but makes its own value from everything, the only possible resistance is the affirmation of other, transcendent values. Capital flows can dissolve everything, but not my God, my land, my ethnic group, my gender. Global media are resisted from historically built systems of meaning. So, resistance identity, constructed with the materials of historical experience, becomes the foundation of the communes of autonomous meaning in this increasingly globalized world in which computer networks and media networks obliterate land rooted institutions. Did it happen in antiquity? Was resistance identity so prevalent and so directly challenging globalization of power and wealth? I do not know, but in any case, this is what is distinctive of our world. Thus, religious fundamentalism is as old as human history, but the global networks of terror erected on the basis of reconstructed religious fundamentalism, and using the same advanced technologies of communication and destruction as the armies of global power, seem to have a historically distinctive character. The dynamics of contradiction between the Net and the Self takes a new meaning in the current technological paradigm, and within the parameters of the new forms of globalization.

Concluding Remarks

So, no, I do not think that there is nothing new under the sun. Because, in social terms, the sun is context, and context is historically, culturally, institutionally, and *technologically* specific. So, networks then and now are not the same networks as I have tried to argue. And identities are used for resistance purposes in this new context characterized by domination imposed by abstract flows of capital, global media images, and unseen guided missiles. Against capital, God. Against mass media, my message, composed with the materials of my history and geography. Against smart bombs, myself (super-smart) as a bomb. Computer networks (and maybe later bio-informatics networks) provide a material infrastructure, and indeed a material culture, that affects the production of meaning and the conflict over it. Thus, in social analysis we must specify the contextual conditions of existence of social forms, such as networks, and of the social construction processes, such as identity building.

Yet, this volume makes, in my view, an extraordinary contribution to general social science by pointing out the importance of both networks and identity, and their interaction, for the understanding of the human experience throughout history. Identity has of course been a fundamental concept for anthropology, psychology, history, and many other areas of inquiry. And network theory is a well-established field for social scientists, with very sophisticated, formal analyses, and a wealth of empirical research (Monge and Constructor 2003). However, network analysis has remained a highly specialized domain, mainly linked to the study of inter-personal interaction. To place it at the center of the analysis of the human experience, including social structure, regardless of time and space, would bring the social sciences closer to the latest developments in biology (Capra 1996, 2002). Networks seem to be the stuff from which the living matter is made. Thus, if we can show empirically, from antiquity to the Information Age, that networks, while conveying different meanings, are indeed essential forms of social structure and agency, we may be in the way of understanding the web of life, including the human life.

References

Capra F. (1996) *The Web of Life*. New York: Random House.

Capra F. (2002) *Hidden Connections*. New York: Random House.

Castells, M. (2000) Information technology and global capitalism. In *On the Edge: Living in Global Capitalism*, edited by W. Hutton and A. Giddens. London: Jonathan Cape.

Juris, J. (2004) Digital Age Activism: Anti-Corporate Globalization and the Cultural Logic of Transnational Networking. Unpublished PhD thesis, University of California, Berkeley.

Mansell, R. (2001) Digital Opportunites and the missing link for developing countries. *Oxford Review of Economic Policy* 17(2):282–95.

Mitchell, W. J. (2003) *Mett. The Cyborg Self and the Networked City*. Cambridge, MA: MIT Press.

Volcker, P. (2000) A sea of global finance. In *On the Edge: Living in Global Capitalism*, edited by W. Hutton and A. Giddens. London: Jonathan Cape.

Zaloom, C. (2003) Ambiguous numbers: trading technology and interpretation in financial markets. *American Ethnologist* 30(2):258–72.

Index

For Product Safety Concerns and Information please contact our EU
representative GPSR@taylorandfrancis.com
Taylor & Francis Verlag GmbH, Kaufingerstraße 24, 80331 München, Germany

www.ingramcontent.com/pod-product-compliance
Ingram Content Group UK Ltd.
Pitfield, Milton Keynes, MK11 3LW, UK
UKHW050756180926
475701UK00007B/1078
* 9 7 8 1 8 4 5 5 3 9 4 7 4 *